IMAGES OF THE WEST

"*ightirab*   separation from one's own country . . . Westernization"—Wehr's *A Dictionary of Modern Written Arabic*.

"To those of us for whom the struggle between Eastern and Western description of the world is an internal conflict as well as an external reality . . ."—Salman Rushdie in a review of Edward Said's *After the Last Sky*, MGW, 19 October 1986.

"The antithesis of *awlad al-balad* [Egyptians least influenced by the West and most traditional] are *awlad al-zawwat*, a term used to designate a person from the upper classes. The stereotype of *ibn al-zawwat* in the popular conception is a highly Westernized person whose lifestyle is European, who is fluent in foreign languages, which he sometimes masters better than his own, who is sophisticated in European manners but ignorant of his own, and who does not follow religious observances and is often a libertine."—Laila el-Hamamsy, p. 57.

IMAGES OF THE WEST
Third World Perspectives

David C. Gordon

Rowman & Littlefield Publishers, Inc.

ROWMAN & LITTLEFIELD PUBLISHERS, INC.

Published in the United States of America in 1989.
by Rowman & Littlefield Publishers, Inc.

Library of Congress Cataloging–in–Publication Data

Gordon, David C.
  Images of the West : Third World perspectives / David C. Gordon.
  p.   cm.
  Bibliography: p.
  Includes index.
  1. East and West– –Public opinion. 2. Public opinion– –Islamic
countries. 3. Islamic countries– –Colonization. 4. Civilization,
Islamic– –Occidental influences. 5. Anti–imperialist movements–
–Islamic countries. 6. Nationalism– –Islamic countries. I. Title.
DS35.7G66   1988   88–20938 CIP
303.4'8217671018– –dc19
  ISBN 0–8476–7603–X (alk. paper)

5   4   3   2   1

Printed in the United States of America

With Ann, in
memory of Victoria

Table of Contents

Abbreviations

AHR	*The American Historical Review*
ASQ	*Arab Studies Quarterly*
AUFS	*American Universities Field Staff Reports*
CHE	*The Chronicle of Higher Education*
CFC	*Contemporary French Civilization*
CSM	*The Christian Science Monitor*
IJMES	*International Journal of Middle East Studies*
JAS	*Journal of Asian Studies*
JHI	*Journal of the History of Ideas*
ME	*The Middle East*
MEJ	*The Middle East Journal*
MM	*Maghreb Machrek: Monde Arabe*
MGW	*Manchester Guardian Weekly*
MESAB	*Middle East Studies Association Bulletin*
Le M	*Le Monde*
MD	*Monde Diplomatique*
MEI	*Middle East International*
MEJ	*Middle East Journal*
MERIP	*Middle East Research and Information Project Reports*
NYRB	*The New York Review of Books*
NYT	*The New York Times*
S	*Salmagundi*
TLS	*The Times Literary Supplement*
WSJ	*The Wall Street Journal*
WPR	*World Press Review*

Abbreviations for publications are only used if it is clear that no confusion will result, and/or if the publication is cited often in the text.

Acknowledgements

While free from any responsibility for the propositions advanced in this essay, Donna Schlagheck, L. Carl Brown, and Richard Koffler are due special thanks for their editorial help and their kind encouragement.

Introduction

In this work, we will consider perceptions of the West that are
commonly held by those in the "East" who have and are experiencing
the effects of Western hegemony. Although they prefer to reject its
influences, they still find themselves enmeshed in the process of
"modernization." To many in both East and West, modernization,
originating as it did in the West, bears the hallmarks of its original
culture. This work is, therefore, a study both of dialogue and confrontation, of acculturation and rejection, of assimilation and decolonization, of dependence and independence, and of alienation and
identification.

Lest my title mislead, it should be made clear at the outset that the
portion of the Third World to be treated in particular, although not
exclusively, is the Islamic world; the reactions of its intellectuals and
idealogues considered here are those involving the worlds of the
British, the French, and the Americans. Such are the parameters of
this study. It is for others more polymathic and more knowledgeable
of other cultures to add to the study of responses to the West by the
peoples of Africa, South America, and Asia, referred to here only on
occasion and in a peripheral manner. The author is well aware that
in limiting his study to cases of a particular cultural complex of the
Third World, he may be doing an injustice to the attitudes of the
Third World as a whole, but his assumption is that much of what is
true of a part of the Third World is also true, in substance, of the
rest. Future studies of course might verify or disprove such an
assumption.

Many works have treated Western views of the "East" or the "Third
World" systematically, but except for two works of Bernard Lewis's
(1982, 1985–86) and several others, few have systematically treated
Eastern views of the West, as Barbara Harlow has pointed out (p. xi).
The present study does not purport to be a systematic study of

Eastern or Third World attitudes, but rather aims to introduce some of the themes such a systematic study might explore.

Broadly, the thesis argued is that the influence of the West has been, and is likely to remain, of major importance to the nations of the Third World seeking to convert formal independence into genuine cultural, economic, and political decolonization. To express the thesis negatively, the West continues to be an obstacle to self-identification among the many who have attained formal sovereignty from the matrix of the almost vanished Western empires of yesterday.

The term "West" has more substance than the term "East." It points to an entity, however ill-defined its borders, however much these may have changed in time, and however variegated its cultural forms and expressions, does have a common reality, at least as myth. The term as used here refers to the modern complex of states and peoples who, however diverse and however often they may have fought against one another, are conscious that they belong to a common civilization, rooted in the classical and Judeo-Christian eras, integrated in the High Middle Ages, and transformed after the Renaissance and Reformation into mainly secular cultures during and after the eighteenth century. The term "East," on the other hand, has been a construct of the Western imagination, an aspect of the West's own self-identification, a term that arbitrarily groups under one rubric different peoples who do not identify with one another, nor have similar traditions, cultures, or values. "East" does not designate any one reality unless used only negatively to refer to a plethora of phenomena that happen to be non-Western, that belong to parts of the world conceived by Westerners as lying in the non-West, the Orient. The nebulous and Eurocentric quality of the term "East" (or "Orient") does not prevent such terms from having enormous psychological and imaginative significance both for the West and for many non-Europeans who have begun to accept Western perspectives.

Identification, both individual and collective, depends for self-definition, reassurance, and reinforcement upon a contrast with the Other; and perceptions of the Other, in turn, are projections influenced and conditioned by one's own self-identification—the two are dialectically interrelated. But all, of course, is not only a play of mirrors; realities intervene, as does the experience of the Other. Perception is not made out of whole cloth, however important a note the imaginary may play. In any case, however false and biased perceptions of the Other may be, they influence behavior and policy and are a part of reality; the converse is true of abstractions such as "West."

It is only recently that the East-West dichotomy has been widely questioned both as having derogatory connotations and as being intellectually unacceptable. Those who have denounced Orientalism, Edward Said in particular, have been right in objecting to the reification in the dichotomy and to the harmful effects of such dichotomies. But, as with either term, East or West alone, the pairing or juxtaposition of the two is, however unfortunately, a binary concept that has played and continues to play an important role in human affairs, indeed a crucial one in the Third World in particular, for good or ill.

The term "Third World" is used here to refer to those peoples and those ethnic groups who, geographically, form part of the East, in most cases after these areas have been freed from direct or indirect political control by one Western country or another. The term is very controversial: some would prefer using it only in the plural, so variegated is the world referred to; others would use it only to indicate the have-nots in industrial as well as in developing countries, all pawns in the world capitalist system; and others would reject it completely as vulnerable to the same criticisms as the term "East."[1] We will use the term, nevertheless, despite the validity of many of the criticisms against it, for purposes of convenience and out of convention. Here the term "Third World" distinguishes peoples (who also so distinguish themselves) from the developed, industrial, largely Western world, and from an "East" that once consisted of strong, coherent, and self-confident civilizations. Today's Third World is yesterday's "East," now independent from subjection to direct or indirect Western rule, but confronted with grim problems and challenges, a legacy of that period of imperialist Western control. These problems and challenges are cultural as well as economic and political and still bedevil the process of genuine decolonization. To the extent that China and perhaps Vietnam, through their options for Marxism, have precisely defined the identification they want, and to the extent that Japan has become fully "modern" following the Western liberal and capitalistic paradigm, these countries are not considered to be part of the Third World. Because Russia, always partly Western and partly not, has fully committed itself to its own version of Marxism *and* has become a modern industrial power, it will be touched upon only incidentally in the following pages. Russia, of course, has faced many of the stresses of identification that now confront the Third World (Raeff, pp. 75, 87).

Contrary to what many people appear to believe, the term "Third World" was *not* meant, in origin at least, to designate a part of the world neither Communist nor liberal-capitalist, but something in between, a third entity. In fact, the term seems to have been coined by Alfred Sauvy, French intellectual and statesman, in an article in *L'Observateur* (14 August 1952) that drew a parallel between the peoples of the world striving for their independence from the Western empire after World War II, and the "Third Estate" during the French Revolution, the masses declared by the Abbé Sieyès in his famous pamphlet, to be not just one more class, but the nation itself, the sole repository of sovereignty. The parallel was tendentious, to be sure; Third World leaders have asked for much but certainly not for everything. Nevertheless, the term has been found useful to distinguish the millions of newly independent peoples and nations seeking to overcome massive problems and to discover an identification to help provide a sense of national unity and pride. The systematic use of the term, according to Peter Lyon, came during the Algerian Non-Aligned Summit in 1972 where it was equated with "non-aligned" and "developing" countries.

Frequent use will be made of the terms "Westernization" and "modernization," terms that overlap, are often used interchangeably, but that are nevertheless distinct. Westernization, in the pages that follow, will be used to designate only *one* model of modernization, that ineluctable and relentless global process that can be avoided only at peril, if at all. Much ink has been spilled attempting to define "modernization," but no one definition, be it a "stages," a functionalist, or a historical definition, has been fully satisfactory to everyone (Geertz, 1968, pp. 57–59). For working purposes, a broad umbrella formulation might be a process of increasing human technical and cognitive control over nature.

As useful as any definition is Charles Gallagher's synthesis of Robert Bellah (1965, pp. 169–70) and Cyril Black (1966), which reads "a process stemming from a rapid increase in the amount of knowledge and information available and the appropriate reactions by a society to such knowledge" (Gallagher, 1968, I:4). Equally useful is Black's definition that reads, "the process by which societies have been and are being transformed under the impact of the scientific and technological revolution . . . a holistic process affecting all aspects of society . . . and involving an increase in the ratio of inanimate to animate sources of power to and past a point of no return as far as the accompanying social patterns are concerned" (Black et al., pp. 3–4). Iran's 1979 Revolution has led some to repudiate the idea of "modernization" completely. Thus Fred Halliday (MERIP, May–June 1986, pp. 31–34) writes that Iran has helped kill "one of the most banal ideological constructions of the post-war world." It remains to be seen if such judgments might not prove to be, over the long haul, too precipitate, at least regarding "modernization" as process, as distinguished from ideology, a distinction to be discussed.

The process of modernization arose first in the West. For this reason, modernization and Westernization are viewed by many as identical; to be modern, it has been assumed, has been to be European in manner and lifestyle. But for example, as the Japanese seem to have shown, one can modernize without adopting everything Western or shedding everything authentically one's own. Having said this, however, one should emphasize that the confusion between the two remains an important factor; there are many who claim they are rebelling against "modernity" when they refuse to adopt Western ways—while on the other hand, there are many who fool themselves into believing that by only adopting Western ways they become "modern." In the past this historical bias may have made good sense; today it makes less and less sense as the significant distinctions of the East and West confront one another and as modernity increasingly becomes man's common destiny and lot. But the bias still remains; the "West" continues to be an important mental construct.

Regarding the Arab world at least, Albert Hourani has suggested that during the period after 1945, which saw the end of the "European Age," the West lost the prestige it once had and peoples began to look for alternative models to the Western ones (Hourani, 1983). Modernization and Westernization can no longer be easily equated without misleading or exposing us to the risk of falling into the sin of "Orientalism."

Ever since the publication of *Orientalism* (1978) by Edward Said, writers on subjects such as the present one, have often felt obliged to show their freedom from this sin, from this Western want to view and discuss the Other through an inherited grid of Eurocentric bias and prejudice, which leads to reification and stereotypification (Gordon, 1982; S. al-Azm, 1980; Zartman, 1983). Without entering into the complicated debate as to whether ethnological study of one people by another is possible or morally permissable, one might simply accept, for both writer and reader, a caveat not to fall into the error of confusing ideal types with concrete realities, nor to make tentative generalizations that serve only purposes of classification and present the risk of becoming rigidly stereotypic.

The focus in this essay will be upon five main themes. One, the West as a cluster of symbols and an assumed reality that has played and continues to play a crucial role in the quest of many in the Third World for identification and full "decolonisation." The West, in other words, must be taken into account culturally, psychologically, and ideologically. Two, there is no single Third World attitude toward the West; there is, instead, a wide spectrum of attitudes (and reaction) ranging from the extremely negative to the extremely positive, from total rejection to a desire to assimilate fully with this West. Between are the views of those who are ambivalent, often "marginal" people whose views, it will be maintained here, are the more creative, and realistic in terms of the future. Three, the search of Third World ideologues for "authenticity" (in face of the Western challenge) often involves them in problematical situations; those considered are the treatment of women, historiography, language, and the media. Four, because of such problems of identity, communities and nations involved with the West often appear "anomalous" in the part of the world in which they find themselves, to many of the "radical" opponents of the policies of their governments. Five, in its relationship with the West, the Third World (along with the West itself) faces three possible future prospects: a catastrophic confrontation between the two; a gradual process of cosmopolitanization as the world drifts into a single cultural mold (inspired largely by the West); or, third and more hopefully, a self-articulation by its various native cultures that, with the Western, will give a single, shrunken globe pluralistic variety and creativity. At present, while the third option is the one preferred, short of an unpredictable catastrophe (confrontation, nuclear, or environmental), the second—world uniformity—appears, sadly, the more probable. But, in either a case of homogenization or of multiplicity, the West will remain materially and psychologically an important variable, one non-Westerners and Westerners alike must confront and come to terms with.

PART I

Western Hegemony

1

The Expansion of the West

Since the sixteenth century, the West has, through direct or indirect domination, played an ever larger role in fashioning the unity of the world and in giving this world many of its practices and values. While the period of domination has been short (a mere three to four centuries), the impact of the West has been extensive and, as outcries against "neo-colonialism" would seem to indicate, persistent. It is this Western imprint we consider in this chapter, along with some of its effects and some of the attitudes and rationalizations that, to Western minds, explained and justified the domination of the West. This imprint in turn influenced Western views of the Other—of the East it had subdued—and the independent nations that emerged from the grip of Western colonialism. In conclusion, consideration will be given to the conscience of Westerners, a conscience that has been either repentant and guilty over the fruits of empire and has sought to make recompense for damages done, or that remains unrepentant for the past and confident that the West's destiny is to bring "progress" to the rest of the world.

The Colonial Imprint

By 1800, Europe controlled about 35 percent of the landed surface of the world, by 1878, 67 percent and by 1914, 84 percent (Headrick, 1977, p. 3). After World War I the percentage rose even higher when England and France established mandates over some of the succession states to the Ottoman Empire in the Middle East. This was the height of Western global hegemony, the culmination of the expansion of the West traceable to the Crusades in the eleventh century and the *reconquista*; but the groundwork for what were to become the great modern Western empires can more accurately be dated from the seventeenth century after which the energies of the West were exported rather than directed to internal discord. In this century the Treaties of Wesphalia brought the Thirty Years War to an end and established once and for all the primacy of secular over religious authority in central Europe (1648); the French finally defeated Spain's struggle to assert her hegemony over Western Europe (Treaty of Pyrenees, 1659); and in England the Civil War came to a conclusion with the Restoration (1660) (Rabb).

Western expansion which, in William McNeill's words, led to "the irremediable collapse of the traditional order of each of the major Asian civilizations" and to the penetration of the West into "the tissue of weaker societies," became progressively more irresistable (1963, pp. 726–30, 653–64). Finally, during the nineteenth century, the last resistance of the "traditional" forces of the Asian civilizations collapsed only later to give way to the resistance of new forces inspired by Western nationalism. In 1850 the Taiping Rebellion was put down in China, in 1853 Commodore Perry "opened up" Japan, in 1858 the Sepoy Rebellion in India was finally crushed and after 1856, while on the winning side of the Crimean War (1854–1856), the Ottoman Empire came progressively under greater Western pressure and control. By 1912, all of Africa, except for Liberia and Abyssinia, had come under Western domination.

Why was the West able to subdue so much of the world? Several reasons have been suggested: the dynamism of the West, for one, that came in part from its very lack of centralized unity; the great prestige and progress of science and industry; and the spirit of adventure of these restless "Faustian" peoples. Such factors, as well as good fortune and sheer luck, gave the West advantages not enjoyed by others.

From roughly the fifteenth century to about 1945, the West enjoyed a clear advantage in the field of military and naval technology. For example because of innovations in ship design by the end of the sixteenth century, refinements in hull and sail construction enabled supply ships to carry cannons and thus to defend themselves successfully from a distant bombardment. Symbolic of the coming of the European age in Asia was the naval battle of Diu (1509) when the Portuguese won a clear-cut victory over the Mamluk and Gujerati fleets and opened the way for the establishment of the Portuguese thalassocracy (Cipolla, pp. 101–2; Wolf, pp. 235–36). One reason for the victory at Diu was the Portuguese possession of new three-masted, square-rigged vessels that were able to remain at sea for months.

Improved technologies of observation and measurement also contributed to the success of the West. The telescope (invented about 1608), the microscope (about 1590), and the thermometer (1592), all became functional by the seventeenth century (McNeil, 1963, pp. 585–91; Hall, pp. 6–7; Landes).

Important innovations that enabled Westerners to survive abroad were the use of sauerkraut in the eighteenth century to prevent scurvy, and quinine prophylaxis against malaria, which made possible the penetration of parts of Africa known as the "white man's grave" in the nineteenth century (Headrick). Other important practices that extended trade and commerce in the nineteenth century, include the gradual replacement of sailing ships by steamships, the digging of the Suez Canal (1869), and the laying of cable telegraph lines, linking, to give one important example, India and England in 1870. Non-mechanical factors were also important, among these pugnacity, recklessness, organization, and discipline, which, according to G. N. Clark, account for the "superiority of Westerners as fighters" (p. 193). In the nineteenth century, war became increasingly more lethal because of a great number of innovations that improved the accuracy and the rapidity of fire-power, for instance the French Minié bullet, the breach-loaders of the mid-nineteenth century (the famous Prussian needle-gun), and the development of the machine gun culminating in the Maxim gun of 1884. Europeans also had at their disposal gun-boats, first used effectively in the Opium War in 1839. As Hilaire Belloc put it, "Whatever happens we have got the Maxim Gun and they have not."

Important as technological innovativeness was in accounting for Western hegemony, fortune also played an important role. Europe was geographically well-endowed with extensive and contiguous well-watered virgin soil. Unlike others, she was spared the destructive scourges of the Mongols and, for reasons about which one can only speculate, others who had the possibility of entering the race for modernity first did not choose to do so. For example, China invented gunpowder, the compass, printing, and civil service exams and might have taken the lead in institutionalizing science and expanding to other parts of the world. She instead remained self-contained and self-satisfied, closed off from the rest of the world after the fifteenth century. But these are might-have beens; it was in the West that an independent and adventurous bourgeois class first developed, that the large-scale exploitation of other parts of the world began, and that commerce first became subject to production, social labor to mechanical power, and modern capitalism and the Industrial Revolution first arose (Wolf, pp. 266–67). First, in the Industrial Revolution, the West had the edge; leader in the early stages of the unfolding of the world economic system, it enjoyed and exploited productive and technological advantages over others (Myrdal; Wallerstein, 1974, 1979). In crude terms, the West became economic master, and the rest of the world it penetrated became dependent, producers of primary goods and raw materials, while England and then the West in general became the "workshop of the world." The whole world after the sixteenth century became a vast frontier for the West to exploit and from which the West derived its fabulous wealth. As Walter Prescott Webb has put it, the West benefited from "the largest frontier in world history" to launch "a business boom such as the world had never known before and probably never can know again" (p. 16). In the process of amassing the gold, silver, and commodities produced by cheap labor abroad, this dynamic civilization, Webb suggests "decrystalized," that is, became less rigid and conformist, more individualistic and economically innovative and even more expansionist. In a sense, the entire world until about 1914 was Europe's oyster. Webb, in his dramatic portrayal of the establishment of the West's economic hegemony, admits that Westerners deserved their good fortune to the extent that they had the energy and the knowledge to take advantage of it. However, the East became the victim of this Western impact; as Elie Kedourie (citing Toynbee) observes, just as the world's intervention in an eclipse makes a shadow over the moon, so the West has helped to create the Third World (1970, pp. 366–67).

The shadow of the West fell heavily on the rest of the world. Its impact varied according to the time the Western presence was first experienced, the depth of its penetration, and the condition of the society when the impact was first felt. In general, the earlier the impact, the more cruel it was, the less inhibitory to Western behavior were conscience and world opinion. For example, the conquest of South American civilizations in the sixteenth century was far more brutal and ruthless than the Western conquest of most of Africa in the nineteenth (Léon-Portilla; Wachtell). In the cases of the conquest of the Incas and the Aztecs by small bands of Spaniards, there was no hesitation on the part of the latter to resort to undisguised lying and to punitive and terroristic massacre. To members of the last generation of the Incas who remembered the conquest, according to Nathan Wachtell, the invasion was a "gigantic cataclysm," a psychological "trauma" (pp. 201–5). Not only had the gods died, but masses of people were shifted to other places to be cruelly expoited. Nature added to this cruelty when perhaps half to two-thirds of the Indians perished from imported diseases. In Mexico many Aztecs died and were traumatized by the ravages of man and by a nature disturbed by human intervention (Léon-Portilla; J. H. Parry, pp. 62–63; C. Gibson, pp. 35, 40–44, 64).

In the case of Africa, during the time of the "New Imperialism" (after 1878), force was used, but partly because of world (and domestic) opinion, hypocrisy played a more important role than outright brutality in the subjugation of the Africans. Where brutality was, in fact, practiced, as in the Congo, and was known about, it received wide public condemnation. A more common practice was to persuade tribal chiefs to agree to treaties that provided for "protectorates" over themselves and then to transform the contractual content of these treaties into de facto direct rule. Similarly, sincere or hypocritical in different cases, the imposition of Western rule was rationalized by benevolent doctrines such as the White Man's Burden or the *mission civilisatrice*. Cruelty, nevertheless, was employed, and Western domination caused serious psychological and cultural damage to host cultures. The cruelty practiced in the Congo by King Leopold and his cronies is well known from Conrad's *The Heart of Darkness*, and from André Gide's later condemnation of the king. In his memoirs, Matungi, a chief in the Belgian Congo, saw the imposition of Western ways as the negation of all that he had been brought up to respect (Turnbull, 1963, pp. 57–70). While he continued to hold on to his own values, he lamented, "for my children it is different . . . the white man fills their head and they doubt. I circumcize my sons, but I cannot circumcize their minds and their heads." The Herero uprising in German South-West Africa (1904–1907), which led to the slaying of thousands of natives by the Germans, was, according to one of the tribal chieftans, a result of the German system of justice. To the Herero, who customarily handled crime through arbitration rather than punishment, the German system seemed ruthless and was "practiced with such vehemence" that it finally became intolerable to the natives (Wilson, Henry, p. 167).

As the treatment of natives by the intruding Westerners varied, so also did the depth of penetration and of cultural transformation. Obviously each case must be judged on its own merits, but one can be on guard against two pitfalls; one, in judging the relative penetration of the West by the values and mores of ruling elites, highly Westernized as these might be; and second, one should guard against basing any interpretation on superficial (and possibly ephemeral) indications such as the popularity of blue jeans and "rock 'n roll," or the fact that in India some of Calcutta's streets are still called Clive Row or Defferin Road.

Among students of Western expansion and of cultural radiation in general, there is considerable dispute regarding the extent and the depth of acculturation. For example, it is uncertain just how "Western" India has become and whether the parliamentary system will survive there; how Westernized is Turkey because of Atatúrk's policies; and, conversely, how final Iran's present rejection of all things Western will prove to be.

Regarding the differing effects of Western influence over different peoples, Harold Z. Schiffrin observes that in China and Japan, intellectuals have sufficient confidence in their cultural heritage to be able to absorb Western ideas and ideals without the "crippling effect" this absorption has had elsewhere (among many Muslims, for example). In addition Confucian scholars, well before the Western influence, had adopted critical and secular approaches to matters much as historical criticism. It is, perhaps, no accident that the first sophisticated attack on "Orientalism" should have come out of the context of the Muslim Arab world (Schiffrin, pp. 253–55).

How hazardous speculation over such matters can be is illustrated by a conversation between Geoffrey Barraclough and the Japanese intellectual Takeo Kuwabara regarding Westernization (WPR, March 1981). On the one hand Barraclough insisted that Westernization in Japan and elsewhere was only "skin-deep," that the short-lived Western hegemony had only produced a technological, not a cultural, transformation, that ethnic identification (even in France among groups like the Basques) outlasted any forced conformity to an Other. But then, in seemingly flagrant contradiction, Barraclough proceeded to deplore the fact that China, in the post-Mao period, was risking the "Americanization" of China and the destruction of "Chinese culture" by its open-door policies; Barraclough, for ideological reasons of his own, was suggesting the possibility of what he had only just called impossible.

The questions just raised can, at best, only be given the most speculative of answers; but while only the future may provide solid answers, there do seem to be some "ideal-type" patterns or ways in which the West has impinged upon the worlds of the East.

Economic Effects

As Europe expanded, there gradually came into being, after the sixteenth century, a world economic system embracing virtually the whole globe and making all parts of the world economically interdependent. The dominant element in this system was the West who inaugurated it, became the first to take advantage of it and, in different degrees and ways, subordinated the economies of the rest of the world to its own (Braudel; Stavrianos; Wallerstein, 1974, 1979). Over time, the economic life of the world was radically transformed to the advantage of the West.

Stavrianos has made the point that Western hegemony produced a new form of exploitation. Alexander the Great plundered but did not transform; the West transformed in order to plunder and in the process vastly increased its wealth and its power over others (pp. 36–37). Stavrianos estimated that in 1500 the disparity between the wealth of the West and of others was in a ratio of 3:1; by 1850 the ratio was 5:1, and by 1970, 14:1 (p. 38). Between 1400 and 1970 he sees four major periods, each characterized by its own particular form of wealth extraction: 1400–1700, when Western colonialism was limited to America, the mode of exploitation was "commercial capitalism;" 1700–1870 was a period of "waning colonialism" when "industrial capitalism" was the mode; 1870–1914 was the era of world-wide "new imperialism" and "monopoly capitalism;" and the period after 1914, especially after World War II, "monopoly capitalism" has been on the defensive. Even if one holds that such a division reflects a Marxist and anti-capitalist (and anti-Western) bias, such a division would, roughly, correspond to the way idealogues of the peoples struggling for independence within the Western imperial framework, and now leaders of the Third World, would tend to view the history of their imbrication with the West.

In one particular part of the new world economic system, the Middle East, whose experience was not very different from other parts of the "East," Charles Issawi shows that the West directed trade toward itself and away from earlier patterns for its own benefit. Under the new dispensation, finished goods were traded for raw materials, local artisan industry was undermined, and Westerners came to control the heights of the economy (except for land tenure), initially working through minorities who tended to dominate the middle levels of the economy (Issawi, 1982, pp. xii, 1–8, 9–16; Batatu, pp. 24, 29).

Albeit with reservations because of their ideological implications, Issawi accepts the term "center" for the West and "periphery" for the "East," terms, along with "semi-periphery," currently employed by supporters of "Dependence Theory." Immanuel Wallerstein, one of the leading theoreticians of this school, has talked of the "structure which today we call a capitalistic world economy" created by a West to incorporate economically over a period of four centuries "all the rest of the earth within its boundaries" (1984, p. 169). This, *mutatis mutandis*, has been the fate of many of the new nations of the present Third World who, molded by the West to a large extent, have entered upon the world scene as part of the periphery, often dependent on their previous rulers and/or other developed industrial powers. One need not accept Wallerstein *et al.* uncritically to appreciate that their reflections contain much truth, if not all the truth. The notion of dependency in a nondoctrinaire sense can be applied, as it will be further on in this work, to culture as well as to economics and politics.

The Social Schism

A consequence of the Western impact, not unrelated to the phenomenon of economic dependence, was the making of a schism between an elite, increasingly drawn into the cultural orbit of the West and tied to it in many economic and political ways, and the mass of the people. The effect of this schism was often to separate leaders from their people in language and manners as well as in terms of political interests, and to divide society into the "Westernized" and the "traditional," corresponding invariably to the division between the haves and have-nots, the rich and the poor. Iran is an example of how this division led to the complete loss of the Shah's and the ruling class's legitimacy, resulting in their overthrow by a new class of leaders supported by the mass of people. In the case of India, the sharp division between the haves and have-nots continues to the extent that some observers speak of "the two Indias" (Stokes, 1978): one, the India of severe poverty, of "traditionalism"; the other a very modern India, capable of producing its own nuclear weapons, and sustaining a sophisticated scientific establishment. This is the India whose families were educated according to Lord Macaulay's prescriptions, in English, using English textbooks imbued with Western values, and disparaging, by implication, native values (J. Walsh). The India of the masses is one of the fifteen poorest countries in the world with an annual per capita income of $190 (1982); half the people can't afford a minimum ration of bread, half the villages have neither electricity nor potable water, and only 36 percent of whose adults are literate. At the same time India is ranked one of the ten largest industrial economies in the world.

Another case is Indonesia as it was reconstituted after the Right defeated and crushed the Communists in 1965–1966. Since then, the United States has been the dominant influence, culturally as well as ideologically, on the elite level. American-trained administrators, especially the "Berkeley Mafia" for example, carry special weight at the University of Indonesia, in Djakarta. Television is fed largely by American programs, and names such as Lucy and Robert are popular—a recent song goes, "She was called Juyu in the village and now she's called Joy." The Indonesia of the masses, according to Erwin Ramedhan, is looked down upon as backward and "traditional." As in much of the rest of the Third World, this "traditional" mass is being mobilized by new leaders on the Left or those representing militant Islam, to whom Westernization or Americanization is equated with domination by the haves.

And then there are those who are caught between the two levels of Westernized and "traditionalist," the marginals who will be discussed in pages that follow. By way of anticipation and illustration, one might cite here the drama of the migrant worker which, of course, has a poignant human side to it, as well as the economic one. Many of the migrant families have no alternative now but to stay in Europe for an indefinite period, bringing up their children there, raising inevitable questions of identity and acculturation. "In Algeria," a young unemployed Algerian is quoted as saying, "I'm not Algerian. In France I'm not French" (NYT, 15 August 1983). Such a person might well know French better than he knows Arabic or, should he be a Berber speaker (20 percent of Algerians), he might never have learned Arabic at all (Le M, 13 July 1983). And his family might very well suffer from the common crisis in which parents try to preserve their native and Muslim customs, while they lose their children to European mores and life-styles.

Alien Strands

The Western impact has been felt in a third way among those states challenged by the West but not, at least not immediately, subjugated, such as the Ottoman Empire and China. Losing territory on the periphery and well aware of Western military superiority, leaders of states threatened with truncation if not absorption decided to protect themselves, and still keep their cultural as well as territorial integrity by borrowing only one strand from the Western tapestry. This strand was usually, although not always, that of military technology (Abu-Lughd, 1963). The assumption was that one could adopt and adapt to such a strain from an alien culture without harm to the integrity of the fabric of one's own culture (Toynbee, 1953, pp. 71–74; 1935–1961, Vol. VIII, pp. 88–629). This, it was soon realized, was illusory; the adoption of one strand would inevitably alter the pattern into which it was interwoven and, to sustain the new strand, auxiliary and supportive strands would also need to be imported. In the case of military technology, these supports were Western science, engineering, and education that, in turn, would call for new habits and new attitudes (Cipolla, p. 109). While Peter I of Russia and Atatúrk realized that partial borrowing would almost certainly require further borrowing, they opted unabashedly for full Westernization. According to Toynbee, some leaders like Gandhi clung to the illusion that borrowing could be wholly selective, that, for example, native industry could be preserved while India accepted political modernization. He was soon disillusioned and was forced to admit, with other leaders who had hoped for the same, that partial penetration by the West almost certainly involves continued penetration, often to the detriment of tradition and of premodern expressions of communal identity. Toynbee was clearly right in suggesting a bias in favor of continuing to import more strands of an alien culture once one was adopted, even if he overstated, as some of his critics have said, the inevitability of absorbing the alien culture in toto. Were Toynbee wholly right then, contrary to the position taken in this essay, Westernization and modernization would indeed be identical. In any case, the adoption of the strand of Western nationalism—a blend of democracy, ethnicity, and the ideal of territorial sovereignty—was to prove particularly disturbing. In the context of the East with its complex mixtures of peoples and variegated religions, languages, and heritages, Western nationalism could only serve to fragment and to pit peoples against one another as, indeed, it did in parts of the West such as the Hapsburg Empire. In India, in the Ottoman Empire and elsewhere, peoples who had in "mosaic" style learned to live together now became enemies one against the other, and the unity of empires eventually gave way to a multiplicity of states, in many of which ethnic diversity still proves to be a serious hurdle to national unity and cohesion.

In Islamic areas, where to the pious the highest loyalty in principle is to the *umma* (community) of all Muslims irrespective of ethnic background, nationalism has been a particularly dangerous and sometimes "heretical" challenge, dividing Iranians, Arabs, and Turks from one another as never before (Lewis, 1964, pp. 70, 73, 78–84), and fragmenting Muslim empires (such as the Ottoman) not only along Christian/Muslim lines but also along ethnic and linguistic lines, thus destroying the unity of the *umma*. Among the Arab succession states to the Ottoman Empire, confusion of identification and loyalty lasts to this day; to many Muslim Arabs, before World War I, for example, it was unclear whether they were primarily Ottomans, Muslims, or Arabs, and to this day there is often confusion between whether one's highest loyalty is to the Arab nation, to the regional state (Syria, Iraq, etc.), to the city, to the extended family, or to Islam.

Another Western strand to go awry when woven into the Eastern tapestry was the constitutional parliamentary system of government. Once considered a sign of progress, in most cases it failed to survive the end of Western control. By 1984, for example, Alan Cowell could find only nine African states in which the constitutional legacy of the colonial period still survived and, allowing for exceptions such as India, the fate of parliamentary government was the same in Asia (NYT, 14 August 1984). Why has this been so? In regard to the Arab world in particular, Bernard Lewis observes that the failure of parliamentary government was *not* the result of any intrinsic incompatibility between constitutional government and Islam. Islam, in fact and contrary to conventional Western opinion, favors toleration, encourages relative social equalitarianism, and, because of respect for law, rejects political despotism. The reasons constitutional government has failed to survive in almost all of the Arab world, with a few exceptions such as Tunisia and Lebanon (to 1975), were because it was originally imposed by colonial decree, manipulated cynically by the colonial power and the local landed aristocracy to suit their own interests, and appeared at a time when the middle classes were weak, when mass loyalties were generally tribal and primordial, and when totalitarian approaches were popular (as in the West in the period before World War II) (Lewis, 1964, pp. 57–62).

A fourth way the Western imprint has been felt is in the weight of its example and its spread by Westerners sure of the superiority of their civilization, confident in its universal value. The ways that

Westerners have viewed themselves, have explained and thought about their imperial successes, have tended to view the Other, and have rationalized or condemned their own actions, has relevance for non-Western views of the West. Western self-congratulation has sometimes persuaded, often fed resentment, and Western self-criticism has sometimes served to induce admiration, but often it has been used as ammunition against Western presumption and Western domination. Jacques Ellul grandiloquently states, "The entire world has been pupil to the West it now rejects" (p. 24). Exaggerated as such a statement might seem, it does point to the intimate Western involvement many of the Third World revolutionary leaders and founding fathers, who most often have been educated in Western school at home or abroad in the West, have had—one only need consult the autobiographies of the Kenyattas, Gandhis, and Nehrus. Western self-perceptions are, in short, one matter of concern to those ideologues who seek to uncover their Third World nation's "authenticity" and true identity. It is these Western self-perceptions that are considered next.

2

The "Superiority" and "Universality" of the West

By the seventeenth century "Europe" as a self-conscious civilization had emerged from the matrix of "Christendom," sensitive to its distinction from the Other—the Asiatic, the Oriental, the Eastern (Anderson, Chabod, Hay). In the seventeenth century, Sully worked out his "Grand Design" for European peace; in the eighteenth century Voltaire spoke of Europe as a *Grande République*, and Edmund Burke could say confidently: "No European can be a complete exile in any part of Europe." In the nineteenth century, Ranke referred to Europe as a "family of nations." Asia as an exotic or negative mirror-image of itself that served to reinforce identity, enhance self-confidence, and feed, through its exoticism, psychological needs, had already been portrayed by Machiavelli as the embodiment of absolutism in contrast to the West's "aristocratic bureaucracy." To Jean Bodin, Asia embodied despotism, in contrast to Western monarchy, which was limited by a feudal aristocracy. This view was to be given its classical expression by Montesquieu in the eighteenth century when he talked of "western liberties" as a precious legacy to be defended against the despotic wont of princes and kings (1949, vol. I). The point made, which continues to be made to this day, is that because of the particular development of feudalism in the West (with Japan perhaps the only parallel), despotism, the hallmark of the Other, could never develop in the West (Anderson, pp. 402–31, 462–594; Hexter; Quigley). Ultimately feudalism, by dint of fragmented sovereignty, the fact that kings had *dominia* (specific rights) but no *proprietas* (property ownership) over territory, and their relationship to the aristocracies below was contractual, laid a basis for the eventual rise of the free town and representative government (Anderson). Much of this analysis of the West can be accepted, but the contrast Westerners perceived between their civilization and the Other was reductive and simplistic.

As the eye of any other beholder sees, the Western observer will see what he wants, what serves his interests, and what provides reassurance. It projects on the Other its own preoccupations, and so often says more about itself than about the Other it beholds (R. Dawson, 1967; Turner in Hussain, 1984). Also, in judging another culture, the Westerner follows a universal habit, dichotomizes in order to classify and better understand—for example, we/them, civilization/barbarism, Europe/Asia, the West/the East. These Western dichotomies can be traced back to ancient Greece and to the Biblical distinction between the land of Japheth (Europe) and the land of Shem (Asia), and are implicit in current notions such as "oriental despotism," the "mechanical penchant to the West," the "aesthetic" nature of the East, and the like. All such notions that are used as part of a defensive or an offensive armory against the Other only widen the distance between peoples. This is also true of exoticism, the use of the Other to derive bemusement or aesthetic pleasure, to satisfy psychic and oneiric needs, and to escape from the everyday. Exoticism, by keeping the Other behind a curtain of mystery, as Norman Daniel says laconically regarding Muslims, makes the East "much more different than need be" (1966, p. 481). Often, efforts to comprehend and employ the culture of the Other, of the East, by American writers such as Emerson, Thoreau, Ezra Pound, and J. D. Salinger (Yu)—present the Other's classical and traditional culture rather than its living present (Jawdat; Graham-Brown). Another pitfall in the use of the Other is the subsumption of complexity and variegation into an oversimplified generalization. This is what the West does when it characterizes the East as marked by political despotism and social stagnation, a generalization that in recent times has given rise to its own acronym, AMP, for Asian Mode of Production. Much energy has been expended debating whether or not this paradigm is useful, and whether Marx did or did not subscribe to it (Wittfogel; Turner, 1978; Avineri, 1968; Gellner, 1983; Anderson). The debates have been useful in generating new insights, but they need not concern us in the present context. Whether the paradigm AMP is valid or not, it was the perceptual formula of the East accepted by many Westerners. This formula, reinforced among members of the Left by Marx in his popular pieces, helps explain why socialists in the nineteenth century attacked the imperialist behavior and motivation of capitalists but did not criticize the fact of imperialism. Together with most observers on the Right, the socialists assumed the East would remain indefinitely stagnant and unhistorical unless aroused by the West (Grimal, pp. 13–39).

But while the model, AMP, influenced Western perceptions, there were many other nuances and exceptions, particularly when the focus was upon one particular aspect of the "East" rather than on the "East" as a single entity. The different visions of China, Japan, India, and the kingdoms of Islam in Western consciousness might alone show the emptiness of the concept "East," except as a force in the imagination of the West.

Richard Dawson, who has devoted an entire book to the subject of the Western image of China, appropriately likens this image to a chameleon, because the perceptions are a reflection of the needs and propensities of China's observers, rather than of China's inherent nature. In the sixteenth century, Jesuits who visited China and reported what they saw tended to be very enthusiastic; some of them saw Confucian ethics as protoChristian, while Dutch merchants tended to regard the Chinese they dealt with as treacherous and amoral. These two diametrically opposite views suggest the old tale of the blind men asked to describe an elephant—each one described him according to that part of the elephant he was able to put his hands upon.

In the eighteenth century, the admiration for *chinoiserie*, Chinese artifacts, and for China herself was sometimes turned imaginatively into a utopian ideal of civilized decorum and wisdom as a criticism of the West. To Voltaire and others who favored enlightened despotism over aristocratic disruptiveness, China served as a positive model. To Montesquieu, supporter of the "aristocratic thesis" against royal absolutism and a fervent defender of liberty, China was a model of despotism. Adam Smith and other early laissez-faire economists saw China in terms of *their* ideological predilections—China was engulfed in poverty because of lack of free trade.

In the nineteenth century the game of elephant identification continued: to Hegel, the Absolute Idea had reached a low level of self-consciousness; to Marx, China represented the AMP; to Max Weber, China was backward because she did not subscribe to the "Protestant Ethic"; and Tennyson, echoing the West's own faith in progress, penned the line in *Locksley Hall* that has now become a cliché, "Better fifty years of Europe than a cycle of Cathay." By the end of the nineteenth century and by the first decade of the twentieth, when it became clear that Japan was becoming impressively formidable, and because of a concern with demography and the belief that

China had vast resources, there arose the myth of the "Yellow Peril," a myth that dove-tailed with other racist tendencies of the nineteenth century.

Anne R. Thurston points out that the "chameleon" is still alive and well (CSM, 1 February 1984, pp. 16–17). In a review of recent books on China, she comments on the extreme attitudes expressed by Westerners regarding communist China. She observes that during the oppressive Cultural Revolution Westerners ironically tended to excuse and defend China, but now that China has been opening herself to the West, descriptions of her tend to be very negative (Butterfield, 1982). The West, suggests Thurston, is only seeing in China what it wants to see—either an ideal model (now that the Russian model has faded) for those inclined to the left, or (because the communist ideal is still attractive to many in the Third World) anathema to those inclined to the right.

While sometimes bracketed with China in Western perception, the West's relationship with Japan has been too different for such identification to be common practice. Before Japan's victories over China in the late nineteenth century and over Russia in the early twentieth, Westerners tended to look upon the Japanese as intelligent and hard-working, with a highly developed sense of the aesthetic, but also as sexually and religiously amoral, imitative, and lacking in originality (Minear, 1980; Kiernan, 1969, pp. 180–186). World War II elicited hostile feelings among Westerners toward the Japanese and, since the war, Japan's economic prowess has caused considerable concern mixed with admiration. As Minear (1980) points out, even among eminent Western scholars of Japan, Basil Hall Chamberlain, George B. Sansom, and Edwin O. Reischauer, dichotomous views of Japan continued to prevail, at least of the Japan that existed before modernization. The dichotomy that persists is that of the West as being more intellectual, Japan as being, according to Sansom, part of the Asiatic pattern, primarily still an "aesthetic" one. But, inevitably, many Westerners today are confronted with the obvious evidence of Japan's modernity, as well as with its competitive edge. Thus, many such stereotypes are stale and out of date.

While romanticized images and Chinese products were favored in eighteenth-century Europe, India, in the nineteenth century, became the focus of a romantic movement to whose protagonists Hinduism had more to offer then than the humanistic and secular teachings of Confucious. Thus Friedrich Schlegel spoke of India as the source of the "Supreme Romanticism," and Baron von Eckstein believed that as

Greece had served the renaissance of the sixteenth century, India would serve the renaissance of the nineteenth century (Chaudhuri, 1978). Even in the twentieth century, Indian lore and the various sects that gather around popular gurus are of considerable interest to many Westerners, for instance, Aldous Huxley. To N. C. Chaudhuri, an astringent critic of his own people, the India the West looks to for salvation is mythical and, despite its "esoteric wisdom," incapable of enabling Indians themselves to cope with modern realities such as mass poverty. Similarly, Salman Rushdie, in a review of Attenborough's *Gandhi*, criticizes this Oscar-winning epic movie for catering to Western tastes, illusions, and "certain longings in the Western psyche" (July 1983). Among these illusions is the view of India as the "fountainhead of spiritual wisdom"; among the longings the thrill of seeing the sacrifice of a "perfect" man in history, and applauding revolutions that are nonviolent and therefore acceptable. Attenborough, Rushdie said, had turned this "crafty Gujarati lawyer" into a "celluloid guru," a "Christ," and in the process mangled history. While one need not accept what Chaudhuri and Rushdie have to say at face value, their views do suggest ways in which, from an Eastern perspective, Western perception of the East might tell more about the West than about the East. Today, as R. K. Narayan complains, the India in which most Westerners are interested remains the India of the Raj, of Kipling, and more recently of Paul Scott. According to Narayan, the West has little interest in independent India and even less knowledge.

Unlike the cultures of Hinduism, Confucianism, and Buddhism, toward which the West has had no reason to feel any strong hostility or sense of rivalry, Islam, ever since its founding and expansion in the seventh century, has constituted a challenge and a threat to the Christian West, at least until the eighteenth century when the West could lay its fears of Islam to rest. Before then, the West and Islam were in a state of physical confrontation—in Spain after the seventh century, in Palestine after the eleventh century, and on the marches of the Hapsburg Empire and Russia through the seventeenth century. The two were in a state of ideological conflict from Islam's inception, paradoxically, in part, because Islam and Christianity shared the same Judaic sources and reverence for many of the same prophets, including Abraham and Jesus. It was as this powerful enemy that Islam helped define Western contours and Western sense of self.

An extreme statement of the role of Islam in the formation of the West's identity was made by Henri Pirenne, the Belgian medievalist (1939). His thesis was that the rise and spread of Islam isolated

Europe economically, forced it upon its own, contributed thus to the spread of feudalism, and then to the rise of the defensive Carolingian Empire. While this theory is no longer accepted by medievalists, certainly not in the unqualified manner it was presented (Havighurst), the Pirenne theory represents an important and influential perception by a Westerner of the role of the Other, in this case Islam, in the making of the West. Although Pirenne gave primary emphasis to Islam, he also considered the inroads into Europe by pagan Hungarians from the east and Norsemen from the north to be important influences in the formation of the West.

Early images of Islam in the West were predominantly very negative, but not wholly so (Sénac; Daniel, 1962, 1966; Hay; Rodinson, 1980; Southern). Roger Bacon, for example, recognized the superior scholarship of the Muslim during the thirteenth century, at a time when much of the lore of Greece existed only in Arabic translation and commentary (Southern, p. 59). The most sophisticated universities were Muslim universities in Spain and North Africa; and it is a well-known fact that Saladin was highly admired as a Muslim leader in the West. Philippe Sénac observes that as the Turkish menace subsided, "One forgot Islam to only see in the Other a political power, a potential ally," and in 1493, when Pope Alexander VI received the Sultan's ambassador, "It was no longer the Christian West which was combatting Islam, but Europe receiving the Orient" (p. 162).

In general and even to this day, Muslims are regarded as "fanatics," cruel to women, licentious (eunuchs and harems are common stereotypic symbols), and despotic. Muhammad has been disparaged as an epileptic and a sensualist. During the Renaissance, "Arab" came to be identified with "Gothic"; both were equally pejorative terms to humanist scholars, and both were seen as aspects of the Dark Ages and of the heritage from which Western thinkers were then trying to break (Rodinson, 1980, pp. 50–51). During the Reformation, both Protestants and Catholics used references to Islam pejoratively in their mutual disparagement, and both Wycliffe and Luther suggested that the state of Christianity was, in their time, so abominable that even Islam was preferable (Southern, p. 75). During the Enlightenment, scholars spoke positively, on occasion, of both Islam and Confucianism; for example, Richard Simon expressed admiration for Muslim moralism; Pierre Bayle admired Muslim toleration; Voltaire saw parallels between Islam and the Deism he advocated (Rodinson, 1980, pp. 68–69), and Gibbon expressed admiration for Muhammad and for the unqualified monotheistic nature of Islam (Vol. 3, pp.

436–44). In this century, Antoine Galland published his monumental translation of the *Arabian Nights* that still enriches the imagination of the West.

In the nineteenth century, the view generally shared by Western scholars, was that Islam was in a state of decline, was even decadent, compared to its golden age before the thirteenth century. The leading Muslim state, the Ottoman Empire, was in a state of anemia, was "the sick man of Europe" who was more to be feared in death— because of Western rivalries over his carcass—than in life. Some alarm, however, was felt in the late nineteenth century, a parallel to the fear of the Yellow Peril, regarding "Pan-Islamism," a "revival" of Islam that might threaten the structure of Western imperial control. This myth has taken on new life since the Iranian Revolution.

Uses of the Other, utilitarian and often disparaging, are common to all civilizations, not only Western ones, and serve to enhance self-confidence as well as to confirm identity. From the seventeenth century through the nineteenth, Western pride and confidence in its own culture grew until the Western civilizations became one, in Western eyes, with civilization itself. To the Dutch philosopher Grotius, Europe excelled in arms and industry, in the gentleness of its customs, and in its liberty. To Gibbon in the eighteenth century, the free West was in the vanguard of the progress that involved the constant increase of "the real wealth, the happiness, the knowledge, and perhaps the virtue, of the human race" (vol. 2, pp. 436–44). And in the nineteenth century, Hegel proclaimed that "The history of the world travel from East to West, for Europe is absolutely the end of history . . . The East knows and to the present knows only *One* is free . . . the Germans would know that *all* are free" (1857, p. 90). Hegel's notion was that Europe had reached the highest level of human self-consciousness and inner as well as outer freedom. Lowest on the scale of civilization was Africa, continent of "the Unhistorical, Undeveloped Spirit, still involved in the conditions of mere nature"; India and China were at intermediate stages in the self-fulfillment of the Idea. And Karl Marx, drawing upon and radically transforming Hegel's vision, although hardly enthusiastic about the capitalistic West, nevertheless put Europe in the vanguard of history, its mission being to awaken the static East, which was incapable of arousing itself from its torpor (Avineri, 1968; Gellner, 1983; Turner, 1978).

One document that makes evident the West's self-satisfaction in the nineteenth century is the eleventh edition of the *Encyclopedia Britannica*, published November 1, 1918. The contributors to the Encyclopedia claimed that volumes contained the general consensus of opinion of "countries which represent Western civilization." This civilization was in the vanguard of progress, and progress, *inter alia*, involved the organic betterment of man, the diminishing of international jealousies (!), the lessening of the amount spent on arms, and the increasing economic unification of the world (Koning, 1981). Clearly, some of the material was written before the World War and was left unrevised. Regarding non-Europeans, this apogee of Western self-confidence, as Hans Koning (1981) calls it, was generally disparaging: Western dominance was the result of lack of grit on the part of others; Negroes have a natural criminal tendency; the Chinese are inferior in character, Haitians are ignorant and lazy; "Mahommedans" are lax and lascivious; the Arab, in particular, lacks an eye for the straight and hence cannot form a right angle; and an Arab servant cannot place a cloth "square on the table." These are among the gems Koning found in his reading of this summation of the nineteenth century.

Other randomly selected illustrations of Western self-confidence might include Bismarck's attitude toward the "Eastern Question" in which he did not think Germany need or should become involved. A delegate at the Congress of Berlin of 1878 said of his view: "Prince Bismarck never misses an opportunity to make it known that . . . the eastern question, in so far as it concerns peoples and form of governments situated, so to speak, outside the circle of European civilization and having no future, ought to have no interest for Europe apart from the consequences that it can have on the relations of the great European powers with each other" (Craig, p. 511). Another illustration is found in Elias Canetti's autobiography. It describes his running into an old acquaintance from his childhood in Bulgaria: "I took him no more seriously than anything or anyone in that supposedly 'barbaric' Balkan period. And now . . . I was astonished at how much he knew, how much he was interested in. He had kept up with the progress of science . . . I expected nothing of the people who lived there and suddenly crossed my path in 'Europe' " (pp. 84–85).

On the eve of World War I, important intellectual developments, in particular the scientific breakthroughs of Freud and Einstein, caused the optimistic world of the nineteenth century to crumble and the "rationality" of man to be questioned. However, the faith in Western superiority, for most Westerners, continued until after World War I. Even after World War II, it made no sense to statesmen of the older generation such as de Gaulle and Churchill to contemplate the end of Western tutorship over the colonized peoples. Churchill declared that he refused to preside over the liquidation of the British Empire and de Gaulle, at the Brazzaville Conference (January–February, 1944), while agreeing that the French empire should be thoroughly liberalized, made clear that under no circumstances would his government contemplate independence for the various colonies. De Gaulle, but not Churchill, was wise enough to soon realize that the winds of change made it imperative to reconsider France's imperial role. He did effectively participate in the ending of the French empire, but only, one suspects, because he felt France's still universal role was now to work with the Third World as senior partner rather than as master.

Almost as sanguine in proclaiming Western superiority as Gibbon was in the eighteenth century has been Hans Kohn in the twentieth. To Kohn, in contrast to "older and contemporary dogmatic and authoritarian ways of life" that encourage "uniformity," the West emphasizes diversity, a critical and practical approach to problems, and the use of science as a means to solve social problems (pp. 31–34). Unlike others, Western civilization is based upon the belief in equal rights for all and in the dignity and humanity of every individual, and it welcomes opposition and criticism—in sum it embodies "the concept of a free man and a free mind in an open society" (p. 37). No previous civilization, Kohn insists, has had such vitality and dynamism, and its very existence has been as important for mankind as the birth of human self-consciousness in what Karl Jaspers calls the "axial time," the sixth century B.C., during which Confucius, Buddha, Lao-tzu, the Greeks, and the Hebrews appeared (Jaspers, 1953). Today, Kohn believes that Western civilization has become global, the common property of mankind.[2]

In the process of empire-building, partly from self interest, partly from conviction, Western policy and theory came to reflect not only this Eurocentrism, but even the racist notion that the Western races as well as their cultures were superior, that non-Europeans were incapable of sustaining a Western way of life, which represented the acme of civilization.

One example of this Eurocentric tendency was the reinterpretation of the idea of a "protectorate." Once viewed as a reciprocal, contractual relationship between ruler and ruled, the protectorate was transformed to include the unqualified domination of the latter by the former; this, in fact, occurred in the course of the absorption by the West of almost all of the African continent (H. Wilson, pp. 83–84; Gong). International law, Wilson suggests, was thus turned into

European law and applied according to Western decision and interpretation. Another case of Eurocentrism was the adoption by some French colonial leaders of the English theory of indirect rule, of "association," in place of the Jacobin universalist ideal of assimilation into French civilization. One reason for this Western shift to ethnocentrism was the influence of anthropologist Gustave Le Bon, who argued that races were distinct in character. The most important treatise on the subject was Jules Harmand's influential *Domination et colonisation* published in 1910. France, he argued, should realize that her colonial charges were culturally different and should so be treated, rather than being considered fully capable of becoming French and European; France should rule them through their own leaders and institutions in a spirit of coexistence. In the context of the times, such Frenchmen who rejected the ideal of assimilation were, in a sense, repudiating their own ideal of human equality and fraternity. For example, in the 1950s Raymond Aron was accused of abandoning French liberal (assimilationist) values by recommending that independence be given to Algeria. This was an unfair criticism because by then, as he pointed out, the rise of Algerian nationalism and the population explosion among the Muslim Algerians precluded genuine assimilation, which he would have supported. Attempts to achieve assimilation would have required exorbitant amounts of money to raise the Muslims to the same economic and social level as the French and the use of genocidal tactics to wipe out those involved in the national movement (Aron, 1957, 1958).

The rationalization for the imperialist control of others by the West was often a confusion between the claim to cultural and to racial superiority—thus Jules Harmand could say that the French had a duty to assist the colonized "because we belong to the highest race, the highest civilization" (1910, p. 156). The distinction between racial and cultural superiority is important because, if the basis for domination is cultural, the native, in principle, can become free by adopting this culture while, if the claim is racial, the native can never hope to transcend his condition. Contrary to professed Christian and democratic principles many Westerners, sadly, came to see their colonial charges in racial and racist terms.

Racism, of course, has not been unique to the West, nor has it been a new phenomenon in the West during the nineteenth century when it became so widespread. What was new was the claim that racial differences were based upon scientific research; science with all of its contemporary prestige was invoked to buttress prejudice and ignorance (Gould; W. I. Cohen; E. Said, 1978). Peoples were now ranked hierarchically, from the inferior to the superior, their position in the hierarchy determined by language, craniometry, skin pigmentation, or intelligence tests, all seen as measures of both intelligence and of character. Paul Broca defended slavery; Cesare Lambroso worked out a typology of criminality; H. H. Goddard, R. M. Yerkes, and Arthur Jansen connected findings of intelligence tests to racial characteristics and ability. As distinguished a scholar and intellectual as Ernest Renan ranked peoples according to the philological characteristics of their language, with Western languages being considered superior to Semitic languages. Count Joseph Arthur Gobineau could claim that the Western races were threatened with decadence through miscegenation. With the same pseudo-scientific self-confidence (Mason), Charles Darwin's theories were distorted to accommodate the social and economic characteristics that supported imperialism and colonial domination. Cecil Rhodes could unabashedly state: "We are the first race in the world, and, the more of the world we inhabit, the better it is for the human race" (Goonetilleke, p. 143).

Racism as a rationalization or justification for imperialism or any other form of behavior persists, of course, on a popular level, but whatever academic or scientific rationale it once claimed has largely collapsed with the fall of Hitler. However, claims to cultural superiority persist. Such claims, even though less ignoble than racial prejudice, can be even less logical as a rationale for empire than racism, especially for a culture that upholds human autonomy and believes with Rousseau, Kant, Hegel, and the Declaration of the Rights of Man, that all men are born free and have the potential to be free. During their revolution against French rule, it was not unreasonable for Algerians to argue that they were simply applying to their condition what they had learned in French schools, or for the Vietnamese, lacking battle hymns of their own, to have sung the Marsellaise as they attacked the French at Dien Bien Phu. It can be argued, in fact, that the reason for the short life span of the Western empires, for the rapidity of the process of political decolonization, was the war-weariness and exhaustion suffered by the European powers. As James Morris regretfully admitted in *Farewell the Trumpets* (1980), imperial control was incompatible with the ideal of self-determination. Ironically, the ideal of self-determination, rooted in the political philosophy of Rousseau, Herder, Mazzini, and later, Woodrow Wilson—denied the Europeans a valid moral argument for maintaining their empires.

Even with the end of the Western empires, however, the belief in Western superiority, while it has dwindled among many, still persists in the notion that the West is the model for the developing world, the prototype of the Third World's future. Denis de Rougement proposes: "Europe since its birth has performed a function that is not only universal but also universalizing. It has aroused the World, first by exploiting it, then by furnishing the political and technical means for a future unity of 'mankind' " (A. Gaspard). Hans Kohn suggests that the unique superiority of the West now seems to diminish only because the Western "revolution has become global" (p. 58). And Jacques Ellul, in an excoriating attack on the decadence of the modern West, still insists: "The end of the West today would mean the end of any possible civilization" (vii) and "all peoples are now "western" (viii). According to one of the fervent practitioners of the fad of futurology, Alvin Toffler, the futurist game is largely a Western one judging by the membership of the World Future Society whose typical member has been white and Western (1972, p. 7). This is perhaps why so much of the material produced by futurists consists of projections made on the basis of the present Western society and its state of technology, the assumption being that the rest of the globe, including the Third World, will be absorbed into a common world evolution, or devolution, determined in the West. In *The Futurists*, an anthology edited by Toffler, the exceptions to the general Eurocentrism of the authors are few. Among the references to the Third World is Eric Jantsch's "For a Science of Man" (pp. 211–32) in which the author pessimistically suggests that, because of limited future resources, only the rich will benefit from progress and the gap between rich and poor will expand to the point of explosion. He proposes that, in the meantime, China and India, among other Asian countries, be consulted regarding ways of handling our ecological problems, because the West has not done a very impressive job. John McHale writes, in "The Plastic Parthenon," a wildly optimistic, futuristic scenario in which all individuals enjoy "psychic mobility" and can choose any style of life they wish. He credits Sarkis Atamian with the notion that Western television programs and movies are preparing the Third World to think "planetary," more specifically, to adopt an optimistic view of history by seeing good guys come to good rather than bad ends, as in their traditional literature! In his *The Third Wave*, Alvin Toffler, himself an optimist and enthusiast, does take the Third World into consideration to an unusually generous extent. His theme, in brief, is that the technology of the Second Wave (heavy industry) is becoming obsolete and is now being replaced by the technology of the "Third Wave" in which new computer processes, a general communications revolution, sources of energy and automation will reverse the processes of urban centralization and create a world of "prosumers" who, instead of holding down "jobs" will be able to devote their time to self-cultivation. The Third World, considered in a chapter entitled "Gandhi with Satellites," can, in this new era, end its problems of indebtedness, mass unemployment, dependence, and general misery, *unless* the West sells it on the cynical philosophy that it should concentrate on small industry and agricultural development. Should such advice be followed, the Third World will be driven back to the primitive level of the "First Wave." However fanciful Toffler may be, he, unlike many of his Western colleagues, is concerned with how the Third World might be integrated into his future schema. This schema, however, a Western one, based on the technological and scientific revolutions of the West, producing a cosmopolitan culture fashioned according to Western values. As André Malraux once said, "Europe still defends the highest intellectual values in the world. To know this it is enough to try to imagine that she no longer exists" (Gaspard).

3

Western Empire: Conscience and Consciousness of the Other

It is not strange that few Europeans before World War I were particularly bothered by matters of conscience regarding their sway over much of the rest of the world. This was as true of the Left as of the Right. Conscience, rather than condemning imperial expansion, condoned imperialism as a way to bring "civilization" to others. As Philip Curtin (1971) points out, imperialism in its heyday was so complicated and variegated a phenomenon that it still escapes easy definition. It can be said that its various expressions were based on the commonly held conviction among many Europeans that they were "civilized," while non-Europeans were not. Most Westerners continued to hold this view well into the twentieth century. While French colonialism tended to be relatively free of racism, this was less true of Anglo-Saxon colonialism. As T. E. Lawrence wrote in *Seven Pillars of Wisdom*, the assimilationist French considered imitation of their ways flattery, while the British regarded imitation of themselves parody (p. 347). Evelyn Waugh obtained much of his humorous effect in *Black Mischief* by treating native ways as parodies of the West (Anne Zahlan, pp. 48–52). In Burgess's Malayan quartet, *The Long Day Wanes*, Fenella, the protagonist wife, when she first joins Crabbe, says in the spirit of the memsahib she is to become, "Where is this glamorous East they talk about? It's just a horrible sweating travesty of Europe" (p. 111). Rushdie in *Midnight's Children* has his protagonist say that in India everything English turns into parody. Nirad Chaudhuri has gone so far as to hold this snobbish exclusiveness responsible for the British failure to truly "Westernize" India (1954).

While Waugh could claim that in the 1930s, when he wrote *Black Mischief*, it was "an anachronism that any part of Africa should be independent of European administration," Conrad, Joyce Cary, and

Forster were already questioning the morality and wisdom of Western imperial rule (Zahlan, p. 52, n. 25). Jonah Raskin, the American radical Black, in *The Mythology of Imperialism*, insisted that there was even among these critics of empire, worthy as they were, a reluctance, certainly regarding Africa, to move from criticism of empire to the advocacy of independence or of revolution. Raskin's belief was that, even among the most sensitive white Westerners, fear of blackness and of the abyss of anarchy dictated their views of the Other. Doubtless, he would feel the same about postludes to empire written by the Updikes and the Naipauls of today. It is also true that in spite of the protagonists' sensitivity and the empathy with the "natives" in classics such as Orwell's *Burma Days* and Forster's *Passage to India*, there are significant reservations, however obliquely presented. In *Burma Days*, reservations about Flory's denunciation of the British empire as purely mercantile and even thievish, destructive of native culture, and leaving a legacy of nothing but football and whiskey drinking, appear in the mouth of his friend D. Veraswami who insists that England has brought social and economic progress to Burma. In *Passage to India*, Fielding, in spite of his love and friendship for Aziz, deplores Aziz's attitude toward women, his fatalism and verbalism, and the multiplicity of gods in whom he believes. As Raskin emphasized, these keepers of the Western conscience could not quite shed their Western identification and their feeling that, in spite of all of its faults, the West was man's best hope. Joyce Cary spoke for many when, in his *The Case for African Freedom*, he predicted chaos for Africa should the British leave and in the foreward George Orwell expressed his agreement.

Conscience

Eurocentric as Western views of empire were even among some of its critics, imperialism did have Western opponents even before World War I, opponents who pointed to the disparity between the values of imperialism and the values of individual autonomy, derived from Western humanism, the Enlightenment, and the Christian tradition.

After World War I, increasing numbers of Westerners began to feel guilty about ruling over others. This mood was exacerbated by the propagation of the democratic ideals of Wilson, the socialist ideas of the Russian Revolution, the fact that thousands of native troops from Africa and Asia had spilled their blood upon the battlefields of eastern France, and the brutality of the war itself, which hardly held up Western civilization for admiration. Western writers were deeply troubled by both the threat of the dystopian potential of the modern West and the hubris of its imperialist pretension, both of which were seen as humiliating to the autonomy and dignity of individual human beings.

Expressions of such loss of faith in Western civilization among Western intellectuals and artists multiplied after the horror of World War I. Already the sweep of criticism had been anticipated by a few figures, including Nietzsche, Spengler, and Burckhardt, but it had become a sign of Western civilization's loss of faith in itself. Even Hans Kohn (1962), while maintaining his confidence in the West, admitted that after World War I "confidence in the validity of Western civilization" had been "undermined and destroyed" for many, that a "spiritual fatigue" had found expression (p. 62). Among the dark prophets were Arnold J. Toynbee; Karl Jaspers (1949) who wondered if modern man had not cut himself off from "being" itself, Denis de Rougement who wondered if Western man had not totally abandoned the essential Christian ground of his own heritage (1977, pp. 139–40); the ever melodramatic Jacques Ellul who pronounced "The West is at its end" for having rejected Agape for Eros (1978, p. 200); and Raymond Aron who, in his posthumously published *Mémoires*, expressed dismay at the feeling of "nihilism" infecting the West, and at the fact that the rest of the world was absorbing only Western technology and not its liberalism (1983, pp. 727–28). Others, less pessimistically, argued that the West needed the East to recover nature and the aesthetic dimension of living. So argued, in different ways, F. S. C. Northrop and Jacques Berque (1964). As for the "dystopian," the H. G. Wells who wrote the optimistic *Modern Utopia* also wrote *The Time Machine: An Invention* (1895) and *When the Sleeper Awakes* (1899). In the latter work, he anticipates Aldous Huxley's *Brave New World*, in which individual autonomy is destroyed by technology.

Among those who have written both dystopias and anti-imperialist novels, are George Orwell, E. M. Forster, Anthony Burgess, and Aldous Huxley. Gone were the days of imperial glorification and self-congratulation—of Kipling whom Orwell (1956) saw as a "jingo imperialist . . . morally insensitive . . . aesthetically disgusting." The imperial venture was now portrayed as a shabby and arrogant affair represented by the exclusive white club; the insensitive memsahib, the Westernized native snubbed, or worse, by the Europeans, his white English friend humiliated or defeated while trying to help him. The empire was now often seen reflecting Orwell's beatitudes in *Burma*

Days: keeping up one's prestige; the firm hand; white men hanging together; even if this last tradition could, on occasion, be racially interpreted by invoking the myth of Ham to justify imperial control.

Before World War I, Western Marxists and other Socialists, while they may have seen imperialism abroad as progressive in arousing the "East" from its lethargy, nevertheless denounced its practices as cruel and ruthless, its motivation, greed, its rationale, to give the ultimately doomed system of capitalism a temporary respite. Political leaders in the tradition of French Jacobinism, denounced the imperialist policies of the Opportunists as did Clemenceau on July 30, 1885 when he condemned Jules Ferry's intrusions into Tunisia and Indo-China as based upon the false code of racial superiority. Its justification—the "civilizing mission"—he said was a hoax that joined "violence to hypocrisy" (Lacouture-Baumier, pp. 51–52). Clemenceau's anti-imperialism was in line with the Condorcets, Brissots, Abbé Grégoires, Abbé Raynals, and Diderots of the Enlightenment and the French Revolution, the liberal political tradition that Vietnamese and Algerians were later to turn against France.

In England, as in France, there was an anti-imperialist minority even during the hey-day of imperial expansion (Kroebner-Schmidt, pp. 221–49). "Little Englanders" included John Atkinson Hobson, John Morley, and Goldwin Smith. Of considerable importance in arousing disgust with the imperial venture was the Boer War, which did so much to tarnish England's tradition of "not giving them an inch, or they'll take a mile," and *esprit de corps*. Literature written between the world wars indicates, if not a "loss of nerve" regarding empire, a loss of enthusiasm. Consider Paul Scott's Sarah Layton in *A Division of Spoils*: "I could finish with India before it quite finished with me, rusted me up, corrupted me utterly with a false sense of duty and false sense of superiority." After World War II, it became obvious that the era of Western imperial rule was over; writers in this anti-imperialist tradition saw those Westerners who remained or returned—Victor Crabbe in Burgess, Mountolive in Lawrence Durrell, the Quiet American in Graham Greene, and the Smalleys in Scott's *Staying On*—as irrelevant, irresponsible, or pathetic.

Parallel to opposition to empire and imperialism on the part of Westerners, has been, on an epistemological level, the phenomenon of Western intellectuals and scholars who have challenged the traditional Western view disparaging of the East and of the Third World. Such scholars and intellectuals have sought, particularly in recent years, to undo the harm done by popular stereotypes and by the skewed and ethnocentric views of earlier and contemporary scholars. In regard to Western public opinion in general, Norman Daniel wrote, "Dominant was the notion that Islam was a sexually corrupt tyranny based on false teaching. It would be hard to show a basic change in opinion in these respects from the eleventh century to the twentieth" (1966, p. xvi).

The opinions and attitudes of Western administrators and officers toward Muslims were usually those of superiority and contempt (Mansfield, pp. 497–99). Some scholars also served as advisors to colonial authorities, for example, Snouck Hurgronje to the Dutch authorities in Indonesia (Grimal, p. 106). In one position paper he advised the government to win over the Indonesian aristocracy as an ally against the "epidemic of Panislamism" among the masses, and more gradually win over the masses themselves through slow political assimilation. Such ethnocentrism has been largely overcome or at least addressed by Western scholars of the East. With regard to Islam, the tendency to reduce the culture of Muslims to that of the "classical" model and then to assume that all deviations from this culture are deteriorations, has been seen as dangerously aberrant by scholars such as Kenneth Cragg, Montgomery Watt, and W. C. Smith, all of whom have written about Islam with sympathy and sensitivity. Smith, in particular, has been congratulated as an anti-Orientalist for refusing to reduce "Islam" to a religion or the term "Muslim" to a noun; "Islam," he insists, is a faith (not a thing), and "Muslim" is an adjective strictly designating one who has this faith (Pruett). All of these scholars would condemn any tendency to homogenize Islam or to reduce it to a single series of dogmatic precepts and would agree with Norman Daniel, who has devoted much of his scholarly life to exposing the intolerance of Westerners, that the record of Western Orientalism has, indeed, not always been one of objectivity and of fairness. Other Western scholars who share this critical view of Orientalism are Roger Owen (1973), Jacques Berque, and Bryan Turner (1978, from a Marxist vantage). With regard to Asia in general, Orientalism is questioned in the essays of Olivier Zunz (*Reliving the Past*), on an even more general level of reflection regarding the possibility of knowing the Other in Clifford Geertz (TLS, 7 June 1985), and in the works of Claude Lévi Strauss, especially *Tristes Tropiques*. A summary of the views regarding Islam now deplored by many regenerated Western scholars is reflected in Peter Brown's words: "Ever since the early Middle Ages, Europe's view of the East has been blocked by a major civilization whose features were all the more disquieting for bearing

so strange a family resemblance to its own Judaeo-Christian and
Greek inheritance . . . As a result, no other non-European civilization
has been so persistently gagged and bridled by European stereotypes
as has Islam" (1979).

Today there are many Western students who would subscribe to the
view expressed by Henri Brunschwig in the conclusion of his well-
known interpretative study *French Colonialism*, that imperial control
had not been needed to introduce the Third World to modernity or
to bring them into the international system of trade: imperial domination only forced the pace of history, made modernization abrupt
and sometimes violent and traumatic; imperialization caused psychic
damage through the humiliation of others; imperialization was a "vast
error," since the West could have expanded just as easily without
conquest; imperialization has left a legacy of exploitation by an
indigenous Westernized class that has, with liberation, taken over
from the European. As categorical is David Lamb in his popular
account of contemporary Africa: the colonial experience in Africa
was "overwhelmingly negative"; it left behind an infrastructure that
Africans had not been trained to manage; it bequeathed dependence,
and left a "lingering inferiority complex, a confused sense of identity"
(pp. 136–64). This perspective is shared by John Entelis regarding
ex-French Algeria (1986, pp. 69–70). In a later chapter, some other,
more positive views of the Western colonial legacy will be considered,
but few would today deny that at least for some peoples and for some
parts of the world the bitterness exhibited by Brunschwig and Lamb
is justified. But whatever judgment is finally made, barely two decades
after the end of World War II and hardly more than a half a century
since 1900 when the Western empires seemed to be solid and permanent, formal Western control over most parts of the world came to an
end.

There were many factors involved in this rapid ending of empire,
among them war exhaustion; the loss of prestige suffered by the
Western powers in the Far East at the hands of Japan; the demographic factor, combined with the moral factor of nationalism among
the colonized peoples; the interests of the United States in opening
new economic empires; of the Soviet Union in encouraging defections
from the international capitalist system; and the conviction of many
Westerners that imperialism was morally and ideologically obsolete
(Barraclough, 1967, pp. 153–98; H. Wilson, pp. 179–85). This obso-
lescence had been apparent even before World War I. The West had
been defied successfully by the Japanese in 1904–1905 when they

defeated Russia, and by Turkey, who emerged as a sovereign republic after World War I in spite of the initial enmity of the victorious Western powers. The end had already been anticipated in Wilson's Fourteen Points, predecessor to the Atlantic Charter of 1941. Both were used to justify the Allied side in the two world wars by solemnly stating values and principles that were, obviously, as applicable to the East as to the West.

But while the bite of conscience led to the West's abandoning her empires and empathizing with the Third World nations emerging after World War I, there still remained sceptics, who have rejected feelings of guilt or shame.

The Unrepentants

At the extreme, these unrepentants consider that those who feel guilt over the West's imperialism exhibit "failure of nerve," are "bleeding hearts," and they insist that, cruelty aside, the West did a great deal for those she once colonized by providing them with Western values and institutions, still precious, still worth protecting and promoting.

A more moderate position is taken by scholars such as Jacques Berque and Maxime Rodinson, who are often critical of the West and sympathetic to the Third World, but who refuse to sacrifice their loyalty to the West, to France (in these particular cases), and to certain Western values, "critical objectivity" in particular (Berque, 1978, pp. 181–82; Rodinson, 1980). Rodinson, in particular, defends as an important Western contribution the critical historical method as a dissolvant of cultural dogmatism, a method by which Western scholars "demystified" their own religious scriptures, and a method that he, Rodinson, could in good faith apply to even as sensitive a subject as the Prophet without being guilty of either "ethnocentric" or "colonialist" intent (1980, pp. 120–21, 142, 152; 1961, p. 14). Similarly, he warns against a new *Jdanovism* that can lead to the suppression of all criticism coming from the Other because this is regarded as "ideologically tinctured" (1980, p. 152).

Exasperated by his critics, Ernest Gellner complains of being beset by "neo-Marxists eager to extend the thesis of perpetual change by young anthropologists keen to defy the functionalist paradigm, by historians anxious to stress the indispensability of their own craft in an age of expansionist social sciences, by nationalists or guilt-expiating Westerners intent on denouncing the stability/stagnation doctrine [Gellner's view] as a piece of colonialist denigration" (1981, p. 83). Other examples of defenders of the West might include Jean Daniel and Raymond Aron, both of whom have argued that one of the best contributions the West could make to the Third World is to remain true to its own best values (Daniel, *L'Express*, 30 November 1962; Aron, 1983, pp. 664–66, 725–26).

At the more intransigent extreme of our imaginary spectrum one might place Jean-Pierre Péroncel-Hugoz who, in a recent popular work with no apologies (except to say he respects "true" Islam), describes present-day Islam as culturally reactionary, obscurantist, sterile, and cruel to women; André Siegfried who was wont to take a similar line, arguing that the ideals of true social progress and humaneness could only have come from the West; and economists like P. T. Bauer who, in the final analysis, hold the Third World and not the West responsible for its own backwardness and poverty. Pascal Bruckner at times waxes racist in his fervent defense of the West: "What's Qaddafi but a Bedouin version of Mussolini? Khomeini is a Robespierre disguised as Ali Baba and a Torquemeda who knows how to manipulate the masses" (p. 141). Not much allowance for what is of genuine Islamic provenance here. And as for Friedrich von Hayek, when he was asked what one should do for the Third World, he answered his interviewer from *La Vie Fran aise* (17 January 1983): "Nothing, nothing, we should do nothing . . . At least we can save the Occident." While it was unclear exactly what Hayek had in mind, one might surmise that he spoke for many Westerners who, in a situation of *sauve qui peut*, would opt for the West with little hesitation. Use was made of Hayek's statement in *Le Monde*, in any case, by an Algerian to lambaste the West by showing its heartlessness in the North-South confrontation (Le M, 21 May 1983).

An obvious source of Western guilt feelings has been the record of Western imperialism; and, as one might expect, many of the unrepentant defend it as ultimately beneficial to the world, however morally checkered it might have been. David Landes, for example, suggests that "Poor countries can learn from, if not copy, the Western example . . . the West is the only successful example around" (NYRB, 29 May 1986, pp. 46–49); and William Pfaff contends that the "Western agenda" is the agenda of the post-colonial world, "whether it likes it or not," and that Third World "conversion" has been to Western values, not only to Western technology (S, pp. 65–81).

One position has it that the chief criticism that can be made of

Western imperialism is that it did not go far enough and that it ended too soon. This case has been made, albeit in differing ways, by Herbert Luthy, James (Jane) Morris, and D. K. Fieldhouse (Luthy, 1955, 1957, 1966; Morris, 1965; Fieldhouse, 1966).

Luthy's thesis, in broad strokes, is that the mission assigned to the West in history was "uncompleted," and this mission was to integrate the world into a united order and into a single global civilization, a *civilization universelle*. The West abdicated this responsibility because of its own inability to transcend diversity and fragmentation and prevent internal civil war. Nonetheless, the groundwork for a universal civilization (and history) were laid as Western-educated and -oriented leaders took over control of the successor states to empire, whether these leaders were Marxists or liberals. In support of his thesis, and in accordance with this thesis, Luthy reviewed G. B. Pannikar's *Asia and Western Dominance* (1955) praising it, in spite of some reservations, for openly recognizing that Great Britain had contributed much to the making of India—the civil service, the groundwork for democratic government, the institutionalization of equality before the law, and English as a common unifying language. In spite of its sins, India, after the days of the Raj, could never return, Pannikar recognized, to its "millenial immutability."

If India had benefited much from the British presence, other parts of the world had not; with the end of empire, the path toward modernization and the adoption of a universal cosmopolitan culture, was still an arduous one, one the West still had a responsibility to abet indirectly if no longer directly, according to Luthy. James Morris, while admitting the uglier side of imperialism, nevertheless has continued to express respect along with considerable nostalgia for the days of the British empire. Angry at American criticism of the empire, he submitted statements in its defense to *The Saturday Evening Post* in 1965 and to *The New York Times* in 1978 (NYT, 4 August 1978). Good government, he argues, which Britain did provide, is preferable to "self-determination" (the latter being the American-sponsored principle that did most to undermine Western empires), and, with all of its faults, the British empire did bring order and progress to much of the world that now knows only chaos.

Fieldhouse, answering some of the Marxist interpretations of empire as a phenomenon of exploitative capitalism, points out that in most cases the Western nations did not benefit economically from the colonies, that profits abroad were not dependent upon colonial control, and that the loss of colonies has not affected the Western imperial nations negatively (from the economic point of view) (pp. 380–90). Like Luthy, however, he does blame the Western powers for having failed, in regard both to "duty and self-interest," to better prepare the colonized to assume the responsibilities of independence (p. 410).

Others who share the perspective of these three are J. H. Plumb (1965), Duignan and Gann, Kedouri (1970) and J. B. Kelly, particularly the latter two who hold the West responsible for abandoning many people, especially minorities, to very cruel fates when they abdicated imperial responsibility. In this context, L. Carl Brown makes the point that if variables such as length of time of imperial rule or relative lightness of the oppressiveness exerted are present, the result, as in the case of Tunisia, can prove fruitful and provide the basis for a genuinely modernizing society after independence (L. C. Brown, 1964). Another special point made in recent years by Third World sympathizers and harsh critics of the imperial experience, such as Jacques Julliard, is that since independence the record of many new states regarding human rights is so bad that one should at least entertain the possibility that the principle of national sovereignty should no longer be allowed to block international intervention, whether such states in question are pro-Western police states, or socialist totalitarian states such as Cambodia, Vietnam, or Guinée under Sékou Touré. Such intervention would of course be denounced as neo-imperialism and gun-boat diplomacy. Julliard would apparently pay this moral price.

Needless to say, to many Third World ideologues those referred to here as "unrepentants," especially the more intransigent, illustrate and prove the continuing hostility of the West and its unabashed "neo-colonialism." This has been even more true of Western attitudes that border on the hysterical and hateful, attitudes that might be seen as a form of nightmare, with the peoples of the Third World as the specter.

Nightmares and the Third World

The vision of the rising of the Yellow Race, and the sweep of Pan-Islamism haunted the late nineteenth and early twentieth centuries. Among those who took the first threat seriously were Rudyard Kipling and Lothrop Stoddard. An American writer about international affairs, Stoddard, within a two year period wrote two volumes, *Tide of*

Color against White Supremacy (1920) and *The New World of Islam* (1921) (Rodinson, 1980; Kiernan, 1969, pp. 170–72).

Today, the threat of Pan-Islamism has been revived with talk of the "rise of Islam" and "the crescent of crisis," following the Iranian revolution. In *The Race War* (1966–1967), Ronald Segal presented the classic statement of the impending violent rise of the peoples of the Third World, ground into misery of starvation in the world system against the West. This would happen, according to Segal, when the "colored" of the world recognized that the common source of their suffering was the West, and that "wealth and want have different skins," that, for example, the average income of an Indian was only one twentieth that of an Australian (p. 393). In Segal's vision, South Africa prefigured the reality of what was to become universal; Japan, only a "satrap" of the West, was irrelevant as a model because it was modernized before being swamped by the population explosion; and Russia, in the final analysis more white than red, would only help the liberal West to try to police the world against the "colored."

There was obviously much to question in Segal's projection into the future—for example, would the "colored" with their often deep mutual hostilities and rivalries be able to cooperate? Colonel Qadhafi might, as he did in Harare (Zimbabwe) during the conference of non-aligned powers, talk of an international army to "spread fire under the feet of America" to the accompanying chant of four women in uniform: "Down, down, U.S.A.!" But at the same time he called the Third World gutless and helpless (NYT, 5 September 1986). Sadly, hatreds and rivalries divide much of the Third World among itself. A survey of 1986 in the *New York Times* (4 January 1987) showed that during the year over six hundred had died in the Punjab as a result of sectarian violence (Sikh versus Hindu); in Karnataka state seventeen were killed in Muslim-Hindu clashes; in north-east India, there were reports of battles and deaths as a result of Gurkha agitation for a separate state; and in Tamil-Nader in the south, riots against the use of the Hindi language led to the death of 19,000 persons. These are only some of the cases of inter-Indian violence. In April of 1985, at an international conference, the "non-aligned," as Kieran Cooke pointed out, were unable to even mention the politically divisive issues of the Iran-Iraq war, Kampuchea, or Afghanistan (CSM, 29 April 1985). In 1987 there were clashes between Sinhalese Buddhists and Tamil Hindus in Ceylon, Christians and Muslims in Nigeria and Egypt, and Zulus and other tribal groups in South Africa. As for Lebanon, the once proud example of inter-sectarian coexistence had, by 1987, long replaced northern Ireland as symbol of fanatic inter-religious violence.

Segal's impending war was related to the extraordinary demographic expansion of the human race, what Kiernan (1969, p. 172) calls the "vertigo of numbers," evoking images of "fecundity" and "hordes" overflowing the "ant-hills" of the Third World. While there are claims that the population explosion of the globe can be handled by science and technology—Herman Kahn's (1970) for example—the figures are alarming, and in an analytical review of current literature on the problem of overpopulation, Jonathon Lieberson concluded that, yes, the problems of overpopulation could be overcome by technology, but only in areas of the globe where development was advanced. In much of the Third World, overpopulation will remain a tragic issue.

For serious socio-cultural and religious reasons, the problem of population increase has not received enough attention. In many areas, the convictions of some Third World leaders, until recently, has been that the West has appealed for population controls only as a means to protect its own dominance by rendering the Third World less explosive and less demanding. John Waterbury contends that this thesis is not all that fanciful (1978, p. 60). Under President Reagan, a reversal has taken place; Third World leaders have been asking for help to curb population growth, and the United States is taking a laissez-faire position except in the matter of abortion, which the Reagan administration is reluctant to support with federal funds. But the statistics will not go away; population growth, so unequal between North and South, can only reinforce the disparity between rich and poor—Segal's nightmare refuses to disappear and was renewed by Geoffrey Barraclough in his pessimistic survey of North-South relations (1978). On the right, John Lukacs sees massive migration of Third World peoples into the United States as a greater threat to national integrity than even the U.S.S.R. In his view, large portions of the Republic are beginning to resemble the Third World (p. 156), and Third World "savagery had already penetrated large areas of the United States" (p. 84). These are apocalyptical statements.

Deeply disturbing is the hostility and cruelty shown by the Western host to the migrant worker. They are unfairly accused of causing unemployment and are held responsible for polluting the atmosphere with their customs and culinary tastes. Distaste and fear are reinforced by pointing to projections from present trends that show, for example, that in the year 2000, 40 percent of the population of

Brussels will be foreigners, that Berlin is becoming the second largest Turkish city in the world, that the number of foreign school children in Germany rose from 165,000 in 1976 to 700,000 in 1983 (60 percent of those were Muslims), that one in every four school children in West Berlin is of foreign ancestry (Gupte, 1984; CSM, 25–27 April 1984).

Millions of migrants and their families are being integrated into European life: about 45,000 young Turks are about to graduate from vocational schools in Germany, and every fifth policeman hired in London is black. Despite this seemingly hopeful sign, hostility toward the immigrants is rising. A 1983 poll in Germany showed that 72 percent of those asked favored the expulsion of the immigrants, 78 percent blames them for unemployment of Germans, and ugly incidents, even murders of immigrants have taken place in German and French cities in recent years. Pejorative expressions such as "Turken raus!" and "schwarz kopf" have become only too common (MD, December 1983, p. 33). Recently, the immigrant presence in France has become an important issue in politics. In the municipal elections of 1984, for example, the rightist leader of the National Front Party, Jean Marie Le Pen, increased his party's vote from 1 percent to over 10 percent partly by denouncing the immigrant presence and indulging in racist rhetoric, typified by his warning that France is being colonized by an "Islamic-Arab wave" (CSM, 25–27 June 1984; MGW, 24 June 1984). On a more sophisticated level, the "new Right" headed by Alain de Benoist (1984) has argued that any assimiliation of non-European races would both harm the West and "marginalize and deculturate" the immigrants, that differences between races should be respected, in the spirit, these neo-Gobineaus seem to be saying, of "apartheid" (Le M, 17 April 1984). Paul Balta, in a bizarre twist on the nightmare theme of race war, quotes from a pamphlet distributed by pro-Shah Iranians in Paris to arouse Western support for their cause (Le M, 12–13 June 1983). "The plan of Khomeini," according to the pamphlet, "is clear: he wishes by using Maghreb workers [in France] to smash both Europe and North Africa, take the Arab Orient from behind, and take over the whole *umma* [Muslim community] by terrorism. Thus, soon, the vice opened up in Tehran can close in Paris."

The real nightmare, however, may not be what Westerners fear *from* the immigrant, but rather what they might someday do *to* the immigrants they once so fondly courted and used.

Not the least frightful of contemporary nightmares regarding the Third World is that of a world nuclear holocaust. This nightmare is, of course, universal, but one version of it is a scenario in which nuclear capability ceases to be under the control of the allegedly more stable developed powers, and falls into the hands of "dangerous" and "irresponsible" Third World leaders—as if the West had not produced Hitler nor dropped the first atomic bombs. One variant involves a mass uprising of the Third World against the West, which is disadvantaged because of its relatively small population and must face the grim prospect of having to use the hydrogen bomb in its own defense. Against the insistence of those who now possess nuclear capability that it not be allowed to proliferate, Third World leaders have argued that this gives the West an unfair advantage, and perpetrates Western dominance in the world (Weissman and Krosney; Spector). It is for this reason that India has refused to sign the Nuclear Non-Proliferation Treaty of 1968, and that, or so it is alleged, Muslim leaders want an "Islamic bomb," one that Pakistan most probably has. Mazrui in the Reith Lectures of 1979, proposed that genuine world disarmament would only be possible after all African nations (and presumably the Third World nations also) are granted nuclear capability as "a new initiation, an important rite of passage, a recovery of adulthood." No longer will the Great Powers be permitted to say that such and such a weapon is not for Africans and children under sixteen" (Weisman and Krosney, p. 324). Regarding the second scenario, the West having to use nuclear power defensively, Segal suggests that there was method in Mao's madness when he called the American atomic bomb "a paper tiger" because should it be used against any nation of the Third World, the "whole colored world," Segal (1967) says, would rise in a "fury of revulsion" against the West. "Is there not also the confidence," Segal asks, "that a society which would kill, as it would have to do if its nuclear intimidation were to succeed, people by the hundreds of millions, must meet the self-destruction of the insane" (p. 427).

There is not much that can be added to so dismal a prospect except, alas, that Third World leaders are not likely to be any more trustworthy than Western leaders if given the instruments of human annihilation. So did Third World leaders feel about other Third World leaders.

Western nightmares involving the Third World have found expression in fiction even as early as Shakespeare's *Tempest* in Caliban's defiance of Prospero: "You taught me language: and my profit on't/ Is, I know how to curse: the red plague rid you,/For learning me your language!" Caliban and his abortive revolt continues, to this day, to represent a myth in colonial discourse. Caliban appears in Robert Browning's "Caliban upon Setebos: A Natural Theology," Percy MacKaye's *Caliban* (1919), and he serves, in a rather patronizing way as the title "Caliban's Children" to Paul Johnson's chapter in *Modern Times* on the topic of African succession states to empire. The Prospero-Caliban relationship also serves as a paradigm in Mannoni's psychology of colonialism (1956). Something of a sequel to Shakespeare's *The Tempest* was Ernest Renan's play, *Caliban* (1878), a whimsical, poetical treatment not to be taken too seriously, but which does contain some interesting and indicative twists. Caliban, here, became the leader of a proletarian uprising against Prospero, who has moved to northern Italy, only this time Prospero's book and Ariel's magic prove impotent. Caliban seizes power but, enthroned, becomes a moderate and benign ruler. Among the reasons for Caliban's revolution have been his *ressentiment* at the loss of his island over which, Ariel points out in dialogue between the two, he held no more sway than a gazelle over the desert or a tiger over the jungle. Ariel also observes that Prospero has taught him the "Aryan" language, that divine tongue, the channel of reason that ungratefully, Caliban has turned into a vehicle of cursing. In this play Renan clearly reveals some of the Orientalist prejudice for which Edward Said takes this famous writer and philologist to task, for example, Renan's view of Aryan languages as vehicles of a superior culture (Said, 1978, pp. 130–45).

Another myth, parallel to the Caliban myth, has been that of the master-slave relationship, which received its classical formulation in Hegel's *Phenomenology of Spirit* (1977, pp. 111–19). The master's identity and well-being increasingly depend upon the slave who, as he realizes this, gains an ascendancy over his master. This theme is also echoed in Nadine Gordimer's *July People* and other of her novels set in South Africa, in the works of Faulkner and Beckett, and in Harold Pinter's screenplay, *The Servant* (1963). In much of the more contemporary use of the myth, the emphasis is upon the weakness of the master over his slave because of his feeling of guilt, and his sense of the incompatibility between his (Western) values and his role as master. One case, however, in which the myth is used as pure nightmare is Rudyard Kipling's "The Strange Ride of Morrowbie Jukes." A civil engineer is entrapped in the sunken city of the half-dead, a stinking hole in which, instead of being shown "the certain amount of civility," he is forced to rely upon a native ex-telegraph clerk who treats him alternately with arrogance and cringing insolence. When

Jukes's horse is eaten by hungry dwellers in the hole, his guide explains, "the greatest good of greatest number is political maxim. We are now Republic, Mister Jukes, and you are entitled to a fair share of the beast. If you like, we will pass a vote of thanks. Shall I propose?" In Kipling, as Angus Wilson observes, only "the Law" as the "Idea" stands between order and savage anarchy and evil (pp. 72, 203). In this tale, which parenthetically ends happily through the *deus ex machina* arrival of a servant of Jukes who has trailed him and pulls him out to safety, the thin screen between order and anarchy has temporarily disappeared, the Westerner has lost his legitimacy as master and has become dependent on his inferior.

A contemporary fictional treatment of the nightmare in which the "Law," and the "Idea" have lost their force is Jean Raspail's *Le Camp des Saints*. Beginning in India, the poor and miserable of the earth slowly and glacially move upon Europe, the Indonesians upon Australia, the Chinese upon Russia, until the whole world except for Switzerland (temporarily), is engulfed by the hordes of Africa and Asia who are joined by the migrant workers in Europe to rise in revolt. The West, reduced to the chaotic misery of the Third World, has been overwhelmed by demography, undermined in its will to defend itself by sentimentality and feelings of guilt, and demoralized by Leftists and do-gooders. Only a brave band of paratroopers remain to resist with a few others who, with self-mocking gallantry, sing Piaf's "Non, je regrette rien," at the end, and fight to the last man in honor of the West. In Raspail's scenario the world has been reduced to a place in which the white Western man no longer has a place.[3]

Raspail's novel touches on virtually all of the themes already encountered in Segal's *The Race War*. These themes also appear in such recent works as William Clark's *Cataclysm* and Pascal Bruckner's *The Tears of the White Man*. To encourage sales, the publisher of the American edition of Raspail's book, on the jacket quoted President Boumedienne of Algeria who, during an interview in 1974, warned the "North" that it must help the "South": "Otherwise no quantity of atomic bombs could stem the tide of billions of human beings who someday will leave the poor, southern part of the world to erupt into the relatively accessible spaces of the rich northern hemisphere looking for survival."

Perhaps such a scenario most closely approaches reality in South Africa, the world Nadine Gordimer writes about. Of her recent *Something Out There*, Salman Rushdie writes of the novella that gives the collection its title, "The haves and the powerful, fearing the uprising of the have-nots and the powerless, dream of them as monsters" (NYT Book Review, 29 July 1984, pp. 7–8). This could apply to Raspail's scenario, one that is rightist and even racist. From a leftist perspective, David Caute's *Decline of the West*, a fictional account of a mercenary band of Westerners who seek, in vain, to destroy a revolution of a Third World African people for independence, is, in part, the mirror image of Raspail—the gallant band in Caute, is a gang of lost souls who end their venture in insane brutality, loss of nerve, flight, and self-pity and guilt. The evil genius, André Laval, an admirer of Spengler who sees himself as the last defender of the West in Africa, is asleep when Amah, a revolutionary leader bound up and about to be killed, appeals to Laval's last companion and, at the end, to his executioner to release him: "Europe . . . has taken the world by the throat, dominated it with cynicism and violence, refusing solicitude and tenderness, yet talking all the while of Man, of courage and death, of violence viewed as historical self-fulfillment or as sexual rediscovery. What terrible sufferings have we endured after each of your 'spiritual' victories over us!" (p. 640). From two different points of view, Raspail and Caute foretell the West's end.

Other fictional works that deal with Western anxieties and fears regarding the Third World are Paul Erdman's *Crash of 1979*, an account of the destruction of the West caused by a paranoiac Shah of Iran seeking to create a great empire by resorting to nuclear weaponry, and Richard Bulliet's *The Gulf Scenario* in which Pakistan, with its large but poor population, seeks to take over the vulnerable Gulf states with their small but very rich populations; the plot is thwarted and the Third World War is narrowly avoided. Perhaps Bulliet's book will be best remembered for the uproarious if somewhat malicious description of one sort of Third World dependence his protagonist suggests: "the countries of the Gulf can best be compared to a group of irascible millionaire paraplegics coasting down 116th Street in Harlem in golden wheelchairs at four in the morning. They're wearing guns they don't know how to use; they're being pushed by poverty-stricken attendants whom they despise . . . The only question is who will do the mugging: the neighborhood bad guys, the attendants, or the police?" (ibid., p. 102).

A final example of the Third World nightmare in the Western imagination is Gunter Grass's *Headbirth*, an alternately ironic and sardonic treatment of Western hypocrisy and insularity in face of the problems of the Third World. At one point in the narrative, Raspail's nightmare is touched upon when one character envisions the flooding of the West by the "damned of the earth," only instead of producing the horror Raspail foresees, mixing and intermarriage between the various races gives a new vitality to a tired and shrinking West. Grass would represent the very "loss of nerve" Raspail deplores, the very consciousness of guilt Segal applauds.

To date, the nightmarish views discussed above have fortunately been confined to minorities in Western countries. The desire to help the suffering peoples of the Third World and help them develop the means to cope with the technological problems they face is a more representative Western attitude. Since the end of World War II, an attitude and a conviction has arisen on the Left that might be considered the mirror image of the Western nightmare—a positive identification with the peoples of the "South," designated "Third Worldism." To many ideologues of the Third World, both impulses, those of the "modernizers" and of the "Third Worlders," seem to be signs of Western generosity; to others, these impulses appear to be signs of condescension and hypocritical disguises for forms of "neo-colonialism."

Modernization

Modernization Theory, or rather "theories," have been rooted in the Western experience and have been, in a sense, projections of the Western conviction that it itself represented the future as well as the highest level of "civilization" to date. Modernization Theory, as it is dealt with here, does not refer to a world process that is clearly taking place, but to an ideological conviction that this process can be manipulated and should be manipulated in a particular direction—toward the Western model. Perhaps the first statement of this conviction meant as a basis for actual policy was made by Thomas Babington Macauley (1800–1859) on February 2, 1835 in his recommendation to the Governor-General in Council regarding the education of India's future elites. Up to this time, the initiative had been taken by Orientalists like William Jones and H. H. Wilson who had encouraged Indians to study their own historical past, had founded the College of Fort William (in 1800) to educate civil servants in Indian culture and languages, and had established the scholarly Asiatic Society of Bengal in 1784 (Kopf, 1969, 1980). Through Macaulay's influence this Orientalist approach was defeated, and the initiative went to the Anglicists or the Westernizers with the encouragement of men like

Charles Grant, William Wilberforce, and James Mill as well as Macaulay. In 1835, under Governor-General Bentinck, Fort William was dismantled, and soon schools were Anglicized. David Kopf points to the statement made by Girish Chandra Gise in 1862, a leading Indian journalist, that the earlier generation of the English had had no hatred for the Indians, while the present generation saw Indians as people without any past worth knowing, as "simply niggers" (Kopf, 1980, pp. 505–6). Kopf also holds that had the Orientalist point of view prevailed, Indians would have been more effectively "modernized" than they were, because through refinement of the vernacular and the development of a nationalistic "renaissance" would have been encouraged. Be that as it may, the future for India was not to lie with the traditionalists, but with the Westernizers of the day who had Macauley's perspective.

Macauley's proposals were simple, dogmatic, unequivocal. Modern civilization required education in modern subjects and in a living modern lanquage (Curtin, 1971, pp. 178–91). The lore of the past, which he sarcastically said taught "the uses of cusa grass and all the mysteries of absorption into the Deity, " or, as in Egypt, "the ritual by which cats and onions were anciently adored," was of no further use. As the Russians had "civilized" themselves through European languages, so India should do the same with English. The recommendations were replete with claims of European "superiority," claims held to be "absolutely unanswerable," and in ringing terms Macaulay declared: "all the historical information which has been collected from all the books written in the Sanskrit language is less valuable than what may be found in the most paltry abridgements used at preparatory schools in England."

If Macaulay's famous recommendation represented the first stage of "modernization" theory, perhaps Albert Sarraut's recommendation to his government after World War I can be taken to represent a second stage. Sarraut, Minister of the Colonies from 1920 to 1924, was a leading figure in the French colonial establishment. He recommended, in his *La Mise en valeur des colonies françaises* (1923), that because World War I had seriously damaged Europe's moral prestige and had encouraged the spread of nationalism, particularly among Asians, and to show gratitude to the colonial soldiers who had served in the war effort, initiative should be taken to consciously and systematically develop the economies and the societies of the colonized peoples. This would assure their loyalty as well as serve to benefit all mankind. Politically, Sarraut called for the establishment of local assemblies and the enlargement of the role of those already in place; this would eventually give way to full consultative representation (although certainly not independence). Like Macauley, Sarraut had confidence in Western progress, in *mise en valeur*, development, but unlike Macauley, there was now in his liberal approach to the colonies a distinct sense of guilt and a sense of France's and the West's vulnerability, should action not be taken. Little, however, was done to refashion the Western empires between the two world wars, and by the time it was realized how swiftly matters were evolving towards decolonization during and after World War II, it was too late.

The third and fourth stages of modernization theory can be said to have come after World War II when the market was flooded with proposals and blueprints as to how the Third World should be "developed" (Lerner, Apter, Huntington, etc.). In the third stage, modernization theorists tended to be unduly optimistic, as it soon became apparent, and held modernization and Westernization to be basically the same; it was soon realized that the fourth stage is marked by the growing realization of the difficulties involved, and a growing tendency to distinguish modernization from Westernization (Eisenstadt).

In stage three, an assumption was made that if sufficient capital was poured into a "developing country," a process could be encouraged that would lead almost automatically, through a number of other stages, to modernization. In the initial stage, sometimes called the "take-off," a society would move from traditionalism, the customs and prejudices that kept society static and stood in the way of progress, to a breaking of the cake of custom. The total process would culminate in making the society in question similar to Western societies. Daniel Lerner, one of the early modernizing enthusiasts could say, for example, "what the West is, the Middle East seeks to become" (p. 47).

The optimistic and Eurocentric stage was followed by a fourth stage as confidence waned in the ease with which the developing world could be modernized. Problems of poverty and dependency remained in most cases as intractable as ever, the world continued to be divided, in the main, between the poor South and the rich North, and the gaps between them seemed to grow larger rather than smaller. In addition, in most of the Third World, liberal institutions of the West gave way to various forms of authoritarian rule or to a preference, sometimes, for the Russian, or later, the Chinese, model over that of the open society of the liberal West. One reason for this was the failure of the developed nations to support efforts to alleviate the plight of most of the Third World. For example, the Pearson Commission of 1969 and the Brandt Commission of 1978, both appointed to study the problems of underdevelopment, proposed that each developed country contribute as least .7 percent of its total GNP to Third World development, if any appreciable change were to result. The West, on the average, came nowhere near to meeting this figure; in the first part of the 1980s aid provided was, on the average, only .38 percent of GNP! (J. Tinbergen). As Stephane Hessel, a distinguished French diplomat and administrator wrote under the rubric, "What can France do for the Third World?" (Le M, 24 March 1982), "One thing is . . . certain; we have not been successful in helping the Third World to emerge from underdevelopment . . . dependence has grown enormously." Why was this so? Because, Hessel insisted, the West had selfishly allowed terms of exchange to deteriorate to the disadvantage of the poor, had insisted upon a banking system that kept Third World states under serious constraints, and had encouraged regional rivalries to sustain the economically sterile purchase of expensive arms. But even were the developed to supply the funds deemed essential by international philanthropists, the conviction was now growing, two decades after decolonization had begun, that modernization theory to date had been inadequate. One criticism was that the modernization theorists of stage three neglected to consider the differences between Third World societies at the point of "take-off," the vastly different heritages, customs, habits, covered by the vague umbrella-term "traditionalism," the assumption, erroneous it was now argued, that all traditions were equally inimical to progress and, conversely, that with progress all traditions would inevitably be undermined and discarded. It was also argued that there were cases of countries that had adapted to modernity and yet had kept many of their traditional ways (Khalaf, 1975). Lebanon, an example sometimes given, may not be all that "modern," as events since 1975 seem to have shown, but Japan certainly continues to serve as a case of the blend of modern and traditional, even to the extent of vying with Europe and Russia as a model for modernization by others (Black, 1975, pp. 8–9).

A second criticism is that the third stage theoreticians worked under the erroneous belief that each Third World nation could be treated as a discrete unit rather that as an element in the total world economic system in which it was "peripheral" and in a state of dependence. Gestures by the developed nations to combat underde-

velopment were hypocritical, a mask for "naked imperialism" according to André Frank, one of the leading defenders of Dependence
Theory (Cockroft, p. 397). Loans, allegedly to combat underdevelopment, in fact, have only deepened dependence, benefited only the
ruling compradore class, and have only contributed to the further
deterioration of the internal situation of the aided nation. Dependence Theory will be considered in a later chapter; suffice it to say
here that the failure of the developed world to seriously help the
Third World does not serve to discredit this theory, vulnerable as it
might otherwise be.

A third criticism has been that the optimism of the third stage
theoreticians is unwarranted, that experience has shown that progress
towards modernization is by no means certain or inevitable, that
"regression" (even, some have said, a "return to the bush") is possible.
The Iranian revolution has done much to cast doubts on all progressive theories directed at the Third World, as several experts at the
yearly meeting of the American Political Science Association in 1979
admitted (CHE, 24 September 1979, p. 7; Benard and Khalilzad, pp.
1–26). This revolution has been interpreted by some outsiders and
some insiders alike as a revolt against modernization, although fairer
would be to see it as a revolt against specific models, the Western or
the Russian, in order to develop a model of modernization appropriate to Islam. In any case, the Iranian Revolution did indicate, as
students of the Third World have warned, that the West to date had
dealt largely with small elites who are in most cases Western in values
and education, and not with the masses among whom the traditional
is still very much alive and who are still to be heard from. Modernization, in short, may be an inevitable part of life in the twentieth
century, survival may depend upon it, but it remains an elusive
process, one still to be fully understood (Emerson; Black, 1966, pp.
151–52).

A fourth criticism of third stage modernization theory is that it has
been overly Eurocentric in assuming that what the developing peoples
would want or should want is to finally become like the Europeans or
the Americans (Khalaf, 1975), and that the only model of the process
of modernization is the Western (the Russian paradigm being considered warped and defective). Cyril Black, for example, who makes this
criticism while he considers modernization to be a universal process
and describes it as holistic, does make a distinction between functions
that are essential to modernity and particular institutions that are not
necessarily so. Thus representative institutions may function properly

only in feudal estate societies, and, conversely, traditional institutions may survive by being given new functions to perform; a language, for example, can be modernized and made to serve progress *or* it might be discarded for an international language such as French or English (Black, 1966, p. 53). There are several different paradigms for modernization—the liberal Western, the Russian, and, a recent addition, the Japanese; of course, in principle, each culture can design its own paradigm. In this vein, Mark Tessler observes that one useful index of modernity originally proposed by Daniel Lerner is "empathy," the ability to see alternative points of view and possibilities, to transcend the exclusiveness of the traditional, and to adopt the broad-mindedness and flexibility of the modern. While Lerner may have interpreted this concept with a Eurocentric bias, Tessler rightly observes that it need not be considered Eurocentric at all. For example, a person with empathy might choose a Western approach, or he might decide, freely and after making comparisons, in favor of a traditional pattern of his own culture, because it is useful to preserve and adapt to modernity for social, religious, political, or purely aesthetic reasons.

In general, then, theories concerned with modernization in the fourth stage are less rigid, mechanical, and deterministic, and less Eurocentric than those developed immediately after World War II. The assumptions of the stage three theorists however still influence popular opinion, and, in both the West and the Third World, many people still assume that modernization and Westernization are essentially the same. One reason for this already suggested is that Europe was the first example of the unfolding of the process of modernization, and that, in recent decades, the United States has loomed large in the consciousness of the world as the most advanced state on the globe. It will be argued in a later chapter that the imprint of the West, in spite of the tumultuous events of our times, remains strong and durable—the pressures to Westernize continue.

Third Worldism

By the clumsy term "Third Worldism," a term adopted from the French for which there is no obvious substitute, is meant an attitude toward the Third World shared by many leftist radicals after World War II, an attitude that is almost the mirror image of that of the modernizers. Third Worldists are those who have rejected the Western and often the Russian paradigm for human progress; they have had faith that, because the revolutionary peoples of the Third World have been only superficially drawn into the Western world, they might "save" mankind by offering a new and purer paradigm and by creating a "new man" as material for a better and more humane future.

The inspiration for this soteriological ideology of Third Worldism can be traced back to the Western utopian tradition and to what Henri Baudet terms the "psychological urge" typical of Westerners, in times of stress and disarray, to deride their own culture as arrogant and domineering and to seek the ideal among others. This rejection of the "decadent" (Western) present appears distantly in Hesiod, and then in Rousseau, Spengler, and many others. From utopian socialism, Romanticism, and Marxism, Third Worldism derives its revolutionary belief that salvation can only come through a radical transformation of man and society. More recently Third Worldism can be related to the aspiration of many young Europeans during and immediately after World War II to see a decadent capitalist West saved by "revolution"; when this failed to materialize, some turned their sights east to the Third World, the victims, to their mind, of an exploitative West. Through revolutionary victory in the Third World, they would weaken the West and find, as well, expiation for its sins. An extreme case of a Westerner turning against his own culture out of a sense of guilt is Jean-Paul Sartre in his introduction to Fanon's *The Wretched of the Earth*, particularly when he proposes "that when a native shoots down a European he kills two birds with one stone, he suppresses an oppressor and frees an oppressed; there remain a dead man, and a free man" (a statement Raymond Aron particularly deplored in his *Mémoires*, p. 722). Among those reinforcing guilt toward the Third World is Toynbee, who felt the rest of the world was right to see the West as a remarkably rapacious civilization (1953), and V. G. Kiernan who indicts the West for having wiped out healthy races abroad in the course of imperialism while establishing hospitals for "deformed infants and idiots at home" (1969, p. 311); for accusing others of savage ferocity while "oftener than not it was European ferocity that provoked them to retaliate" (ibid., p. 313). J. M. Elliott remarks that the feeling of guilt pervading contemporary historiography of empire has helped to replace a Eurocentric view of the world with a sympathy for the "Other," and has even led Western historians to "doubt whether European civilization was much good even for Europe" (1984). This doubt has even been extended to expressing anguish over destroying forms of another's culture while having little confidence in the superiority of one's own (H. Wilson, p. 117; Aron, 1983, p. 117).

One of the most eloquent and influential voices of Third Worldism was Frantz Fanon, a French-educated black psychiatrist from Martinique, protégé of Jean-Peal Sartre and a member of the inner circles of the Front for National Liberation of the Algerian Revolution. His *The Wretched of the Earth* was probably the most fervent and comprehensive statement of the position of many of the Third Worldists ever made. The world of colonialism was portrayed by Fanon in purely Manichaean terms, the evil colonizer/the have-not colonized, the master/the slave, evil/purity. In the *cri de coeur* with which the book ended, Fanon described the European as a dynamic, successful, but a cruel culture that was now meeting its nemesis; Europe was torn between "anomic and spiritual disintegration," her "game is over," especially in the magnified and blown-up version of herself that was the United States with its "frightening dimensions." The Third World, declared Fanon, should neither fear, envy, nor imitate the West. "Let us," he pled, "invent total man which Europe has been incapable of doing . . . For Europe, for ourselves, and for humanity, comrades, we must grow a new skin, develop new thought, attempt to put on his own feet, a new man (*un homme neuf*)" (ibid., p. 242). This new man, it should be emphasized, would be the product of a dialectic between the colonizer and the colonized; he would not be the product of a revival of any particular past or of any particular tradition or history; he would be neither eastern nor western, but universal man, his full powers and qualities finally fulfilled. The concept of the "new man" emerged, as suggested, out of a Western secular utopian tradition; and this is one reason why to nationalists intent upon reviving their own traditions and customs, corrupted or suppressed under colonialism, Third Worldism appeared as an alienating force of Western provenance— almost a continuation of Western empire even if under a red rather than a national standard. In some cases where Third Worldists took over power after independence because of their genuine contributions to the revolutionary movements, these Third Worldists were subsequently eliminated from power by forces more attuned to the traditions and aspirations of the masses. This was true of the Algerian case, for example. Here the secular radicals (and their French allies, the *pieds rouges*) who initially claimed the Revolution against France for their own, were finally eliminated from power when the first president, Ahmed Ben Bella, was overthrown in 1965 in part for seeming too "Castroist," and too indifferent to Islam—and Fanon's

name began to fade from memory.[4] Better known now is the name of
Ahmad Ben Badis, the founder of the Muslim revivalist movement
under which the Algerians sought a return to a reformed Islam and
the renewal of the use of Arabic as the language of education and
culture. This impulse gave the revolutionary movement on a mass
level its dynamism, and assured that the pristine Third Worldist goals
of many leaders of the Algerian revolution have not prevailed, even if
they remain in a more modified form as part of independent Algeria's
identity (Gellner, 1981, pp. 149–73; Berque, 1978, pp. 67, 70; Gordon, 1966).

Today Third-Worldist enthusiasm has largely waned. Soon after
World War II, when the concrete as opposed to imaginary lives of the
new Third World nations began, faith in the soteriological mission of
the Third World gave way to disillusionment and disappointment.

Third-Worldist enthusiasm peaked in the years 1954 to 1962,
culminating in the victory of the Vietnamese against the French at
Dien Bien Phu (1954); the Bandung Conference of Third World
leaders in Indonesia (1955); the Suez crisis of 1956 when Jamal Abd
al-Nasir (albeit with U.S. and USSR support) stood up to the French
and the British in alliance with Israel; the humiliation of the United
States at the Bay of Pigs in 1961; and the conclusion of the eight-
year-old Algerian Revolution in 1962 (Gorce; Chaliand, 1977, 1984;
Sorum). Later moments of glory—the address of Yasir Arafat to the
United Nations in 1974 and the fall of Saigon in 1975—were inspir-
ing, but too much had happened in the Third World in general to
encourage a revival of Third-Worldist enthusiasm. The Arabs had
been deeply humiliated by their defeat in 1967; in 1970 Abd al-Nasir,
the Arabs' modern Saladin, died just when Lebanon began its path
toward disintegration; the killing of "Che" Guevara in Bolivia in the
same year was a serious blow to the spread of "Castroism" in South
America. The radical rise of the price of oil in 1973 further emphasized the fact that the Third World was being increasingly divided
between the rich and the ever poorer. In 1978 China invaded Vietnam
and ended any hope for Asian solidarity, and in 1982 the PLO lost its
one remaining base on the borders of Israel when their armed
presence in Lebanon was virtually eliminated. Gérard Chaliand, once
a Third Worldist himself, has noted that, politically and socially, none
of the Third World nations have met the expectations once placed in
them. And, except in the case of some of the Third World states that
benefit from self-development (Taiwan, Singapore, for example) or
from the sheer luck of oil-wealth, (the Gulf states, for example), the

gap between the rich developed world and the South has been growing ominously. At the same time, sadly, the rhetoric of Third Worldism has grown thin as once exemplary leaders of Third World-ism have failed to meet their promises. Two cases of such leaders have been the late Ahmed Sékou Touré of Guinée and Julius Nyerere of Tanzania. Each at one time was held to be the exemplary exponent of Third Worldism and leader of a progressive Third World nation.

Sékou Touré was the one leader of French-ruled black Africa to openly defy President de Gaulle and refuse to remain within the French community by opting for immediate independence from France in 1958. Fanon, who admired Touré, headed his chapter in the *The Wretched of the Earth* with an epigraph from Touré and warned against the betrayal of the revolution by middle-class leaders. Fanon also discussed Keita Fodeba, Touré's appointed director of Guinée's Ballets Africains, as the African artist who had most successfully produced art that both condemned colonialism and inspired its cultural transcendance without resort to the folkloric (1961, pp. 155, 169–74).

Upon independence, Sékou Touré declared Guinée to be "socialist," its chief enemies, "imperialism" and "feudalism," and its goals to erase the "esprit du colonisé" and to produce the "new man" (Lacouture and Baumier, pp. 84–86; Jean-Claude Pomonti, Le M, 24, 25, 26 May 1984; CSM, 3, 4 April 1984; NYT, 4, 6 April 1984). By 1984, however, this last leader of the famous Bandung generation had become a travesty of what he had promised three decades earlier. Upon his death in April 1984, illiteracy was 80 percent, the educational system was so bad that experiments with native languages as mediums of instruction were abandoned in favor of a return to French, the prisons were full of political inmates, the economy was in a disasterous state, and there was almost no one to mourn him. His closest colleagues were rapidly eliminated from positions of power, and the reign of his Guinean Democratic Party, accused of (pro-Malinké) tribal racism, was ended.

As for Julius Nyerere, upon being awarded the Third World Prize in New Delhi in 1981 he gave his full support to four policies close to the hearts of Third Worldists, to force the North to make concessions to the South; to develop agriculture rather than industry in order to first get rid of poverty; to strengthen bonds between the Third World countries; and to refuse to imitate Western patterns and values (NYT, 23 February 1982). Today, sadly, Tanzania cannot but contribute to the waning of Third-Worldist utopian enthusiasm; its leaders have exposed the Third World to easy criticism among unsympathetic Westerners and also to self-criticism among Third Worldists themselves. Western criticism of Third Worldism ranges from the sardonic to the sympathetic, but skeptical. Sardonicism appears in the pages of Paul Johnson's *Modern Times* in chapters 14 and 15 of "The Bandung Generation" and "Caliban's Kingdoms." Charles Issawi has said, under a title "On Gods that Failed," "the Soviet Union, China, Vietnam, Cambodia . . . It is understandable, and pardonable, to have worshipped a God that failed. But a whole Pantheon?" (Princeton Alumni Weekly, 4 April 1984). Jean Daniel, French liberal journalist and writer who has been sympathetic to the Algerian and other Third World causes, in a review of Fanon's *The Wretched of the Earth* wrote that perhaps the West should collapse for its sins, as Sartre urged in his introduction to Fanon's book, but the fact was that it continued to survive and to prosper, and that while it should feel guilty for much of the past, it could not be held responsible as Fanon thought for all the ills—tribalism for example—that plague the newly independent nations. Rather than reject the West totally, Daniel concluded, the Third World should seek its assistance (*L'Express*, 30 November 1961). Albert Memmi, Jewish Tunisian author of many works denouncing colonialism in terms similar to Fanon's, nevertheless took Fanon to task for his "revolutionary romanticism" and his belief that a "new man" could emerge from the sequels of colonialism (1968, p. 66). No new nation to emerge from colonial rule—largely because of colonialism to be sure—could claim any purity, said Memmi. Most were dominated by a selfish "national bourgeoisie" who had no interest in genuine social progress, possibilities, it should be said in all fairness, Fanon himself had anticipated with concern. Among the fiercest critics of the class corruption of the Third World revolutionary movement have been Third Worldists themselves. Again we turn to the case of the Algerian Revolution.

Among the large body of literature that treats the Algerian Revolution as a disappointing failure, as one might expect, have been works by Marxist radicals and other Third Worldists. Among these works are Daniel Guérin's *L'Algérie caporalisée?*; T. M. Maschino and Fadela M'Rabet's *L'Algérie des illusions: la révolution confisquée*; and Gérard Chaliand's *Revolution in the Third World: Myth and Prospects* (pp. 69–74, 109–11).

Guérin's thesis is that a positive reply must be given to his question; Maschino-M'Rabet's thesis is that Algeria is dominated by a lower middle-class using Islam and Arabization as smoke screens to remain in power; Chaliand, in his analysis summarizes what most of the other critics have to say. Once a Third World enthusiast, now disillusioned with virtually all of the Third World regimes, he holds Algeria's leaders, in particular, responsible for never having confronted the question of the social content of independence, for having lacked any "ideological ground," and for having failed, as Fanon had urged, to mobilize, ideologically educate, and so transform the peasant class. The only leader who might have done this, Abane Ramdane, was assassinated by his colleagues. The peasants were used and then neglected; the victors were the urban petit bourgeoisie with their "revolutionary rhetoric and conservative ideology." Writes Chaliand (1977): "Traditional ways of thinking are not changed by armed struggle, unless armed struggle *as a movement* promotes a modernizing and revolutionary ideology, one which, while exalting the sense of national identity, can also prune the socially and culturally conservative elements out of the national tradition and free the energies of the greatest number of people." Speculating on what Fanon would have thought had he survived the revolution, Irene Gendzier concludes that he would have been disillusioned: the strong mass party, separate from the state he had envisioned, never materialized, and he would have deplored the present emphasis on "Arabic" and "Islam" as obfuscatory (pp. 269–70). Elsewhere as well as in Algeria, Third Worldism, by the mid 1980s, had not met the test of time. P. M. de la Gorce summarized this disenchantment as follows: "socialist experiences have turned into tropical dictatorships and capitalist experiences into cosmopolitan corruption" (1984). As for the attitude of many Third World ideologues, except for those who were Marxist international revolutionaries, Third Worldism before the 1980s had long come to seem an expression of Western arrogance and presumption. Even as close a friend of the French as Léopold Senghor, first president of independent Sengal and member of the Académie Francaise, stated in 1950: "I know of no people more tyrannical in its love for mankind [than the French]," and in 1963 "The French left-wing is still not decolonized. It secretes a mixture of "Jacobin" spirit and missionary spirit, typically French. This left-wing wants to impose its *máitre á penser* on us; above all it refuses to let us think by ourselves" (Andrew, p. 338).

PART II

Third World Reactions and Responses to the West

4

Patterns of Response

The influence of the West upon the East has been discussed in terms of the varying degrees of Western penetration, the tendency to transform areas of the East into peripheral parts of the Western-dominated world economic system and to split the elites from the masses in terms of interest and culture, and the manner in which a single strand detached from the West and introduced into an alien culture can produce unexpected and sometimes dangerous results. The West's influence has also been considered in terms of Western self-images and pretensions to which Third World ideologues have reacted. In this chapter, the discussion will focus upon Third World images of the West and upon the role that such images have played and will continue to play in the quest for authentic decolonization and identification.

Each discrete entity of the East coming under the Western influence, obviously, reacted in its own way in terms of its own traditions as well as according to the historical circumstances of its confrontation with the West. The general Chinese pattern was to attempt to reinforce traditional isolationism, which was psychologically buttressed by a sense of cultural self-sufficiency and superiority. Even when forced by gun-boat diplomacy (the Opium Wars of 1839–1842) to open herself first to Western financial penetration, then to cultural penetration, China has, so far, managed to preserve the masses of its people from Western influences before and after the communist victory of 1949. William McNeill may argue with cause that "really intimate confrontation between Chinese and Western civilizations therefore still lies in the future" (1963, p. 785), but the ideology of communism itself serves as a powerful Western dissolvant of traditional culture, as does also China's current flirtation with forms of capitalist competition.

This flirtation in the 1980s has been erratic and troubled, ranging from what has seemed a genuine opening to freedom of individual expression and action, to strong reactions against such an opening on the ground that it has given license to forms of Western corruption. This is reminiscent of the crushing of the "Hundred Flowers" encouraged to bloom in the late fifties. In 1983 the government denounced the "cultural pollution" coming from the West, and in 1987 began to denounce Western "bourgeois liberalism." Both moves to suppress what had been released were evidence of the clear association made by China's communist leaders between the West and individual autonomy, freedom of expression, a free market for ideas and ideologies as well as with pornography, license, and decadence.

Japan's experience has been quite different from China's. For a number of reasons, which will be discussed later, Japan was in a particularly favorable condition to respond positively, rapidly, and, finally, deeply to the Western impact and to Westernize effectively enough to ultimately rival the West itself (Anderson; Black, 1975). As for Hindu India, Western hegemony and the spread of Westernization provided Hindus with the means to compete with the previously dominant Muslim sector, to finally benefit from the unifying administrative and economic structure built by the British and from the adoption of Western nationalism as a rallying force to win its independence in 1947.

The Islamic world, here considered less briefly than the other Eastern entities, shared with the rest of Asia an indifference to the small Christian civilization developing in the remote corner of Europe, even while engaged in combat with it and ruling, through conquest, parts of its territory until, in the seventeenth century, the Western impact could no longer be ignored. Bernard Lewis cites as not unrepresentative the view of the West of Sa'id ibn Ahmad, the Qadi of Toledo, Spain in the eleventh century (1982, pp. 68–69). To him, Europeans were more "beasts than men," lacking "keenness of understanding and clarity of intelligence," overcome by "ignorance and apathy, lack of discernment and stupidity." In contrast to such barbarians stood the Arabs, the Jews, the Byzantines, the Indians, and other peoples concerned with science and learning, and on a somewhat lower plain of enlightenment, the Chinese, renowned for their aesthetic taste, and the Turks, renowned as horsemen and warriors. But this attitude began to be significantly modified after the Ottomans were obliged to abandon their plans to conquer Vienna, to sign the Treaty of Carlowitz (1699), the first treaty in which the Ottomans made important concessions to the West, and to suffer the invasion of

Egypt by Napoleon (1798). Further east the disasterous reign of Aurungzeb in the seventeenth century over the Muslim Moghul Empire of India, and the Afghani revolt of 1709 against the Persian Safavids, marked the decline of the other two great Muslim states. It was now admitted that Islam had much to learn from the "West," however unenthusiastically the prospect might be greeted (B. Lewis, (1964), pp. 32–33). It is significant that the first two works printed on the first Turkish printing press set up in 1729 were the Turkish ambassador's description of France and a treatise on European military arts. This interest in the culture and technology of the West was, however, short-lived since the press was closed down in 1742 because of traditional disinterest in Western science. But the flood-gates had been opened and increasingly members of the Ottoman elite learned European languages, sent their children to study in Europe, established military schools, and tolerated such foreign missionary schools in their midst as Robert College (founded in 1859) in Istanbul, and the American University of Beirut (founded in 1866).

While the heartland of the Ottoman Empire was experiencing the Western impact, Egypt, increasingly autonomous under the rule of the dynamic Muhammad 'Ali, was now being opened to the West (Abu-Lughod, 1963; Hourani, 1983; al-Husry, 1966). Intent upon protecting his domain from the West as well as weakening the power of his master the Sultan in Istanbul, Muhammad 'Ali appreciated the need to learn the secrets of the West and in this spirit sent groups of students to Europe to study. One such group had as its *imam* Rifa'a Rafi' al-Tahtawi, a perceptive observer, who later headed an Egyptian bureau set up to translate Western works into Arabic. His account of Europe (1826–1831) is an important source on the initial responses of Muslims—at least educated and thoughtful Muslims—to the Western impact. The response was generally positive, touched with admiration and the recognition that outside the sphere of religion the West enjoyed superiority over the East. Tahtawi's interest, it should be observed, was by no means limited to the military and the technological; he also showed an interest in and an admiration for the French system of justice, and for its system of limited constitutional monarchy. Remarkable for the time, he displayed an awareness of the connection between the advanced culture of France and the education of women.

The relatively unself-conscious and favorable response of Tahtawi to the West was not unique. While threatened on the periphery of its empires, Islam still held sway over much of the world and had little reason to yet doubt the strength of its traditions or, more importantly, the superiority of its religion. In regard to the Arab subjects of the Ottoman Empire, Ibrahim Abu-Lughod has concluded that matters began to change about 1870, when the Arab world began to appreciate how deep were the inroads the West was, in fact, making into the world of Islam (1963, pp. 135–36, 154). The warning of Butrus al-Bustani, a Lebanese intellectual and writer, was indicative of the danger of *tafarnuj*—becoming Westernized in lifestyle—and so losing one's own roots and authenticity; the serious concern of the Egyptian intellectual Hasan al-Marsifi with the once alien concepts of "nation," "state," "patriotism"; and the proposals of the young Islamic reformer Muhammad 'Abduh to partly modernize the venerable Islamic university of al-Azhar in Cairo. About this same time, Abu-Lughod observes, there appeared the first examples of the distinction made even to this day among non-Western spokesmen between a "materialist" West and a "spiritual" East, a distinction clearly indicating a degree of self-conscious defensiveness. First, in Lebanon where the Christians had close ties to the West, and in Egypt, Western ways penetrated ever more deeply into the fabric of Muslim Arab society. The pattern, in general, was for educated opinion to move toward religious revisionism and increasing secularism under the influence of the West and, then also, toward Arab nationalism, particularly when Arabs, after 1908, lost faith that the Turks would continue to provide them with political equality within the Turkish-dominated Ottoman Empire (Sharabi, 1970, pp. 129–36; Hourani, 1983; al-Husry). As Hisham Sharabi puts it, there appeared to be "an irreversible westernizing and secularist direction" to educated Arab opinion and, on the whole, this opinion was friendly to the West and liberal in its values, assuming that the Arab nation-to-be would enjoy a parliamentary and constitutional policy. In spite of the double frustration resulting from the refusal by the Allies to grant the Arabs independence after World War I, and the promise of a "homeland" to Jews in Palestine, Arab nationalism remained liberal with the West still the model for most of those active in politics between the wars.

During and after World War II, however, Europe lost its moral ascendancy and its role as a model of *mimesis* (Hourani's term) among the Arabs; Arab militants increasingly turned to less liberal and more "integral" and radical ideologies, such as those of the Ba'th Party and Muslim Brotherhood. Modernization and westernization were no longer equated, the West-East dichotomy was losing its credibility, and the Westernized Levantine bourgeoisie began to lose its influence to mass political movements; a greater emphasis was now placed on social and economic justice rather than, as before, on political justice and individual freedom (Hourani, 1983, pp. 344–54). Among the reasons for this "loss of face" on the part of the West were the internecine nature of World War II, the occupation of much of the European Asian empires by Japan, and the creation of Israel in 1948—an affront to all Arabs and a tragedy for the Palestinian Arabs. Intellectuals who had once been in the Western camp ideologically now began to re-examine their values and commitments as was the case with figures such as Taha Husayn, Abbas Mahmud al-Aqqad, Sayyid Qutb, and Ahmad Amin, for example. Sayyid Qutb, in particular, was to become one of the important inspirations of the "fundamentalist revival" of the late 1970s.

In the post-war period, after the 1952 overthrow of the monarchy in Egypt, a leader emerged who embodied the hopes and aspirations of Arab nationalists as no leader had done before; this was Jamal 'Abd al-Nasir. His popularity reached a climax in 1955–1956 when he defied the West and nationalized the Suez Canal Company and then stood up to the Israelis in alliance with the French and British in the second Arab-Israeli war. While saved by the USSR and the United States at the last moment from total defeat, in fact, 'Abd al-Nasir emerged with renewed prestige for having fought and survived. But Nasserism, which swept the Arab Muslim world of the Middle East, then suffered the humiliation of the Six-Day War of 1967 and, increasingly, the Arab world seemed to become divided, pragmatic, and materialistic. To the revolutionary and militant, only the Palestinian movement now offered hope of any Arab renewal until it too seemed to flounder as it ran afoul of political realities in Lebanon (1975–1982). It was not strange that all Western-derived ideologies—nationalism, liberalism, and Marxism—should seem to have come to grief in the Arab context. Militants now wondered if, perhaps, the fault might not lie in having abandoned Islam. Perhaps the answer lay in a return to religious faith, they now reasoned, with Iran after 1978 setting the pace.

Following the discussion of Nicki Keddi (1983), an Iranian pattern of response to the West that might be traced, calls to our attention four revolts against established government, which culminated in the revolution of 1978. In each case, the nature of the revolt was largely defined by the enemy against whom it occurred, and, in each case, the West played a major role. The first revolt was against the Qajar Shah in 1891–1892 for granting a tobacco monopoly to a British company; in this case the enemy was the foreigner seeking further economic penetration into Iran. The second revolt of 1905–1911 was against a weak Shah unable to resist the domination of most of Iran by Russia and Britain; in this case the Shah was forced to accept a constitution—a Western institution—as a means of strengthening Iran. The third revolt of 1951–1953 was against a Shah who was perceived as having sold out the national oil interest to Western companies. The leader of the revolt, Muhammad Musaddeq, was a secular nationalist; thus, the ideology of the revolt was of Western provenance even if it was against Western political (and economic) control. The Iranian oil industry was nationalized until Musaddeq was overthrown, and Muhammad Reza Pahlavi, Iran's last Shah, was returned from exile. The fourth revolt in 1978–1979 dethroned this Shah who was perceived to be a tool of the West (the United States in particular) and to have sold out to the West not only politically and economically but also socially and culturally. With this revolt Iran became "the liberated part of Islam" in the eyes of its leaders and of many other Muslims within the "house of Islam" from Morocco to Indonesia (Mabon; Brière).

The Middle Eastern part of the Islamic world has thus responded to the Western imposition and the Western challenge in a variety of ways, with the general trend being, at least from the vantage of the mid-1980s, from first seeing the West as a model for progress to Islam's hostility toward the West and rejection of it as an object of *mimesis*.

The Spectrum of Muslim Response

Various efforts have been made to make sense of the responses of the middle-Eastern Islamic world to the Western impact by classifying these into ideal-type categories. Of course this procedure, as does any study in mass psychology, runs the risk of reification and over-simplification, but, handled carefully, it has proven of use in bringing some order out of confusion and serving at least introductory purposes.

Classifications of Arab opinion regarding Western confrontation have included those of Abdallah Laroui and Saad Eddin Ibrahim (Ibrahim, S. 1982b, pp. 1–25; Laroui, 1976). Laroui sees as archetypical those "moments of the Arab consciousness" of the "cleric" whose answer to Western challenge is the reinforcement of traditional faith;

the "politician" who accepts the secular and liberal West of the Enlightenment (no longer identified with Christianity) as a model and holds it to be compatible with Islam before this religion was corrupted by "Turkish despotism;" and the "technocrat" who believes salvation lies in applied science and industry and the rule of experts such as himself. To the cleric the West is a distressful threat, to the politician a political model, and to the technocrat an inspiration and eventually a rival—the first would keep his people in a state of obscurantism, according to Laroui, the second would provide only political, but no social change, and the third, the technocrat, completely blind to historical realities, would produce cultural disaster. Laroui's general classification is obviously combative, while Ibrahim's is more purely descriptive of the effect of the process of modernization in the Middle East of the last decades. His types are the "mechanized Beduin" (who replaces his camel with a jeep); the "lumpen capitalist" (who derives his wealth from being little more than a sponsor of imported workers, technicians, and financiers); the "veiled medical student" (who seeks to combine her Islamic integrity with her modern profession); and "the angry Muslim militant."

Other terms of classification are "new men" for modernized and modernizing entrepreneurs who have broken with tradition and are bringing economic and social progress to their cultures; and "Levantine" (a term first used by Albert Hourani to designate an "Easterner," usually of minority status, who is often multicultural and multilingual and moves with equal ease between his native culture and the Western but usually with roots in neither. The Levantine has served in the past as at least a bridge between the East and West. A different classificatory scheme has been proposed by Yvonne Haddad who specifically designates Muslim responses to Western challenges to the religion of Islam (Haddad, 1982). Holding these views are the acculturationist who accepts Western norms; the normativists (who abide by traditional Muslim norms); and the neo-normativists who interpret Islam in a militant and radical manner. We will encounter similar typologies in the discussion of militant Islam, as well as in other recent coinages such as "neo-Shi'ism," for example, which corresponds to Haddad's "neo-normalists." A final classificatory scheme one might consider is that of Toynbee's four types of rebels against an imposed alien culture: the Zealot who totally rejects the alien culture; the Herodian who fully assimilates to this culture; the Archaist who seeks salvation in a return to his own past; and the Futurist who seeks salvation in a radically new future—the latter two, in Toynbee's philos-

in Toynbee's philosophy, courting disaster through their escapes from present reality (1935–1961, vol. *VIII*). While recognizing the epistemological hazards involved, we will make use of some of these classifications and terms in the following discussion of attitudes of mainly Middle-Eastern Muslims toward the West. The classification used here, however, while it draws upon elements from the classifications discussed, is the author's.

The Assimilationists

In one sense there have been no assimilationists (Toynbee's Herodians) among those who have wanted the emancipation of their people in modern times, if by assimilationist one understands a person who wants the full and unqualified assimilation of his people to the polity and society of the conqueror. Even those North African leaders—the Young Tunisians, for example, or the Algerian liberals like Farhat Abbas who before 1954 denied there was any Algerian nation—insisted that they keep their own legal status as Muslims upon assuming full French citizenship. Even an extreme Europeanizer such as Kemal Atatürk, founder of modern Turkey, assumed that the Turks, after adopting Western "civilization," would preserve their basic "culture," following the distinction made by Ziya Gökalp, father of the ideology of modern Turkish nationalism. But in a broad sense, Abbas, Atatürk and others with similar views might be considered Herodians. Atatürk, for example, was convinced that the "Oriental mind"—and Islam—stood in the way of the progress and the modernization of the Turkish people and that the answer was to fully adopt Western civilization and completely free the state from the control of religion (Kinross, pp. 54–57, 390, 434). It was in this spirit that the intellectual Abdullah Cevdet made the often-quoted statement: "There is no second civilization; civilization means European civilization, and it must be imported with both its roses and its thorns" (Kinross, p. 57). It was in this spirit that Atatürk exorted his people to become "civilized" through Europeanization.

Assimilationists such as the liberal Algerian Ferhat Abbas, in a famous article in 1936, rejected Algerian national identity as a delusion and declared the modern Algerians to be "the children of a new world, a creation of the French and of French energy" (Gordon, 1961, p. 44). Only the refusal of the French to grant the full rights of citizenship (except to those who renounced their Islamic status) led

Abbas, and other *évolués*, with a heavy heart at first, to join the revolutionaries of 1954.

Elsewhere in the Muslim world, one would find, in India and Egypt and once in Iran, pro-Western sentiments as deep as those of Abbas. In the case of Iran, Roger Savory relates that during the constitutional revolt of 1906–1907, while a *mulla* could call for the death of any pro-constitutional young men "who have drawn their education from European sources," wear a starched collar and carry a cane, one could also find a Sayyid Hasan Taqizadeh strongly defending the constitution and declaring: "We must Westernize ourselves, body and soul!" (in Lewis *et al.*, 86–87). In the case of India, one could point to the distinguished Muslim leader, Sir Sayyid Ahmed Khan (d. 1898) who founded the Anglo-Oriental College of Aligarh modelled upon Cambridge, convinced as he was that "true Islam" was open to "modernity" and "modernization" (Ruthven, pp. 300–302; Rahman, pp. 49–52, 55–56, 74, 78, 79).

In the post-World War I period a number of young, romantic, Muslim Egyptian intellectuals and writers made what was something of a pilgrimage to Europe, Paris in particular, and returned more enthusiastic about the West and more critical of their own culture than when they left. Sometimes they expressed their views in novels as did Taufik al-Hakim, for one, in his romantic *Birds of the East* (first published in 1925). Through the thin disguise of the protagonist, al-Hakim expresses both his positive and negative reactions to the West and, by comparison, to the "East," which he sees darkly: "There is no more East," he says. "It's become a jungle," one in which the natives imitate everything European, "like monkeys." The West, on the other hand—and he has an unhappy love-affair with a French girl—he finds to be full of "arrogance" and "heartlessness." His dream is of a synthesis—of a West filled with the warmth of the East, and an East revived by the stimulation of the West.

Less critical of the West during the same period than al-Hakim was the influential blind poet and intellectual, Taha Husayn, who held a different view as a young man following World War II. To Husayn, Egypt stood with the West in the confrontation between West and East. Egypt had, he said, "acquiesced most reluctantly even to Arab domination." In the politics of the day, between the two world wars, he defended the Western parliamentary system and the Western educational system Egypt had by then adopted. Husayn's only limit on full assimilation with the West was that the Egyptians should be selective and not accept everything European indiscriminately. It was to this younger Husayn that Fouad Ajami points as an illustration of his thesis that two hearts beat in the bosom of the Egyptian and that one of them is a pro-Western (today pro-American) heart (1981, pp. 108–22, 169–72). Ajami argues that, in spite of the tumultuous events in the Middle East to this day, this feeling is, unfortunately, still deeply rooted, because it leads to "levantization" and "dependency" as occurred under the leadership of the Khedive Ismail in the nineteenth century and Anwar Sadat in the twentieth. There is a *boutade* that Egyptians have Russia in their pocket-book, the United States in their heart; one could amend this to say that, under Sadat, they had the United States in both pocket-book and heart. Among Laroui's "politicians" and "technicians," there are still many Arabs in the various conservative and more traditional establishments who remain deeply committed to and dependent upon the United States regardless of what public rhetoric might dictate. For the novice, however, pro-Western sentiments must be disguised and veiled; the Herodian moment of the pre-World War II period has given way to other moments, much less friendly to the West.

Islamic Reformist Apologists

By "clerics" I mean Islamic reformist apologists who, sensitive to the Western challenge and impressed by Western "superiority" in many spheres, have sought to reform and revive Islamic society, the *umma*, through partial modernization along Western lines (Kerr, 1966). At the same time, and here they are "apologists," the clerics insist upon the superiority of true Islam and its adaptibility to modernity, even claiming that Islam has anticipated many modern inventions and scientific theories. Their movement, whose moment of prominence came before World War I, has led to reforms in the educational system of the venerable theological university of al-Azhar and, in general, to a greater receptivity among many Muslims to modern ideas. Their leading proponents were Sayyid Jamal al-Din al-Afghani (d. 1879), a Persian, and Shaykh Muhammad 'Abduh (d. 1905), an Egyptian. Their tradition was continued by such figures as Muhammad Rashid Rida (d. 1935) and Amir Shakib Arslan (d. 1946), both Lebanese, and 'Ali Abd al-Raziq (d. 1966), an Egyptian, each of whom gave this reform movement his own particular imprint. Al-Afghani, a mysterious and dramatic figure, probably of Iranian origin, travelled widely in the Islamic world and became involved in the political life of a number of Islamic regimes (Donohue and Esposito, 1982, pp. 16–19). His motives were as controversial as his career, but he did influence the emergence of "Pan-Islamism" as an ideology, and he did significantly challenge the hold of the conservative *'ulama* whom he accused of having stifled the scientific tradition that flourished in early Islam. Islam, his message was, could and must experience a revival through modernizing its ideas and its institutions; only so could it meet the challenge of the modern West. Shaykh Muhammad 'Abdu, al-Afghani's disciple in many ways, was a much less controversial or political figure (Abduh, 1966; Donohue and Esposito, 1982, pp. 24–28). Sharing al-Afghani's main ideas, he saw that the West was able to discover and institutionalize "the fundamental principles of modern civilization" after the Reformation, a movement whose fundamental principles were, he believed, the same as those lying in the heart of Islam properly understood, principles now needing to be rescued from the dead hand of traditionalism.

To traditional and conservative Muslim leaders, and to militant fundmentalists, these liberal-minded reformist apologists had made too many concessions to the West and dangerously exposed Islam to corruption and disruption from within, accusations not wholly without reason (Benard and Khalilzad, pp. 89–95). As Albert Hourani has pointed out, in interpreting Islamic concepts in terms of Western ideas, Muslim reformists, while intending to defend Islam, were by way of secularizing it; *maslaha* (the good of the community), for example, was interpreted as "utility," *ijma'* (the opinion of the community) was "public opinion," and so forth (1983, pp. 344–45). In short, the tendency among these reformers was to subtly turn Islam into something resembling liberal Protestantism.

But whatever their faults, the reformist apologists had offered an alternative approach to modernization, one that continues to provide a bridge between West and East, and one compatible with constitutional and liberal nationalist values.

Liberal Nationalists

Arab liberal nationalists, whose moment of prominence came during the years before World War II, generally believed in the Western ideals of individual freedom, parliamentary government, and constitutionalism. In contrast to later socialist and integral nationalists, they intended to emphasize liberty over social equality and justice; education and the ballot box over mass violence as the means to effect progress. While in their struggles for independence they combatted Western powers, they were for the most part friendly to Western values and institutions. To later and more radically prone generations, these liberal nationalists appeared to be overly dependent upon the West, politically, economically and culturally, and their constitutionalism was dismissed as a smoke screen to avoid rapid social change and to defend the exploitive interests of large landlords and bourgeois compradore capitalists.

The cultural content of the nationalism of the liberals was the Arab Islamic heritage and language, in the main, but most of them favored a secular rather than an Islamic state and so intellectuals like Nabih Faris, a Protestant, and Costantine Zurayk, a Greek Orthodox, could join Muslims like Sati al-Husri as ideologues of Pan-Arabism.

While they wanted to revive their own culture and language—the movement they identified with was the *Nahda*, the renaissance—they saw themselves as moving into a Western-like modernity, so much so that some of their recent critics have wondered if the *Nahda* was little more than an expression of Westernization, with only Arab trimmings. Parallel to the *Nahda* during the struggles of the North African states for independence against France, rebel intellectuals often stated that they were fighting for values they had learned in their French schools, the values of the French Revolution. In this spirit, Moroccan satiric playwright Mohammad ben Shakrun saw his work as a weapon against the traditional and the obscurantist in native traditional mores and institutions, which were, he believed, props by which the French dominated and controlled a backward and superstitious Moroccan people (Reichard, pp. 92–97). Thus, Western values were being used to undermine Western political domination, and Western domination was being resisted in the name of Western values to fulfill these values institutionally on native soil.

Although yet today shades of fascism sadly darken the scene, perhaps the most successful Arab liberal nationalist has been Habib Bourguiba of Tunisia until his senescence and unceremonious deposition in November 1987. This French-educated lawyer led his nation to independence in 1956 and established a relatively liberal polity and an open society, which was something of a model, to many Western scholars at the time, of what a Third World nation should be. To this day, Bourguiba and his followers have maintained that Tunisia's cultural legacy is *not* only the Arab and the Muslim, it is also the French and, even more distantly, the Roman, and Tunisia's elite remains bilingual and bicultural on an educated level without self-consciousness or embarrassment. Bourguiba gave his point of view in a speech on April 2, 1956: "The colonial regime was the whiplash of our renaissance. Without it, we would not have reached the present state of our journey. . . . Now that we have shed all complexes, we are duty-bound to say it: 'it is to France that we owe our liberty'" (Lacouture and Baumier, pp. 97–98). While Bourguiba may have had no serious grudge against France and the West, and while most liberal nationalists hoped to base their nations upon Western models, there were early nationalists who could express strong hostility toward the West. One of them, in fact a man often credited with having been the first Arab nationalist, was Abdul Rahman al-Kawakibi (d. 1903), a Syrian Muslim writer and intellectual (Sharabi, 1970, pp. 98–100). While eager to modernize his own society, he had scant affection for the West or for Western models. To him, Teutonic and Anglo-Saxon Westerners appeared as "hard-headed materialists," fierce and exploitative, using science to make wealth rather than to advance human progress. He viewed Latins as "mercurial," immodest, prone to find glory in conquering others. In contrast to these predatory and untrustworthy Westerners, Easterners tended to be compassionate, merciful, and morally motivated. *Tafarnuj*, cultural imitation of the West, should be avoided at all costs because Western civilization was only a veneer, he believed, covering an inner spiritual emptiness and despair; Westerners, moreover, were full of hatred for the Muslim.

Al-Kawakibi, atypical as he might have been of the early Arab nationalists and, while reflecting in spite of his secular vision, anti-Western sentiments of the orthodox and traditionalist Muslims, did anticipate attitudes toward the West of both later integral nationalists and of "fundamentalists."

Integral Nationalists and Marxist Socialists

By "integral" as opposed to "liberal" nationalists is meant nationalists who emphasize society more than the individual, egalitarianism more than libertarianism, the mobilization and integration of the masses more than an open society dominated by middle-class values. In extreme cases, integral nationalism is equivalent to fascism or other forms of national socialism.

Integral nationalism has taken a variety of shapes in the Middle East, ranging from the Kata'ib Party of the Lebanese Maronites, to the pan-Arabist movement known as the Ba'th (Resurrection). The first focuses upon Lebanon as the object of final national loyalty, the latter sees the whole Arab world as the object of loyalty, an Arab world to be united and modernized according to the norms of "Arab socialism." To Michel Aflaq, considered one of the founders of the Ba'th movement, the West is to be condemned for having culturally corrupted the Arab world, for having undermined its cultural specificity, and for having "Europeanized" Islam (Donohue and Esposito, 1982, pp. 107–112; Batatu, pp. 722–48). Islam, in his secularist philosophy, is an integral part of the Arab heritage but more as culture than as faith—Aflaq was himself a Greek Orthodox Catholic. Today both Baghdad and Damascus, even though hostile to one another, claim to be Ba'thist ideologically, and both—certainly compared to Iran in the 1980s—appear to be secular and pragmatic in their social policies. Iran, at war with Iraq since 1980,has denounced the Iraqi ruler Saddam Hussein as an "infidel," an "atheist," and the whole Ba'th philosophy as inimical to Islam because it is a form of nationalism and divisive of the Islamic *umma*. To the present regime in Iran, integral nationalism such as Ba'thism is as "Western" in origin and as alien to Islam as is liberal nationalism. Both types of nationalism are as much anathema as is Marxist Socialism, also of Western provenance.

Marxist socialism finds expression in the Third World in a variety of movements including, of course, communism and also romantic Third Worldism. To be sure, Marxism, or socialism more broadly, has taken many forms that often reflect the particular area that has adopted this ideology and has made it an intrinsic part of its political culture, for instance Russia's Leninism or China's Maoism. Nevertheless, Marxism as an ideology of Western provenance, reflects a particular type of Western thought, one hostile to traditionalism and religion, and one resting upon belief in the Idea of Progress. It is this secular and historically dynamic aspect of Marxism that Third World conservatives, both militant and traditionalist, see as dangerous to them as Western bourgeois liberalism, even if Third World radicals who have embraced Marxism feel it to be and consider it to be, autochthonous. William McNeill has suggested that Marxism has had a strong appeal in much of the Third World precisely because it has been a Western "heresy;" it has offered a way of defying the liberal bourgois West and at the same time legitimizing modernity (1963, p. 782). This interpretation may seem patronizing to ideologues of the Third World, but, in any case, the adoption of Marxism does constitute a rejection of the Western European and American paradigm of an open, liberal society. Objections that even Russian Marxists have made to liberal Western influences are often the same as those made by both integral nationalists, local Marxists, and even, as we will see, Muslim fundamentalists. Recently, for example, Victor Mishin, head of the Russian Komsomol (the Communist Youth League), denounced anomic youth behavior as resulting from "propaganda of the Western way of life and the propagation of political indifference, skepticism, spiritual emptiness and a consumer mentality" (NYT, 9 September 1984). These very words might have appeared in the lectures of Ali Shariati, perhaps the most influential of the Muslim radicals, who is discussed in the next section.

Muslim Radicals

The term "Muslim radicals" is used here to refer to ideologues who combine the thinking of the fundamentalists and of the Third World-ists, giving to the former a progressive, modernist content and to the latter a religious content. In recent years their moment of preeminence came with the outbreak of the revolution in Iran in 1978, but they were soon forced into the underground by the conservative Islamic Republicans of the Imam Khomeini. Their leading spokesman has been Ali Shariati, who died under uncertain circumstance in 1977 on the eve of the revolution. The height of his influence probably came with the lectures he delivered at the Hosainieh-ye Ershàd, a mosque teaching complex, closed down by the government in 1975 (Shariati, 1981, 1982; Tabari and Yeganeh, pp. 11–12; Hanson).

Shariati saw himself as combining the progressiveness of secular modernists, the *raushanfikr* in Farsi, and Shi'ism rid of the obfuscatory and debilitating "traditionalism" of the Islam of the *'ulama* of Iran. His goal was a revival that would transform Iran into a pure and revived Muslim state, but one, at the same time, progressive and modern. He admired many Third Worldists such as Aimée Césaire and Fanon, and even translated Fanon's *The Wretched of the Earth* into Farsi, but he insisted that their inspiration be subordinated to the "national values" of Iran, which he saw as basically Shi'ite. In his writing and his public lectures in Teheran, he often quoted from Fanon and other Third Worldists. His favorite symbols came from Islamic scriptures, for example, Cain and Abel, the first symbolizing the established rulers and monopoly ownership of wealth, the latter symbolizing the oppressed and the system of primitive socialism.

As a modernizer, Shariati wanted Iran to benefit from Western scientific and technological accomplishments, but he strongly denounced Iranians who were mesmerized by the West and became "needy slaves . . . clients . . . clinging imitators" as a result of Western cultural imperialism. Not only should Western cultural imperialism be opposed, but Iranians should realize that even the Western writers many of them properly admired—Sartre, Brecht, Camus, among them—were addressing problems that were those of the West and not of Islam and of Iran. These Westerners wrote "with a full stomach," and yet out of an existentialist despair, one inappropriate to Iranians who had their Islamic faith by which to live, a faith, which renewed and properly interpreted, formed the basis of a culture inherently superior to the Western. Shariati's militant stand against imitation was anticipated by a number of other Iranian intellectuals. Among them, Samad Behrangi (d. 1968) denounced *Amrikazadegi* (Americanization) in education and the use of English as an affectation of rich bourgeois families; Jalal Al-e Ahmad (d. 1969), translator of Camus and Sartre into *Farsi*, denounced *Gharbzadegi* (blighted by, infatuated with, the West).

Regarding the West—and he was educated in Paris—Shariati had some peculiar and often confused opinions; these are some of the ideas he believed in and preached. One, since the Middle Ages the West has been dominated by the bourgeois class and the bourgeois spirit; science has been subordinated to power, not to the search for truth; Western culture has been materialistic, hedonistic, and individualistic and has placed utility over value, rationality over religion, "living for" over "for living;" Western eyes have rested on the "stomach or below," not upon heaven, and power and consumption have been preferred to truth, beauty, and choice (*khair*), i.e., free will. Art has been reduced to depicting "futility" (as with Beckett) or to titillation and propaganda. While the revolution against the medieval culture did produce temporary progress, it soon gave way to Western man, "the world's most menacing beast," becoming slave to the "demon of money," and a victim of "consumerism." Two, Westerners boast of their superiority over the East—thus Renan, Siegfried, and others—but this is only a superiority over an East the West itself has corrupted. In fact, the modern West has been the creation of the Reformation which, Shariati argued, was in turn the result of the progressive Islamization of Christianity beginning with the Crusades! Three, the West developed according to a complicated cyclical pattern in which the break-throughs made by "stars" have soon been corrupted by inferior intellectuals and spread among the masses as superstition. Thus, for example, the insights of such "stars" as Leonardo da Vinci were corrupted by the likes of Francis Bacon into crass materialism. Today, the "stars" such as Franz Fanon, Martin Heidegger, and several others, in a most curious grab bag of names, will revolutionize the West once more and presumably transform it from an enemy to a friend of the Third World until corrupted again by Western intellectuals. Inevitably, Shariati had to confront the issue of the role of women in his idealized revived Shi'ite state to come; his answers, unsatisfying to either Right or Left, will be considered in the next chapter.

Although *sui generis* in many respects, Colonel Qadhafi of Libya can be considered to be as much a Muslim radical as was Shariati (Qadhafi; Meyer). Although he presents himself as the defender of the *umma*, his behavior has been unorthodox, at least from the point of view of the traditional *ulama*, who, in Libya, he has alternately ignored and harassed. It is not strange that in Libya the "fundamentalist" trend has expressed itself in defiance of Qadhafi's unorthodox reliance on the Koran alone (and on his own private interpretation of it); to militant Islamists, Qadhafi's *Green Book* is, in effect, heretical (François Burgat, Le M, 30 December 1986).

In his Islamic program, which he calls the "Third Way," he advocates the adoption of a policy that is neither communist nor capitalist-democratic, but lies between the two. Based upon his later idiosyncratic reading of the *Quran*, and rejection of the *Sunna* and the *Hadith* (the practice and the sayings of the Prophet), he has devised a theory according to which the polity comes under the direct rule of the mass of people and in which men and women are completely equal in all respects, and here he has gone further than even Shariati. Today, in spite of the conservatism of most of Libya's people, women have equal educational and professional opportunities with men; in this, and in the radical causes abroad that he supports, Qadhafi can be considered something of a Third Worldist like Shariati as well as a radical Muslim, also like Shariati. Colonel Qadhafi remains a unique phenomenon as a leader in the contemporary Islamic scene. As for Ali Shariati, his influence has been eclipsed for the time being by the forces of militant religious conservatism in Iran.

Militant Muslim Conservatives: Fundamentalists

The phenomenon now to be considered is one that has been labeled
in a variety of ways, "fundamentalist revival" among them. However,
such a phrase is subject to criticism because it suggests misleading
parallels with fundamentalism in Christianity, and because revival
implies to some people that the mass of Muslims have heretofore
lacked piety and religious devotion. What can be agreed upon is that
the phenomenon involves militancy and that its proponents seek to
restore Islamic norms as the sole norms of political and religious
behavior as when, they believe, Islam was under the early reign of the
prophet. The label "conservatism" is used in the present context with
some reluctance; in some ways the militant movement that now
dominates Iran and is making itself heard throughout the Muslim
world is radical in its aggressiveness and single-mindedness. But if
one compares the programs of Ali Shariati or Qadhafi to the Imam
Khomeini and his followers, the term "conservatism" does seem
appropriate; Shariati would doubtlessly have preferred the term
"reactionary." It has been observed that the militants have transformed Shi'ite symbols—the "Kerbala paradigm" for example involving the martyrdom of Hussein, the true Imam—from passive ones to
defiant and militant ones. Hussein, thus, has become a symbol of the
struggle for justice instead of the lamentable martyr of injustice
(Ajami, 1986, pp. 136–43). Both Ira Lapidus and Bassam Tibi have
maintained that the ideology of the militants is not of traditional
Islamic provenance but is a case of the politicization of Islam by the
employment of a Western-type ideology to mobilize the masses. If so,
and there is much to be said for this argument, we have the paradox
of a defiantly anti-Western movement paying tribute to its opponent
by resorting to its own weapons (also true of the use of tape-record-
ings and television to mobilize the masses).

Georges Corm denounces Khomeinism as morbid and schizo-
phrenic in its negative dependence upon the West for identity, an
obsession that makes it closed, intolerant, and reactionary (1986, pp.
184–95).

It might be observed that some purificational movements, Wahha-
bism for example, were once militant but have, in recent times,
become relatively static and defensive, and that past militant purificational movements, the Kharidjites in the seventh century, the Qar-
mations in the tenth, for example, indicate that Islam has in its legacy
anticipations of the movement considered here.

The term "militant" before "Islamic Conservatism" is used to distinguish the movement clearly from what might be called simply "Islamic Conservatism," a term which could be applied to establishment and governmental Islamism in Pakistan or Saudi Arabia where, from the point of view of the militants, Islam is merely used as a disguise for nonreligious political control of the people by a regime or a family. One distinction often made is between *al-Islam as-sha'bi* (populist Islam) and *al Islam al-rasmi* (establishment Islam). The latter tends to be, if not pro-Western, at least Western-dependent and America-dependent in particular. The second, in contrast to the first, tends to be national in orientation, whereas militant Islamic conservatism rejects nationalism in principle as divisive of the ummah or Islam (Halliday in Cole and Keddie, p. 92). Nevertheless, in the one state where militant conservative Islam rules—Iran—if for tactical reasons alone, while the principle of Islamic universalism has been adhered to, appeals are made to national Iranian feeling (the Arabian Gulf is called the Persian Gulf for example). One might compare the use of "nationalism" in Iran today to Stalin's similar use of it against Germany in World War II. In both cases, "nationalism" has been stimulated by government tactics and a genuine feeling of national engagement—in the Iranian case, against Iraq.

This return, not to Islam, but to the adoption of Islamic norms exclusively, finds different expressions in the contemporary Muslim world. Such expressions include the revivalism of radical Muslims like Shariati, the conservative traditional and non-militant "orthodoxy" of Saudi Arabia, the pattern recently applied in Pakistan and the Sudan of "Islamization" from above (to opponents of the government a case of opportunism), and the pattern of militancy and doctrinal expansionism dominant in Iran today and making waves from one end of the Muslim world to the other, from Indonesia to Morocco and Senegal (Mortimer).

Militant conservatism is, of course, directed against all Western influences that are held responsible for having corrupted the Muslim world and weakened its faith. Those accustomed to Western life styles in Iran can now enjoy Western ways only abroad or behind curtains, as Youssef M. Ibrahimi has testified (WSJ, 17 January 1984). Women returning from foreign flights bedeck themselves with gown and veil before landing, and men appear without neckties and with scruffy faces. Ali Merad, who refers to this revival as the "ideologisation of Islam" sees an emphasis upon *asala* (authenticity) and upon the rejection of *taghrib* (Westernization) as fundamental to the movement.

Merad suggests that the views of Nizam Ajmir Mohamed, are representative of the militant conservatives who hold that the West speaks of liberty while imposing the cruelest imperialism in history; talks of peace and justice while fighting the most devastating wars of all time; "emancipates" women while exploiting them "as a means of destroying the home and the family." In sum, in an article published in April, 1978 entitled "The Impact of the West on Muslims," Mohamed is quoted, "Western civilization claims to be the only avenue of enlightenment and progress while it actually leads straight down the road to moral ruin and suicide." Yvonne Haddad observes that the first organization of a militant and integral (fundamentalist) Islam to view the West not only as alien, but as *the* enemy, was the Muslim Brotherhood (the Ikhwan al-Muslimin), founded in Egypt in 1928 by Hasan al-Banna, an Egyptian sheikh who was assassinated in 1949 (1982, pp. 24–25). Banna's was also the first important modern organization to seek to establish through political means a totally Islamic state governed according to the *Quran* and the *Sharica* (Haddad, 1982, Mitchell; Ibrahim, 1978a; Ajami, 1981, pp. 60–62). According to Banna, Westernization has proven a failure and is "incapable of offering to men's minds a flicker of light, a ray of hope, a grain of faith, or of providing anxious persons the smallest path toward rest and tranquility. Man is not simply an instrument among others." Western life, in short, has become a "materialistic poison." Today the West is on the defensive, and the future belongs to a revived and powerful Islam, one that combines the virtues of both communist egalitarianism and Western democracy and is fired by faith (Karpat, pp. 118–122; Donohue and Esposito, 1982, pp. 78–83). Westernization still remains a threat, however, its individualism threatens the integrity of the *umma*, and its educational system, which serves to laud Western achievements and disparage those of the Islamic world, rests upon a materialistic view of history and upon a methodology that threatens to undermine the sanctity of scriptures and so destroy faith.

Another Egyptian to disparage the West is Mustafa Mahmud, who has spoken of "the psychological emptiness and malaise which occurs in opulent European societies like Sweden or in socialist atheistic societies in the East where we find the highest proportion of insanity and suicide despite the abundant guarantees of life for all" (Donohue and Esposito, 1982, pp. 155–59). Particularly influential among groups that are, today, even more militant and xenophobic than the Muslim Brotherhood, has been Sayyid Qutb who, in many publications, has preached that someday a demoralized, spiritually bankrupt

West would succumb to a renewed Islam, and that to imitate the West in any way was not only apostasy but also disasterous because of the West's false values and its erroneous reading of history and of reality (Haddad in Esposito, *Voices of Resurgent Islam*, p. 90). Sayyid Qutb, a fiery critic of the establishment in Egypt, was executed in Cairo in 1966, but his influence today is greater than during his lifetime.

The hostility of the Ayatollah or Iman Ruhollah Khomeini to the West is too well known to need elaboration here, but a few observations might be made (Khomeini, 1979, 1981). As the charismatic leader in the revolution against the Shah, Khomeini led his followers, the Islamic Republicans, to victory over radical groups such as the communists and groups influenced by radical ideologues like Ali Shariati. In the mid-80s Iran was in the main what Khomeini says it was; those who disagreed are either in exile, in prison, or in the underground; and although in most ways highly traditionalist, he has placed his own individual stamp upon Iran. His establishment of the *wilayat i-faqih* (Guidance of the Jurisprudent) as the supreme governing body of Iran (in the absence—*ghaybat*—of the twelfth successor to Muhammad, the Imam now in a state of occultism), is innovative (Keddie, 1983). Such direct, rather than advisory, rule by the *'ulama* is new and not in accordance with orthodox Shi'ite consensus. Second, his adoption for himself of the title "Imam" gives to his own person a prestige and legitimacy that is unusual and suggests a cult of personality the Muslim Brothers, for one, would oppose (Hudson in Esposito, *Islam and Development*, 1980, p. 11). His purpose is to assure that Muslims live by the true faith now rid of the corruption it suffered originally at the hands of Jews and later at the hands of the West. Another claim original to Khomeini is that Islam is intrinsically opposed to monarchy (Nahid Yeganeh in Cole and Keddie, p. 122). Opposition to many of these interpretations can be found in the very heart of Shi'ite Islam, in the figure of another Ayatollah—Hajj Sayyid Abulghassim Moussavi Khoy of Najf in Iraq—who, among others, denounces Khomeini's unusual assumption of the title "Imam" as heretical. The title, he claims, is meant only for the Shi'ite leader now in a state of occultation (Péroncel-Hugoz, Le M, 11–12 May 1986).

The Iranian religious revolution has had, clearly, a strong impact upon Muslims throughout the world; it has increased suspicion and even hatred of the West, and it has forced even governments closely aligned with the West to attend to the challenge of Khomeini. Whether directly influenced by events in Iran or only reinforced by them, the return to Islamic norms is evident in most Muslim states, among them the following, considered here as illustrative cases.

In Turkey the now ruling Motherland Party of Turgut Ozal takes the line that Turkey must return to its Islamic values that were abandoned or neglected too long under Kamalism, the ideology of Atatürk, and strengthen bonds with the rest of the Muslim world. Limits have been placed on where liquor can be sold; female tourists have been prevented from parading topless at beaches; and penalties have been imposed for insulting Allah or Muhammad. Thomas L. Friedman reported that in 1984 in West Beirut, the once cosmopolitan playground of Lebanon, the atmosphere was being "Islamized" by the pressure of militant Shi'ism. There were cases of women being forced to cover bare parts of the body, of bars being smashed up, and Khomeini's picture was omnipresent (NYT, 31 May 1984). Symbols of the United States, of course, have been threatened and destroyed; Americans have been kidnapped, and the President of the American University of Beirut was assassinated. In the Sudan, probably as a desperate attempt to save a tottering regime, President Jaafar Nimairi ordered justice to be based upon the Shariah; hands have been cut off for theft, an Italian priest was flogged for possession of alcohol, and the unity of the country was even threatened by efforts to impose Islamic law upon the animist or Christian south of the country. In Pakistan, whose original *raison d'*être was, of course, to provide Muslims with their own state, original rule of "modernists" in the last years of the reign of Zulfikar Ali Bhutto (1970–1977) was giving way to a policy of growing Islamic identification and practice (Esposito, 1980; Mortimer, pp. 186–229). Under Zia ul-Haqq, sole ruler since 1977, the emphasis has been upon the full application of the Nizam-i-Islam (the Islamic dispensation); the *hudud* (penalties for breaches of Islamic law) have been strictly imposed, and *riba* (usurious interest) has been abolished as part of a revised banking system.

On a popular level, militant Islamic conservatism has spread widely in the Muslim world. Examples of the new conservatism from the late 1980s include the condemnation of twenty seven Moroccans condemned for plotting against the king and the wide circulation of *Essaraya*, published by Abdelaziz Naamani, a leading militant in exile. Appeal was not yet widespread because, in part, of popular belief in the *baraka* (religious charm) of the king and in his religious leadership (Le M, 16 October 1985). Among the PLO, Islamic militancy was growing to the dismay of many secularists who had prided themselves on the tolerance of the organization that included a membership that was 20 percent Christian (MGW, 18 May 1987; Le M, 17 November 1986). In the Gaza strip, for example, the militant students at the University of Gaza were able to carry 70 percent of the vote in student elections (WPR, January 1987, pp. 56–57; NYT, 30 April 1987). In Malaysia, it was reported that 90 percent of the girls now wore veils (MGM, 25 May 1986). In Egypt, indications of militant pressure were the sponsorship by secular parties of religious magazines, their public concession that law should be based upon the Shari'ah, a new toughness on the Christian Copt community, and a move by the rector of the famous Muslim university of Al-Azhar to have a commission appointed to pass on the publication of all books in Egypt. Among the slogans of the faithful militants were: "neither Jewish nor Christian . . . neither socialist nor capitalist . . . neither eastern nor western . . . Islam!, Islam!" and "No to the West. No to Zionism. No to the Crusades." Decals appeared on cars reading "To God, Religion is Islam." In 1986, riots led to the destruction of Western symbols, video stores, liquor shops, and discotheques. At Assyut University all sports except karate were banned "by student pressure"; biology professors alluding to Darwin were reported to be subject to harrassment; Khalid Islambouli, who assassinated Anwar Sadat, and Suleiman Khater, a policeman who in 1985 had opened fire on Israeli tourists and killed some of them, were considered popular heroes. In Lebanon, the Shi'ite Hizbollah represented Iranian policies and interests, and many members of this loosely-knit party advocated turning Lebanon into a Muslim state, while a part of the program of the Sunni militants in Tripoli read: "Lebanon does not exist! Only Islam, which resolves all problems and frees man, counts" (Le M, 16 March 1986, p. 16–17). In the late 1980s, the prospect for a Muslim state in Lebanon, if only in a part of the country, was stronger than anywhere else outside of Iran.

How lasting and how universal to Islam the new militancy will prove to be is, inevitably, a subject of heated controversy among scholars of the Islamic world. There are those who see it as only reactive, a mark of frustration rather than a positive ideology likely to prevail for very long (Ajami, 1981, pp. 176–78, 183–87, 199–200), and some still insist, as does Jacques Berque, that overall, "evolution is tending to the profane, and progress is experienced as temporal" (1983, p. 44). There are others who see the new militancy as having major significance for the future as well for the present; one Iranian expert maintained at the 1984 yearly conference of the Middle East Institute in Washington, D.C. and then in print that the new military is the most significant development of our time (J. Bill, FA, Fall, 1984).

Whatever the future should prove, it is not insignificant that many, if not most scholars of the Middle East, were surprised when militant Islamism began to get the upper hand in some parts of the Muslim world and to threaten others with subversion. William Polk, for example, openly admitted his astonishment, having assumed that the trend would continue to be in the direction of secular modernization (p. xiv). This lack of vatic foresight on the part of so many regarding Islam in general and Iran in particular (Benard-Khalilzad, pp. 12–24), myself included, was clearly the partial result of a tendency to view the future of Islam too much in terms of Eurocentric assumptions.

In regard to Iran, Hugh Trevor-Roper tells of a conversation he had in 1960 with an Iranian engineer in charge of a newly opened oil well near Qum who, glorying in the dream of a new modern society in Iran, pointed to Qum, whose mullahs, he proudly said, "will have no place, they will not even be imaginable in our brave new world" (TLS, 25 July 1980). It was once conventional among Polish communists to believe that with industrialization and modernization, the industrial workers would shed their Catholic ways and commitments (Davies, 1986, p. 12).

While prophecies might encourage greater humility, it is by no means certain that those who still believe the future of the Muslim Third World to be profane and secular will be proven wrong in the long run (L. C. Brown, 1980, 1987). Probably, the truth as to the future of militant conservative Islam lies between those who downplay its thrust and those who hold it to be the crucial development of the time. While the phenomenon of this militancy is evident in almost all Muslim or partly-Muslim countries, there are factors in each case that stand in opposition to it. Countervailing forces that can be cited, even within Iran itself, are those ayatollahs who oppose Khomeini's extremism but who are, for the nonce, relegated to the sidelines, and the pragmatism of some of his supporters who, upon his death, might seek to preserve the accomplishments of the revolution by relying on a more flexible policy in regard to external pressures and constraints. There was already some indication (in the late 1980s) of a less rigid policy towards the United States (MERIP, Jan.-Feb. 1987, 5–8; Le M, 15 March 1987). To the extent that Kemal Karpat is right when he claims that the phenomenon of militancy is, at heart, a way of mobilizing the lower classes as well as a way of enabling them to enter the political scene (1986), it may prove to be that the symbols of Islam are more tactical devices rather than as indications of any terminal commitment.[5] Finally, as Fred Halliday has observed, militant Islam in only one dimension of the Iranian character; the secular modernist dimension as well as the traditionalist and the baazari (traditional mercantile) are still alive albeit eclipsed at the present ("The Other Irans," TLS, 20 June 1986, p. 667). Other realities limit militant Islamic expansionism; e.g. the Arabic speakers among the majority Shi'ites of Iraq have not aligned themselves (as of 1987) with the Khomeini revolution, and Shi'ites elsewhere are either nationalist and not Islamist in their orientation (the Shi'ites of Lebanon, for example, who align themselves with al-Amal rather than the pro-Iranian Hizbollah), or are even more secularist and progressive, in their ideological commitments, than the host Sunnis (in Turkey, for example). The view of Islam as monolithic is clearly absurd; so also is the view that the world of the Shi'ites is one and uniform (Cole and Keddie, pp. 20–24).

Opposing the new Islamic militancy are the ideologues and leaders committed to varieties (and degrees) of progressive secular rule, the Ba'th regimes of Iraq and Syria (in the late 1980s). In 1985, Gerald Seib reported that in its lively night life, Baghdad seemed to flaunt "the contrast between its version of Islamic life and the puritanical one espoused by Iran's Ayatollah Khomenini. Iraqi leaders apparently believe that their people will be more eager to wage the good fight if they can periodically taste the wordly pleasures that would be deprived them by the "fanatical" mullahs across the border" (WSJ, 1 March 1985). In Turkey, to the military and much of the civilian establishment, militant Islam is regarded as a threat to the secularist heritage of Atatürk (and a form of heresy, *irtica*). In Egypt, too, there is strong establishment opposition to a movement (one clearly divided into many groupings) that cost President Sadat his life and that threatens to upset the policies of Sadat and his successor President Moubarak. In 1986, the regime did not hesitate to close down "pirate" (non-government owned) mosques and to arrest many leaders from among the militants. As *Le Monde* put it, "The government has turned to the offensive against the Muslim extremists" (5 November 1985). Informed observers of the Egyptian scene have questioned the likelihood of militant Islam winning out. P. J. Vatikiotis sees "Egyptianism" as a "continuing barrier to Arabo-Islamism" (TLS, 14 Feb. 1986), and Youseef M. Ibrahim sees Egypt as "too old and too rich in culture, history and beauty to drift into the Middle Ages" (WSJ, 28 May 1985).

It can be noted that some "modernizers" of Egypt in recent history have been eminent intellectuals like Ahmad Amin and Taha Husayn who have strongly advocated that the future of Egypt lay in a synthesis of the best of the East and West (Hourani, 1983). Finally, as a countervailing factor to militant Islam one could include that of the many intellectuals and writers in "modern" or Western-type environments who are important among the makers of opinions and values (some of whom will later be discussed as "marginals"). At a medical conference in London in 1985, Drs. Ghada Karmi and Zaki Badawi, both Arabs, warned against the harmful notion that there was such a thing as "Islamic science distinct from Science as such" (ME, April 1985, pp. 64–65). In Algeria, the government held firm to its decision to declare the end of Ramadam (the Muslim month of fasting) in 1985 on Wednesday, June 19th rather than, as the militants insisted on Tuesday the 18th when the new moon was seen in Mecca. The official APS news service declared that the government would not support "a vision that contradicts scientific calculation" (Le M, 20 June 1985).

Many artists and intellectuals in the Muslim world, educated in "Western"-type schools and milieus, have adopted many of the values militant Muslims themselves denounce as Western. They have expressed distaste at the narrowness and intolerance of the militant wave as in the case, for example, of Farag Foda's best-selling *Before the Fall*, an unrelenting attack on Islamic militancy. The liberal and progressive Arab intellectual might be "embattled," as Judith Miller put it, but he has not yet cried uncle (June 1985).

5

The West Impugned: Resentment and Ressentiment

Some of the concerns discussed have been peculiar only to Muslims, but two concerns that cut across the whole spectrum of Third World opinion are, first, those of Western economic and cultural neo-colonialism and, second, Western racism, a term broadly used to include attitudes and behavior of cultural condescension as well as assumptions of biological superiority.

Third World ideologues who accuse the West of "neo- colonialism," or "neo-imperialism," two pejorative terms for the same thing, have already been encountered in these pages; the indictment has generally been that the West has continued to dominate the economy and the culture (and so the polity) of Third World nations even after formal independence has been granted. Representative complaints made in this regard have included the following: C. G. Weeramantry, a Sri Lanka judge, states that to nations such as his own, which became independent rapidly, there has occurred a "slide back to dependence," there was not sufficient time to develop trained expertise and to encourage genuinely democratic habits (CSM, 17 February 1978). Rex de Silva, a journalist also from Sri Lanka, interprets the United State's refusal to sign the Law of the Seas Treaty, already signed by one hundred nations, as a manifestation of "economic colonialism"; the aim of the United States is to seize underwater wealth before others have the sophisticated "vacuum cleaners" it alone now possesses (WPR, February 1983, p. 46). "The losers," de Silva states, "will once again be the impoverished Third World" K. B. Lall, an Indian, quotes Arnold J. Toynbee in saying that the West has been the "arch aggressor of modern times" (WPR, June 1979, pp. 26–29). Sana Hasan (p. 147) quotes Mohammed Hassanein Heikal, the well known Egyptian journalist who says that his greatest fear resulting from Anwar Sadat's "opening" to the West was that Egypt would become "another Costa Rica." Even leaders of a nation like Tunisia, whose colonial experience has been relatively benign and whose attitudes have been relatively pro-Western, can harp upon this theme. Thus, in October 1983, Mustapha A. Filali, Tunisian delegate to the Permanent Maghreb Consultative Committee, described North Africa as having been severely wounded by French rule (Le M, 27 October 1983). He stated that upon independence agriculture was in an unhealthy state: wine production, fruit tree cultivation, and market-gardening, all were geared to serve metropolitan interests; by being tied to the French franc, North Africa was dependent for 70 percent of its exchanges with the EEC, upon remittances from migrant workers in the EEC zone; and France has tended to encourage tendencies that divide rather than unite the Maghreb. Other critics of the West point out that, for purposes other than rhetoric, the West does not anymore intend to help the Third World significantly enter into the world of development (Catherine Goybet, MD, December 1984, pp. 8–9); Jogdish N. Bahwati, (quoted in NYT Book Reviews, 3 March 1985, p. 11) maintains that "a quiet requiem" is in order for any future prospect of Western aid to the Third World. Philip Ochieng, Kenyan newspaper editor, lambastes both superpowers for continuing an arms race that endangers the Third World as much as themselves (WPR, January 1987, pp. 36–37). He holds it an absurd rationalization that the United States seeks to preserve and extend liberty when, in fact, it supports oppressive regimes in "Chile, Central America, Palestine, South Africa"; that the U.S.S.R. intends to replace imperialism with socialism when "its own state monopolist conglomerate is sucking dry the Vietnamese, the Burmese, the Eastern Europeans, the Afghans, the Ethiopians, and others."

The litany of accusation is familiar enough, but there are some ironic twists given to this subject every so often. Two Indians, Mario Turpo Choquehuanca, a Peruvian, and Edilberto Soto Angli, a Mexican, both express outrage that their authentic culture is falling victim to "Westernization," not at the hands of Western "imperialists" but at the hands of their own ruling class (MD, October 1982, p. 30; Le M, 2 July 1982). To compound the irony, Gabriel Garcia Marquez argues that South Americans were lucky to have had the Spanish as colonizers, that through Spanish influence the South Americans have been able to effect a "cultural revolution" and, unlike Africa, complete "a clear process of cultural decolonization" (WPR, April 1982, p. 61). Regarding this irony Mario Vargas Llosa observes that the "Spaniards" are even now unfairly indicted for what "they" did to the Indians. "Did "they" really do it? We did it. We are the *conquistadores*, . . . our parents and grandparents." He admits that the treatment of the Indians by his own over the centuries to this day is no better than the Spaniards treatment of the Aztecs and the Incas (TLS, 30 January 1987, pp. 110–11). A different twist is given to the subject of cultural decolonization by Mouloud Achour in *El Moudjahid*, Algeria's major newspaper (Le M, 2 July 1982). He expressed his gratitude that the French colonizers had only "neutralized" Algerian culture rather than, by granting full French rights to his people, imposing the "suicidal trap" of assimilation. This *"erreur salutaire,"* Achour says sarcastically, saved Algeria's culture from disappearing and gave it the possibility of revival. A third twist made by Sisa Le Bernard, a Central African philosopher, is that young Africans have been so seduced by socialist-Marxist models that they are neglecting their own proper culture. To them, he complains, culture means "Prague" rather than France's massive invasion of Chad! (Le M, 28 August 1980). On the other hand, Daryush Shayegan, an Iranian intellectual expressed a concern in 1979 that the influence now pervading the tired and spiritually empty liberal West with its "lucidity of nihilism" would spread moral entropy and a deadening "philosophy of good digestion" (a phrase taken from Dostoevski) among the youth of the Third World.

The issues of cultural and economic decolonization are of great and serious importance among the peoples and nations of the Third World. Blaming one's problems upon the West, and upon imperialism and neo-colonialism, is often only a rationalization, a kind of smokescreen; it is also evident that the pressure of the West and of an evolving global cosmopolitan culture are factors that militate against individual people's molding or "recovering" cultures that are unique to themselves, and are merely symbols and guarantees of final decolonization.

This concern with the Western threat to identity goes back to the early years of the 1870s when such influence became widely perceptible. In 1871, at the same time that some Arab intellectuals in the Levant began to parody compatriots who adopted Western styles of dress, Kanagaki Robun in Japan satirized those Japanese who were "beef-eaters," scented their hair with cologne, wore calico under their kimonas, carried gingham umbrellas and pocket watches, and pretended they were helping Japan to become "a truly civilized country" (Duus, p. 87). In recent times, the same lament has appeared in the poetry of Aimé Cesaire to make the point that is is without any shame that Africans can admit that Western political forms might not be suitable for them: Africans are "Those who have invented neither powder nor the compass/Those who have tamed neither gas nor electricity;/Those who have explored neither the seas nor the skies . . . My negritude is neither a tower nor a cathedral;/ It plunges into the red flesh of the earth." In a different context but with similar intent, the Moroccan writer Abdelkebir Khatibi writes, "we want to uproot Western knowledge from its central place within ourselves" (even if this uprooting is to be done with the aid of Jacques Derrida!) (Barakat, p. 13).

A related form of resentment often expressed is that the West tends to judge others by its own standards and arrogantly holds these standards to be of "universal" applicability, and disparages those who, given the chance, want to be other than Western—such people must be, the Western logic goes, "fanatical" or the tools of others (the Russians, most often). Anouar Abdel-Malek, who expresses this resentment, also remarks in passing that the term "decolonization" itself reflects Eurocentric arrogance as a *"vocable occidento-centriste privatif,"* by which he means that the term implies only a negative process, and one that presumably once completed will provide a status identical with that of the free West (1972). Along the same lines, Onwuchekwa Jemie Chinweizu in a work entitled *Toward the Decolonization of African Literature* attacks Western literary critics for having applied Western categories to African literature by imposing Western "cultural hegemony," and, in the process, debasing this African literature. In this spirit, demands have often been made by Third World ideologues in favor of the decolonization of history, sociology, and anthropology. Among Western scholars held by Third World ideologues particularly guilty of disparagement, in this case of Muslims and Arabs, have been Bernard Lewis, for allegedly explaining all contemporary Arab behavior as motivated exclusively by religion; and Gustave von Grunebaum for his alleged Western chauvinism and his tendency to disparage Islam as in his statement, for example, that the "dominant feature of . . . [the Muslim's] . . . identity is membership in the 'umma,' . . . and that it took the Western impact to open the inner life as subject and problem of literary endeavor" (*Modern Islam* pp. 134–135).[6]

One could argue that while it is true that the West has often been arrogant and supercilious in its dealings with others, these attitudes are no different from those of other civilizations in their dealings with the West as well as toward one another (Benard-Khalilzad, pp. 86–87). A Third Worlder might very well answer that while this claim is, of course, true, other civilizations have not laid claim to being "universal" and "humanistic" as has the West. But more importantly, no civilization has had and continues to have as deep an impact on others as the West.

In 1956, when Sir John Bagot Glubb was dismissed as commander of Jordan's Arab Legion following nationalist agitation against him, he was asked what the West had done wrong; his answer was "superciliousness" (Dean, p. 261). This perceived superciliousness, or condescension, or even racism, of Westerners continues to anger many in the Third World and poison relationships between it and the West.

There are many examples. One is the case of K. S. Kua, a Malaysian who objected to an article on his country written by Anthony Burgess (MGW, 1 February 1981, p. 2). The article, Mr. Kua said, was full of the "predictable, subjective observations . . . which may sound cute in a novel or a tourist's diary, but of which concerned Malaysians are sick." To Kua, Burgess's most irritating cliché was that the Chinese do the work and prosper, while the Malaysians govern and produce nothing. Another case is that of Saidou Bokoum, an African *metteur en scene*, who complained that in France African culture is considered marginal because of the "mépris occidental;" African artists are treated as "Harkis" (Algerians who fought for the French in 1954–1962) (Le M, 6 August 1982). Similarly, the well known Nigerian novelist, Chinua Achebe, complains that Western myths oblige Blacks to say nothing about their own experience or else no longer be considered authentic Africans! The black man is limited to making strange sounds; the Western assumption is that only the white man can speak for and explain the native (TLS, February 1980).

Edward Said's *Orientalism* constitutes one long diatribe against the West for its prejudices. His indictment has come in the context of an awakening among Arabs in the West, in the United States in particular, to the fact that they are, according to James Zogby, executive director of the newly found American-Arab Anti-Discriminatory Committee (ADC), "the last minority to stand up for its rights. The blacks have done it, the Jews have done it, the Hispanics have done it, but the Arab-Americans haven't—until now" (WSJ, 30 August 1984). Arab-Americans like Zogby and Said and Arab students in the United States—there are presently about three million of both in the United States—were especially embittered by the open display of hostility to Arabs and to Muslims in general after Israel's founding, and particu-

larly after Israel's triumph in the Six Day War of 1967. This resentment was exacerbated when, with the radical rise of oil prices after
1973, Arabs were abused in caricatures and as stereotyped villains on
television shows. When Khomeini seized power, Iranians were confused with Arabs and both were indiscriminately branded fanatics.
Today, Arab-Americans are better organized than before, but they
hardly have the influence of their main rivals, the pro-Zionist and
pro-Israel political action committees. Consequently, Arab-Americans
continue to be bitter and often to feel treated as racial inferiors
(Ghareeb; Suleiman; Shaheen; Mansfield, pp. 490–502, 503–54; Curtiss).

More recently, as Magda Abu-Fadil points out, Arabs have been
insulted by a host of anti-Shi'ite jokes (as in the song "Chicken Shi'ite")
and by references to the "tribal barbarism" of a whole people held
guilty for the terrorism of some of their extremists (ME, August 1985,
pp. 19–20). Juan Carolos Lerota spoke for many South Americans
who resent Western attitudes that view South America "as the back-
yard of the United States" (S, Spring-Summer 1968, no. 70–71, pp.
152–54).

Particularly painful to migrant workers in Western countries, are
the pejorative views of themselves held by various sectors of the
European country in which they live. They are exposed, for example,
to the vulgar lucubrations of the rightist politician Le Pen: "tomorrow
the immigrants will be in your home, eating your soup, sleeping with
your wife or daughter" (*Journal Herald*, Dayton, 22 March 1985), to
the sophisticated sophism of the French intellectuals of the rightist
movement, Le GRECE, who urged the migrants to go home in order
to preserve their own identity (MD, April 1986, pp. 10–12). They see
statistics used to show, for example, that half of the school children
of Amsterdam are non-Dutch, and that one fifth of them are black
(mostly from Surinam) (NYT, 6 August 1986), and that unless something is done in the United States, by the year 2000 the number of
alien immigrants in the country will rise to such figures that "our
compassion to share what we have will destroy what we have" (Lamm
and Imhoff). Since the increased tempo of terrorism in Europe and
elsewhere in the 1980s, anger in the West has often dissolved toleration, and Arabs, in particular, have felt very uncomfortable in Europe
(WSJ, 16 September 1986), even in cities like Paris (Le M, 10 May
1986; WPR, December 1986, p. 40). The prominent contemporary
political figure Michel Poniatowski is quoted as having said regarding
immigration: "If you want the ideas of Ayatollah Khomeini or Colo-

nel Gaddafi to take root in France, all you need to do is let in another million Algerians . . . It's up to the French to decide whether they want a French society or a strife-ridden society where Europeans and Muslims are pitted against each other." The prime minister, Jacques Chirac, has warned that in thirty years "it will be impossible to prevent men of the south from marching northwards" (MGW, 18 May 1986). One Algerian who has chosen to stay in France and become fully French reflects that, "Yesterday we were despised, today we are feared, tomorrow we will be simply respected" (Mustapha Kharmoudi in Le M, 4 November 1986). Well might one hope for the arrival of such a day. First however, solutions will have to be found to the causes as well as the symptoms of unemployment and terrorism in the West. To those without jobs or to those who are frightened, toleration does not come easily. Tragically, those to whom one expresses intolerance and fear are, in turn, not likely to respond with charity.

It might be argued that Western "racism," biological or cultural, is no different from similar racism on the part of any civilization to its neighbors, but it is the West that, in the modern world, has had the power and the means to implement and give concrete expression to its presumptions by subduing and suborning others through force or by "neo-colonialism;" the Third World is thus the victim not only of "racist" disparagement but also of racist behavior and deed.

The final expression of resentment at the West on the part of ideologues of the Third World to be considered here is the current wave of attack upon "Orientalism" on the part of Western-educated intellectuals and scholars with roots in the Third World. These critics, who often make use of Western ideas and techniques in their criticism, are to be distinguished from both the reformist apologists (Al-Af-ghani and Abdu, for example), and dyed-in-the-wool traditionalist *'ulama* with their criticism of Western scholars of Islam, in particular, the "Orient." The critics in question here have much in common with Western critics of "Orientalism" discussed earlier.

The most spectacular and influential attack upon Orientalism by these "modernist" critics has been Edward Said's *Orientalism*, a work that in certain circles has been almost Koranic in its prestige. According to Said, Orientalists, to one degree sinfulness or another, have created for the uses of the West, practical, imaginative, emotional, exploitative, images of the "East" that suffer from stereotypification, oversimplification, and reification. The variegated has been turned into the identical, the human and individual have been transformed into the abstract, the typical, and the "exotic," if not the "primitive"

and the "uncivilized." According to Said, the chief victims of Orientalism have been Muslims and Islam, this because of the fact that
Muslims have been closest to the West as neighbors, challengers, and
enemies in the past.

Animus towards Islam on the part of Westerners, even eminent
scholars of the field, has been easy to illustrate. The Lebanese historian Marwan Buheiry observes that at the turn of the century, to take
only one example, a symposium was conducted in the fortnightly
review *Questions diplomatiques et coloniales* (15 May 1901) to consider
prospects for Islam in the coming century. (Buheiry). Speaking for
many of the Western scholars represented was the eminent Orientalist
Baron Carra de Vaux, who wrote that, except for Persia with its
"Aryan" spirit, the prospects for progressive change among the
Muslims was minimal. "Islam is today vanquished," he went on to
declare, "its political decadence was inevitable . . . and in regard to its
temporal destiny, Islam is finished as a religion." To destroy any
threat from Pan-Islamism, he then advised one need only play Muslims against one another by encouraging Muslim heresies and the
Sufi Orders against the mainstream and use nationalism to divide the
various Muslim ethnic groups from one another. Amidst expressions
of these hostile sentiments, an Algerian intellectual, Muhammad Ben
Rahal commented, not surprisingly, that "hostility is the dominant
note in Europe's sentiment toward Islam; if the Muslim defends his
home, religion, or nation, he is not seen as a patriot but as a savage;
if he displays courage or heroism, he is called a fanatic; if after defeat
he shows resignation, he is called a fatalist." Edward Browne, an
English scholar, was considered heretical enough to be called an
"islamophile" by the symposium editors for protesting against stereotyped and intolerant perceptions of Islam by a West he described as
driven by social Darwinist "rapacity and materialism." Regarding the
Orientalist's definition of "true" Islam, Said has argued that a Catch–
22 situation prevails in that a Muslim who fails to conform to it is
considered to be a bad Muslim, and if he adopts "Western revolutionary ideals," he is considered a fanatic. As for the case of Muslim and
other "Easterners" who study their own culture in Western institutions
and are sometimes exploited to bear witness to the truths of Orientalism, these, Said proposes, have been brainwashed and have, so to
speak, joined the enemy as what we have called Assimilationists; with
them the Orient "participates in its own Orientalizing" (1978, p. 322).
One might conclude that in the view of the anti-Orientalists, Orientalism can thus be a form of Westernization.

It is evident that even eminent Western scholars of Islam and of Islamic peoples have been guilty of genuine hostility toward the subjects of their study, but in recent years this indictment has been extended to virtually the whole scholarly establishment of Western "Orientalists." The most extreme statement of this has probably been that of Aziz al-Azmeh (1981).

According to al-Azmeh, Orientalism rests upon a "dyadic topos," a false dichotomy, that of Orient/Occident, of which the Orient is reduced to the mirror image of the West and so is reified and disfigured. This whole enterprise, one assuming that the Orient as a whole is a proper subject for a single discipline, he maintains, should be abandoned. The peoples and regions involved should be studied within the traditional disciplines of economics, history, and so forth. Orientalism, in other words, is an illegitimate discipline—even one of its most distinguished products, *The Encyclopaedia of Islam*, is nothing but a "temporal elongation of essences," and Edward Said, al-Azmeh has concluded, has been too timid in asking only for the refinement of Orientalism rather than for its total abolition. Other Westernized Muslim critics of Orientalism are Abdallah Laroui (1976), A. L. Tibawi, Anouar Abdel-Malik (1963), Rana Kabbani, and the editors of two anthologies, T. Asad and Hussain and Olson. The journal that best expresses the anti-Orientalism point of view is the *Arab Studies Quarterly*, a publication of the Association of Arab-American University Graduates, an editor of which has been Edward Said. Inevitably, the attack on Orientalism has proven controversial and has inspired considerable disputation, some useful, some giving only sterile results. On the positive side, the anti-Orientalists have raised valid points, and they have served to sensitize scholars to the dangers of seeing the Other through ethnocentric lenses. On the negative side, however, there has been a tendency to encourage a sort of self-justifying apologia that has been detrimental to self-criticism (Nakhleh; Gordon, 1982; al-'Azm, 1980). Thus Sadiq al-'Azm has warned that while "ontological-Orientalism" is to be deplored, there has been a tendency among many Muslims influenced by Said and others to reject valid criticism and even to glorify Islam as uniquely different from and superior to the "materialistic" West. This is the same error of which Orientalists themselves are accused.

But whatever the merits of the Said challenge to Oriental scholarship might be, and however hostile to the West the critics might be, they are part of the West in their methodologies and in many of their values.

6

Ambivalence and Marginalism

Even among many of those Western-educated Third World *évolués* who have turned against the West and denounced it, there remains an ambivalence toward the West, a "love-hate" relationship and, often, a willingness to admit that the indictment comes not because of a dislike of Western values but rather because the West has disregarded such values, and so has failed both itself and others. Even Frantz Fanon, ferocious in his litany of hatred for the West, admits in his peroration, *The Wretched of the Earth*, that the West has accomplished wonderful things. Edward Said confesses that, as a child of the West as well as a Palestinian, he is deeply opposed to Western Orientalism and to the West's treatment of the Arabs. "In many ways," he says, "my study of Orientalism has been an attempt to inventory the traces upon me, the Oriental subject, of the culture whose domination has been so powerful a factor in the life of all Orientals" (1978, p. 25). In a derivative statement, David Kopf compares Said, a "marginal man," to Nirad Chaudhuri and Jawarharlal Nehru, as I have also done in a different context (Kopf, 1980, p. 492; Gordon, 1980, pp. 223–26). The "marginal man" of concern here is the intellectual of Third World origin who has been Western-educated, is genuinely bicultural (and usually bilingual) and, as a result, often enjoys unusual insight into both his original and the Western cultures. He may opt to identify with the Third World (Frantz Fanon) or with the West (V. S. Naipaul), or become an independent critic of both (Sadiq al-Azm). But whatever choice he might make, the "marginal man" usually deserves a careful hearing in both worlds (Gordon, 1962, pp. 47–53; 1966, pp. 164–76; 1968, pp. 46–50; 1978, pp. 167–70). Said has much of value to say about the condition of marginalism in *After the Last Sky* and in "The Mind of Winter: Reflections on Life in Exile" (*Harper's Magazine*, September 1984, pp. 49–55). In the latter he suggests that seeing the world as foreign "makes possible originality of vision," even if it encourages a tendency to "dissimulate" in order to seem at home in any part of the world, an achievement that is "both wearying and nerve-racking, a mind of winter" (to borrow a phrase from Wallace Stevens).

An area that has been particularly productive of "marginal men" because of the very deep imprint of French culture has been North Africa; and of the three states, Tunisia, Algeria, and Morocco, it is Tunisia that comes closest to what one might call a "marginal nation," committed, under the leadership of Habib Bourguiba, to biculturism. In recent years, however, there is evidence of change; the ambivalence of some members of Tunisia's establishment toward the West has begun to sharpen, to seem less normal and more troubled than heretofore. By the middle of the 1980s student and worker disaffection had become a disturbing feature of the national scene, and there were signs that in Tunisia, as elsewhere, militant Islamic elements were growing and, like other more secular radical groups, objecting to Tunisia's French cultural dimension and to her general political alignment with the West. As Islamic militants told a correspondent of the *New York Times* (9 January 1984), Bourguiba was now held responsible for the "colonization" of Tunisia that continues to provide the West with cheap labor and facilities for its tourists. Bourguiba, they said, still regarded France as his fatherland.

To date, the regime has, often with unfortunate severity, stood firm against militant Islamic as well as secular, radical opposition, but without the self-assurance it once had. Prime Minister Mohamed Mzali expressed ambivalence on a new Franco-Tunisian cultural agreement, a project criticized by opponents as an example of Western cultural "neo-colonialism" (Le M, 27 October 1983). On the one hand, he said, Tunisia was concerned about its Arab authenticity while, on the other hand, it favored an "*ouverture sur le monde*," an opening on the world. Overall, he favored a French initiative such as the cultural agreement, provided that such "overtures are not subject to any ambiguity." Mzali, already publicly in favor of increasing the Arab quotient in Tunisia's bicultural spectrum, was speaking, in his uncertainty, for today's Tunisian establishment, bilingual and bicultural as it has been.

Hélé Béji is a Tunisian "marginal" person, not involved in politics as a public figure but deeply concerned with Tunisia's political future. In her essay, "National Disenchantment: Essay on Decolonization," she expressed the sentiments of many Western-educated intellectuals both toward the West and toward her own country, Tunisia, and its culture since independence.

Regarding Tunisia, she finds the promises made by Bourguiba and his colleagues during the struggle for independence only partially fulfilled today. On balance, the treatment of Jews and of women has been favorable, but while Tunisia has not become "totalitarian," it has become an authoritarian state, manifestly clear in 1978 by the brutal suppression of students and union workers. Today, Hélé Béji believes that Tunisia is dominated by a new class that, under the mask of a nationalistic ideology, holds Tunisia in a strait-jacket; terms such as "development," "cultural identity," and "national entity" all serve to camouflage this political reality and to legitimize the suppression of criticism. The initial *éblouissement*, sparkle of independence, has given way to a *glacis intellectuel*, an intellectual freeze. Only popular lethargy, an inheritance from colonialism, allows the ruling class, which has long since lost its legitimacy, to remain in power; and the only cultural identity fostered today is a sterile and artificial folklorism useful only for tourism.

To Hélé Béji, the West, with its liberty and intellectual vitality, provides a sharp contrast to the sterile intellectual atmosphere of present-day Tunisia. Even though the West provides no substitute for the affective life, the *"doux et irrationel"* of the motherland, even though the West is too well-organized, too *"réfléchi,"* "égoiste et terne," *"mesquin et étriqué,"* too self-conscious and rigid, Hélé Béji seems destined to live her life between Tunisia and Paris.

An even more complicated case of Tunisian marginality is the triple marginality of Albert Memmi, a Tunisian Jew who was a leading ideologue against colonialist oppression before independence in 1956; because of his Jewish identity, he found that he was as little at home in Tunisia after independence as he was in Tunisia under the French. Because of his particular background and views, he found himself on the defensive in his largely pro-French Jewish world as well as in the nationalist Muslim Arab world whose interests he defended. The view from the outside of both worlds, he claims, gave him the insight to understand both the world of the colonized and the world of the colonizers. "I was," he says, "a sort of half-breed of colonization, understanding everyone because I belonged to none" (1965, pp. xiii–xiv). Today he writes books about oppression of all sorts, including that of minorities and women, but he lives in France along with other Western-educated *évolués* who braved the French in the struggles for independence but have now opted to live in the West where they feel they enjoy greater personal freedom.

A third Tunisian is Hichem Djaít, who has written extensively on the problem of the West and Islam. The heavy hand of the West on Islam, he argues, is becoming a thing of the past as Europe, which "once defined modernity," is becoming "winded," "tribal," increasingly "specific" and no longer the "world's axis" (pp. 5, 41, 95–96). "A great passion [the creative search for the truth] has," he maintains, "been snuffed out" with only a "possessive desire" remaining (p. 153). The result has been that Muslims now have the chance of a "tranquil return to God" (p. 72) and to their own authenticity. At the same time, however, he believes that Islam, as well as other cultures and the West itself, are threatened by a common force that we have called "cosmopolitanism," which is discussed in the conclusion of this essay.

There is evidence of similar ambivalence and marginality in the other two ex-French North African states, Morocco and Algeria. There are Moroccan and Algerian writers, once revolutionaries against French colonialism, who have today opted to spend the rest of their lives in France because they find the contemporary Arab scene oppressive, in need, as Elbaki Hermessi has put it, of "a new vision" (Barakat, 1985). Others find themselves caught between a desire to migrate to France and their "dreams of childhood," as Mohamed Berrada has put it (Barakat, 1985). This is also true of writers Mohammed Kheireddine and Khatibi, and poets Ahmad Majati, Mohammed Sarghine, and Mohammed Khammar.

The Algerian writer and theater producer, Kateb Yacine, should be included in this list of "marginals." Until 1971, he wrote, in French, remarkable plays and novels, which revolved around Algeria's past and its revolution against France; he then returned to Algeria to create and direct a traveling theater group that presented plays in the vernacular Arabic. In an interview in 1985 (MGW, 8 September 1985) with Tahar Ben Jelloun (a writer and Algerian marginalist), Yacine described the way young militant Muslims forced him to close down his play "Mohammed, Pack Your Bags!" (a play about migration to France) on the absurd grounds that it cast aspersions on the Prophet. He then denounced the government for encouraging fanaticism by suppressing the "forces of progress" and for ignoring Berber culture and language and the rights of women. Reluctantly, he added, he might have to return to France again to breathe freely as an artist. "I rebel against an Arab Muslim Algeria," he said.

Ambivalence toward the West has also been a hallmark of many

Black African intellectuals and ideologues. Chinua Achebe (1982) has confessed to feeling both Western and "traditional" (Nigerian Ibo). Although, he was planning to write a play in Ibo, English was his usual language of communication as a writer and, while he denied any obsession with Europe, he admitted that he needed its values and its inspiration.

Wole Soyinka, winner of the Nobel Prize for Literature in 1986, favors Nigeria (and Africa as a whole) adopting Ki-swahili as its continental language, but he writes in English with no sense of guilt. He dismisses the accusation sometimes levied at him, of being a Europhile as a form of "neo-Tarzanism" (NYT, 17 October 1986; WPR, December 1986, pp. 60–61). He raised a storm among African intellectuals and ideologues by dismissing Leopold Senghor's notion of "négritude" with the *boutade* "A tiger doesn't need to go around proclaiming his tigritude."

In "The Song of Lawino," the Ugandan exile poet Okot p'Bitek has expressed his own marginality by juxtaposing the simple life of an uneducated African girl with the life-style of her sophisticated *évolué* lover. In this poem, she mocks his white man's suit, which looks absurd after an African downpour, while he advises her to give up "smelly goatskin skirts," nose-rings, and amulets "that dig into the skin" (Anthony Smith, pp. 38–39). In an unusual twist to the cliché of "cultural colonialism" directed against the United States, an East African editor, in an interview with Anthony Smith, was asked how he felt about the controversy in UNESCO over America's domination of the worlds media; he answered that freedom was to him more important than the fight against Americanization, that those Africans who were attacking the United States simply wanted to dominate the local media themselves for political purposes (p. 39). Another twist of the conventional appears in an article by Femi Ojo-Ade attacking Leopold Senghor, one of the first African ideologues to defy Western political control but to defend both Western and African values ("négritude"). Senghor, once president of independent Senegal, has been honored both in Africa and in France, where he is a member of the French Academy, as an intellectual and a poet (in French). To Ojo-Ade, whose opinion need not be taken as gospel but is representative of a type of radical African opinion, Senghor's alleged synthesis of the African and the Western is a myth because Senghor has been totally assimilated into the Western camp. His *"négritude,"* Ojo-Ade argues, simply means seeing the Africans from a Western vantage point as "exotic," and has served politically as a tactic of obfuscation to help keep the French-speaking *évolué* elite in power by shifting debate from real economic and social problems to the false issue of cultural identification.

Since the Iranian revolution, there has been a striking change of heart among many once-pro-Khomeini, anti-American Iranian students and exiled ideologues in the United States and elsewhere in the West. They now obviously need to rationalize their disillusionment and their present stance. Shaul Bakhash discusses two such rationalizations: the followers of Ali Shariati maintain that there have been "two Islams"—one dynamic and progressive—the other, now in power, reactionary and suppressive. On the other hand, secularists like Babak Bamdadan and Shahrokh Meskoub blame Islam itself, a monotheistic, "irrational" religion, imposed upon the cultivated Persians by the more primitive Arabs. Both groups, like exiles of many other revolutions, now lead a marginal life, away from a motherland whose leaders they condemn, and in the liberal West whose values they often deplore.

One of the "human arrangements" to emerge from the colonial experience is the condition of "marginality," the bicultural character of natives who, through exposure and education, became Westernized and bicultural. A Eurocentric French term for such peoples is *évolués*, those who have evolved into a state of "civilization." "*Évolués* have already been encountered as leaders and ideologues of Third World liberation movements. They have been among the most fierce and perceptive critics of Western colonialism because of the insight they have as both insiders and outsiders in assessing the weaknesses of Western culture. Among them are Frantz Fanon, Aimée Cesaire, and Albert Memmi. But there have also been some who have concentrated their talents criticizing not the West but the Third World itself, from different perspectives and for different motives, and they have done so by Western standards and in terms of disparate Western values. Among such intellectuals and writers are V. S. Naipaul, Fouad Ajami, Sadiq al-Azm, Nirad Chaudhuri, and Salman Rushdie. They deserve to be considered among the "unrepentant" in regard to Western values, although not with regard to Western policies or behavior. V. S. Naipaul, a "virtuoso of the negative," has a social vision "deeply marked by the contradictions, if not incoherence, of personality." He sees modern man as rootless like himself; in exile "in a free state" (title of one of his novels), and he has been seen as a tough-minded critic of the Third World who has refused what he calls "the great lie," the refusal to apply critical standards to the non-Western world

(Goodheart). It is as critic of the Third World that Naipaul is of interest in the present context. In *The Overcrowded Barracoon* (1972, p. 76), Naipaul writes: "The West is alert, many-featured, ever-changing; its writers and philosophers respond to complexity by continually seeking to alter and extend sensibility; no art or attitude stands still. India possesses only the unexamined past and its pathetic spirituality . . . India is simple; the West grows wiser." This regard for the West and this disregard for India and the rest of the Third World marks much of Naipaul's fictional and nonfictional work. It is not strange that, in spite of his remarkable literary talents, his work should antagonize many in the Third World as well as flatter the collective ego of the West. Some statements verge on the outrageous—one feels they are often made only to provoke reactions rather than to express conviction—for example, in his island of birth, Trinidad, "all values" have collapsed; some Africans are beginning to return "to the bush"; India is led by "stupid men"; and India, with its vast population, should be ashamed of itself for "offering the world nothing but illegitimate holy men." Upon Indira Gandhi's assassination, he referred to the "old barbarism" of traditional India, stupid in religious identification (NYT, 3 November 1984).

Fouad Ajami, a scholar of Lebanese Shi'ite origin, shares much of Naipaul's bluntness and irony and quotes him frequently. Ajami's *The Arab Predicament* is as severe an indictment of the Arab world as Naipaul's *A Wounded Civilization* is of India (1981). To Ajami, the bourgeois Arab world is now infected by materialistic and pragmatic concerns and *tharwa* (riches as value has replaced *thawra* revolution). Ajami quotes the distinguished journalist, Mohamed Heikal, who says that Arab leadership has embraced the West without its culture in the form of "Levantization" and "technicalism," while the Islamic masses react with the fury of fundamentalism, an expression of emotion without a viable program, the "rage" Naipaul has spoken of (Ajami, 1983, pp. 153, 170–72, 195–96). "The Arab world," Ajami summarizes, "had long ceased to be culturally autonomous. No political-cultural movement had given it the distance from the outside world that political orders need if they are not to break down and lose their autonomy" (p. 169). The West, which mesmerizes so many Arabs, "is to be bought without its anguish, its troubles, its creativity, its cultural freedom" (p. 169); the West, and here Ajami quotes Naipaul again, "is as difficult to enter as to return from" (p. 234).

In his indictment of the Arab world, Fouad Ajami makes considerable use of the writing of another "marginal man," Sadiq al-'Azm, a

Western-educated academician and ideologue of Muslim-Syrian origin who has remained in the Arab world as a gadfly to religious as well as radical institutions and movements, often at considerable personal risk (Al-'Azm, 1968; Scudder). Al-'Azm, like Naipaul, judges the culture of his own people by Western standards, although in this case drawing upon the radical tradition of Marx. To al-'Azm it was the humiliating defeat at the hands of Israel in 1967 that revealed how deeply flawed Arab culture was with its "retarded mental habits, bedouin and feudal values, backward human relations, and obscurantist, quietistic world view with an aura of sacredness." The only hope, al-'Azm believes, is to submit Islam to rigorous (Western) higher and historical criticism and to shake the paralyzing hold of the past—a point Naipaul made about India.

Two other acerbic critics of their own societies, again by Western standards, are Nirad Chaudhuri, an Indian Hindu of the older generation, and Salman Rushdie, the inventive novelist who identifies himself with Pakistan. Chaudhuri, well before Naipaul, lambasted his fellow-Indians for their lack of moral energy, their materialism and racism, and for a "paralyzing bondage to the past" (1953, pp. 153, 124, 160, 427–28). Rushdie, whose two novels *Midnight's Children* and *Shame* are exuberant, gothic, often phantasmagoric accounts of life on the contemporary Indian peninsula, spares no class or institution from his satire. As a solution to the present plight of Pakistan, in which Islam is being used only to shore up a corrupt dictatorship, Rushdie proposes, in *Shame*, to simply adopt the Western triad "liberty, equality, fraternity."

Needless to say, the "Naipauls of the world" (a phrase used by Michael Thelwell in the New York Times Book Review, 24 June 1979) are anathema to those who sympathize with the Third World. Thelwell, a professor of Afro-American studies at the University of Massachusetts, wrote to protest a favorable review of Naipaul's *A Bend in the River* by Irving Howe. Thelwell dismissed Naipaul as one more of the "assimilados . . . seeking signs of sickness, rot or anything they may mock, parody and patronize [in the Third World]" Africa, he said, did not need these "Gunga Dins" to help solve her problems. Reactions to the works of Thelwell, to Edward Said (for whom Naipaul's work is "ignorant, illiterate and cliché-ridden" (S, Spring-Summer, 1986, pp. 44–64, 53)), and to the Nigerian novelist Chinua Achebe, are understandable. There is something troubling about the testimony of the "Naipauls of the world"; it can seem to serve to demoralize rather than to encourage, to feed Western arrogance and even to abet Western "neo-colonialism." On the other hand, one can argue that similar criticism and self-criticism of the West has contributed to its advancement and strength and that much of the criticism of the Third World is justified, if over-stated. Rather than react negatively, the Third World might listen to "the Naipauls of this world." Of course, in many cases, the Third World has and does listen, but in many other cases the pain from the bruises of the past is still too strong, the resentment too deep—irony at the Third World's expense is seen as condescending cruelty.

A final case of marginality to be considered is that of Jawaharlal Nehru, independent India's first prime minister. Deeply educated in English culture, Nehru remained ambivalent about India and about the Great Britain he had combatted for so many years as a revolutionary. "And yet I approached her," he wrote of India, "almost as an alien critic, full of dislike for the present as well as for many relics of the past that I saw. To some extent I came to her via the West, and looked at her as a friendly westerner might have done" (1951, p. 34). So did Chaudhuri, see India; in his autobiography, he wrote that Great Britain had "conferred subjecthood on us but withheld citizenship." Yet, "all that was good and living within us was made, shaped, and quickened by the same British rule" (1951).

To its detriment, the West has lost the allegiance of many marginal people it has helped to produce; to its credit, these people continue to be witnesses, in both senses of the term, to Western values and serve as a bridge between two civilizations precisely because they have asked the difficult questions both of others and of themselves.

By now, Western empire in any formal sense is almost completely a matter of the past, and the political decolonization of its subject peoples is over if one judges by the trimmings of sovereignty, one's own airline, and a flag in front of the United Nations. But economic and cultural decolonization often remain processes that are still not complete, and political decolonization is often only a formal rather than a real accomplishment. The Western presence has proven much more durable than anticipated, sometimes for good, often for bad, and while modernization and Westernization are not the same, the West still often plays a crucial role as bridge and conduit to modernity, and remains, in the eyes of peoples of the Third World, a source of frustration to the recovery of national identification, to genuine self-determination, and to the ending of dependence.

PART III

The Perdurability of the West: Dependency and Problematics of Identification

7

The Shadow of the West

The empire of the West has declined rapidly since the end of World War II. The world has continued to shrink, peoples have become increasingly interdependent, yet the West continues to play a role of continuing importance, both materially and psychologically, in the Third World's quest for complete "decolonization." Among the ideologues of the Third World, even anti-Westerners bear unwitting witness to the West's influence in their often obsessive denunciation and rejection of all things Western. They often protest too much.

Evidence of the Western imprint, on at least a superficial level, has been the spread of cosmopolitan culture to all corners of the earth, a culture marked with the stamp of the United States—its Hilton Hotels, blue jeans, rock and roll music, and Jane Fonda exercises, the sex-permeated luxury and family tribalism of the Ewings. Even in Russia there is evidence of an invasion of American youth cults (*Time*, 27 February 1984, pp. 43–44). E. J. Dionne, Jr., reports that at the height of civil strife between West and East Beirut's rival television stations agreed to show a new episode of Dallas simultaneously (NYT, 21 March 1984). A Beiruti noted that J. R., Lebanon's most popular man, was the only person able to bring the two sides together. One of the most popular foods in Nairobi recently is the hamburger, available in local establishments called Brunchburger, Buffalo Bill's, Burger Chef, Wimpy, Fast Foods, and Burgerland (WPR, November 1981, p. 18). This is yet another indication of the spread of superficial cosmopolitanism.

A number of years ago, Geoffrey Barraclough proposed that the practice of studying the history of the world by focusing mainly upon the European experience should have ended with the Battle of Stalingrad in 1942, that in developments since then and under way well before this epochal battle, the role of Europe has shrunk, and the "action" has taken place increasingly beyond Europe's borders

(1956). In rebuttal to this thesis, Christopher Dawson made the point that Europe continues to deserve special historical study, beyond as well as within Europe, because it was through Europe that the world has become one; through European initiative and with Europe as a model, movements such as nationalism, which have transformed the world, were born (1956). Today, the common cosmopolitan civilization that marks modernity is to a large extent an extension of the West, whether liberal capitalist or communist. Even Toynbee, sympathetic to Barraclough's point of view, conceded that the "spiritual history" of Europe needed to be known by all modern men because, he implied, this history is an intrinisic part of everybody's modern history.

While the spread of the West's cultural, particularly its American forms and shapes, is obvious, it might be emphasized that the extension of Marxism is also an important case of the impact of the West upon others. It is not for nothing that the Imam Khomeini denounced both the United States and the U.S.S.R. as satanic—both capitalism and communism have served to batter down the "Chinese walls" of "tradition" and to contribute to the desacralization of the universe. As George Lichtheim puts it, Russia and China, as much as the liberal West, have spread "Westernization" and contributed to the "technical unification of the world" (1974, pp. 404–5).

One other way in which the West has contributed to the making of the modern world has been through the creation of the "Third World" itself, by undermining native artisan industry, dividing elites from the masses, and providing the technology that has made the population explosion possible. It has been the awareness that the Third World is a projection of the West—perhaps even its creature in many regards—that has fed the West's sense of guilt and responsibility and the Third World's post-colonial resentment for its dependency on the West.

"Dependency theory," in part a reflection of Western guilt-feeling regarding the Third World, is considered here because it serves as a link to a discussion of relationships between the West and the Third World. While the theory may be too mechanical, too deterministic if taken literally, it does serve to suggest ways that Third World nations are, in fact, dependent, and some reasons for this dependency.

The theory, in broad terms, holds that the world system started by the capitalist West during the sixteenth century, embraces virtually the whole world today. The capitalist, Westernized nations at the center of this system skim surplus value from the less developed nations, making the rich richer and the poor even poorer. While industrialized nations at the center of the system produce increasingly expensive manufactured goods, satellite nations on the periphery produce relatively cheap, primary goods. This relationship of economic domination has changed little from the days of colonialism and survives today in a changed form; multinational companies enjoy the support of "compradore" governments in the Third World countries, and of the governments of industrialized nations (Cockroft et al.; S. Amin; G. A. Amin; Wallerstein, 1974, 1979, 1984; Stavrianos). The only escape for the dependent is socialist revolution, at least a temporary withdrawal from the world system. The theory, of course, is based upon Marxist principles, and it assumes West to be "neo-colonialist." It was in the light of this theory that Kwame Nkrumah, who led Ghana to independence in 1957, reworded Lenin to say "neo-colonialism is the last stage of capitalism" and a Brazilian Marxist was led to declare, "General Motors, General Electric, those are the generals who count!" (MGW, 17 April 1983, p. 14). Dependency theory was first developed by Latin Americanists. It is now generally applied to the Third World and, in the case of Bryan Turner, an anti-Orientalist already cited, has been a weapon turned against Orientialism.

Critics of the theory have argued that it fails to account for the success of countries outside the West, such as Japan, Taiwan, Hong Kong, Singapore, and South Korea, who have been able, in part through their own initiative, to industrialize and to prosper in the world-system (Tony Smith; Rouquie). Other critics hold that the theory tends to treat peoples of the Third World only as puppets and interprets the politics of the Third World too exclusively in terms of the policies and interests of the great powers, thereby failing to appreciate the importance of local interests, rivalries, and initiatives (Kerr, 1975; L. C. Brown, 1984; Tony Smith). A third criticism holds that dependency upon a socialist power can be as or more constricting than dependency upon a capitalist power.

Dependency theorists, to be sure, have answers to many of these criticisms. However, the purpose here is not to debate the theory but simply to introduce it schematically as prolegomenon to a discussion of various cases of persisting ties between the West and the Third World—both economic and political ties that often involved a "dependence" less complete and inexorable as dependency theorists would have it.

Economy and Polity

Post-independence change and "modernization" have characterized many new nations, but have not always meant a better life for the masses. In 1980, William Polk (1980, xi–xvii), compared conditions in the Middle East to those extant shortly after World War II. Changes in all spheres of social activity were striking. "In 1945" he observed, "the number of Arab scientists and engineers would hardly have filled a conference room; today these would populate a small city" (xi–xvii, xii). Charles Issawi has observed that, in 1945 there were five engineering schools in the Middle East; by the 1980s, there were 34. In 1945 there were 400 pupils in school in Trans-Jordan; by the 1980s, there were 40,000 Jordanians in universities at home and abroad (1983).

But, as Polk also observed, the population of Egypt—28 million in 1965—had risen to 41 million by 1980! At approximately the same time (1977), Charles Gallagher, in a survey of the world population question, concluded that the "developing" Third World, with its 2 billion people in 85 different nations had a combined GNP of $870 billion ($435 per capita), while the 22 industrialized countries had a GNP of $4,555 billion ($5,800 per capita) (1979a). On the average, the disparity between the rich and the poor has not diminished since then but has widened. In 1984, the World Development Report of the World Bank estimated the population of the world to be 4.8 billion; by the year 2150, this figure is projected to rise to 11 billion and, while it would then stabilize, population in developing countries would continue to rise to 80 million a year into the twenty-first century (Atlas World Bank; CSM, 11 July 1984). Robert McNamara writes that only in China has any real effect been had on the fertility rate; he projects that India's population will double in the next forty-five years, Bangladesh's will triple, Kenya's will quintuple! (NYT, 29 July 1984). By 2050, the population of the developing countries, 3.3 billion in 1980, will be 8.5 billion. The rate of growth in Europe is under 1 percent a year, of the United States and Canada less than 2 percent, while the rate of growth of most of the Third World is 2.5 to 3 percent. Lester Brown of the Worldwatch Institute has observed that where the rate of population growth was 3 percent (as in much of Africa), and where the rate of growth of the food supply was only 2 percent (again, as in Africa), disaster, evident by the winter of 1984, loomed (NYT, 8 May 1984). Since he retired as prime minister of West Germany, Willy Brandt has devoted himself to world problems and has dramatized the plight of much of the Third World with the following facts: one baby out of four in the poorest nations dies before its first birthday, and half have no chance to learn to read during their lifetime; one-quarter of the world's population possesses nine tenths of manufacturing industry and four-fifths of the world's income; and the world's military bill is $800 billion, while official development aid is less than 5 percent of this amount—one jet fighter ($20 million) could pay for 40,000 village pharmacies.

Of the 34 poorest countries (with a population of 2.2 billion, one half of the world living on one fifth of the land), the GNP per person was $410 per year (*Economist* survey, 24 September 1983, p. 46). Life expectancy (China excluded) was 58 (compared to 75 in the industrialized world), and the 1980 literacy rate was 52 percent. Projections were even more appalling (Gallagher, 1979b). By the year 2000, world population would be 6 billion, and by 2500, population would be 12 billion, and most of the increase would come in the Third World. The number of those in a state of extreme poverty would increase from 800 million to about 1.5 billion. The ever-increasing rate of urban immigration would greatly multiply the cost of imported food, which, from 1979–1982 alone, rose in the Third World from $53 billion to $84 billion (MD, February 1984, p. 12).

Geoffrey Barraclough, a leading spokesman for the Third World who had defended the New International Economic Order proposed by the Non-Aligned states under the leadership of Algeria (1967), and had seen some hope for the Third World when the price of oil quadrupled in 1973, had become very pessimistic by the end of the 1970s (1978). He now concluded that the Third World was worse off than before, and as Samir Amin (1977), a dependence theorist, has stated: "Any development policy that accepts the framework of integration into a world market must fail." As for the non-aligned "77" (by 1979 there were 119) who had signed the Charter of Algiers in 1967 in favor of a new economic order, they had long split up and no longer served as an effective counter of the South against the North. Some of them had become fabulously wealthy because of oil, and many were engaged in rivalry and even war with one another. The North could, for the nonce at least, ignore the pleas of the Brandts of this world to radically increase aid to the Third World.

One of the reasons for the plight of much of the South is the unfavorable terms of trade with developed industrial nations. As Barraclough noted (1978), twenty-five tons of natural rubber purchased six tractors in 1960, while in 1975, it purchased only two.

Nations that are forced to rely on a single crop are particularly vulnerable to a fall in the value of this crop—in 1979–1982, the price of sugar fell by 37 percent, cocoa by 50 percent and coffee by 20 percent (E. Jouve, MD, February 1984, p. 12). Because of the world recession in 1982, imports from the Third World declined by $42 billion (Le M, 18 September 1983). For nations in the mid-1980s with large populations, such as Nigeria or Mexico, even oil was no guarantee against disaster. The already desperate plight of the Third World states has been made even worse by their wont to purchase expensive but unproductive military equipment—the Third World spent $27 billion on arms in 1970, $117 billion in 1980 (MGW, 2 October 1983, pp. 16–17). Many of the Third World states have become heavily indebted to the industrialized nations and to the international banking institutions they largely control. This dependence, which reached dramatic proportions in the 1980s was reminiscent of the indebtedness to the West of countries such as the Ottoman Empire, Tunisia, Egypt and Morocco in the nineteenth century, an indebtedness that led to ever greater interference into their internal affairs and, in some cases, to political domination (Issawi, 1982, pp. 64–68). Many indebted countries are now in the desperate position of having to borrow more and more merely to pay off the interest they owe (MGW, 2 October 1983, pp. 16–17). According to the Morgan Guaranty Trust Bank, had new bank loans not been increased by 29 percent to a number of Third World countries in 1981, their growth rate in subsequent years would have fallen by 3 to 5 percent. One trouble, however, is that to obtain fresh loans, governments are required by the World Bank and the IMF to cut down on public expenses, which, in turn, involves the suspension of social services and food subsidies, which are often the only means available to mitigate mass misery and social dissension.

Originally, many Third World states were encouraged to borrow heavily from Western banks and governments because of a number of assumptions that turned out to be wrong. Some of these assumptions were that Third World modernization and industrialization would progress at an even pace; that the West itself would keep growing economically; and, in states rich with resources such as oil, prices would generally hold. Insufficient attention was paid to factors such as rapid population growth (a hurdle to rapid industrialization), or to the historical legacies of particular peoples that would make any fast "take-off" unlikely. In any case, by the 1970s, when the international debt rose from $8.7 to $35 billion, it was clear that the financial world faced a major crisis, one that has only been exacerbated by the fall of oil prices in the 1980s in the case of indebted oil producers like Mexico. As early as 1972, economist Tibor Mende showed that the effort to help the Third World nations out of their distress through large and generous loans only led to the further financial dependence of these states upon the industrialized nations and opened the way to what he called "recolonization" and a world-wide "apartheid" between the poor of the South and the rich of the North. Aid was used, as Joan Robinson said, "to perpetuate the system that makes aid necessary" (Stavrianos, p. 800) and "to integrate the former colonies into the Western economic and value system" (Amin, p. 54). One need not accept what these statements say about motivation to agree that they point to an evident consequence.

Oil, the contemporary equivalent of Spain's gold and silver in the sixteenth century, has proven, for Arabs at least, even after the quadrupling of its price in 1973, no guarantee against dependence; in fact, in some ways, it has increased dependence, as oil has been almost the sole source of income for the area. In the Arab world as a whole, 94 percent of all exports are raw materials; 87 percent of these are oil (Ibrahim, 1982b., pp. 163–67). Saudi Arabia is dependent upon the United States for military protection and, together with other developed countries, for technological expertise. The result has been at least clandestine Westernization among the richer and more powerful and a growing vulnerability to the accusation, made increasingly by Islamic militants, of corruption and even heresy (to most of the princes and businessmen of the Gulf states, the Iranian revolution represents a nightmare) (Ibrahim, pp. 1–25). Whatever they might claim in public, this fear only makes these states dependent upon the United States and, in this vicious circle, more vulnerable to criticism from their enemies. As Malcolm Kerr has written of these Gulf states: "The hegemony of mere money unsupported by manpower, cultural attainments, military strength or industrial development may be something of a mirage" (Kerr-Yasin, 1982, p. 11).

As for states responsible to large populations, the drop in the price of oil in the early 1980s has proven grim indeed. This has been particularly true of Mexico and Nigeria where ambitious projects, laced with corruption, led the two governments into phenomenally heavy indebtedness. One result of the needed retrenchment and the growing unemployment has been the collapse of democratic government in Nigeria, which relies for 90 percent of her national revenue upon oil, and the assumption of power by Major General Mohammed

Buhari and the military (WPR, December 1981, pp. 30–31; NYT, 7 January 1984).

In the case of Mexico, her once booming economy was based upon exports, 67 percent of which consisted of oil. After the drop in the price of oil in 1981, almost overnight her public debt rose from $14.9 billion to $48.7 billion, and she was forced to devalue the *peso*, cut back on sorely needed social services, and see many of her dreams for development go up in smoke. For states like Mexico, as well as Indonesia, Venezuela, and Nigeria, and for Saudi Arabia and other Gulf states, there today is something illusory about the fabulous promise of oil wealth, as was the glitter of gold and silver to the Spanish four centuries ago.

Another sort of dependence lies in the phenomenon of massive labor migration from the South to the North. In Europe, the presence of several millions of migrants from Turkey, Yugoslavia, Morocco, and Algeria, among other countries, is the result of the post-World War II boom experienced by a Europe that needed labor, especially labor to fill less skilled jobs. These migrants played an important role in helping Europe to prosper. For example, it is estimated that in France, one car out of four and one highway kilometer of three were built by migrants, and that even with the recession, many jobs of a more humble sort would remain unmanned should the migrants all leave (Le M, 1 February 1984). Today, there are about twelve million migrant laborers and their families in Europe; about four million of these are in France, the rest are in West Germany, Great Britain, Scandinavia, Belgium, Switzerland, and Holland. The largest group in France is the Algerians with some 850,000; the largest group in Germany is the Turks with 1.5 million. In Great Britain where the figure includes many who have migrated permanently from the Commonwealth as full subjects, there are some 2.5 million immigrants. During the 1980s, because of a recession, foreign workers (the *"Gästarbeiter"* as they are called in Germany with some irony) are no longer wanted; they are blamed for unemployment, for crime, and for a host of other social ills. As one might expect, many are in desperate straits. Between 1976–1981, six of ten migrant-held jobs in France were suppressed and 225,000 lost their jobs; in West Germany 15 percent were unemployed, 40 percent of them Turks (Le M, 1 February 1984).

In the nations from which these migrant workers originate, dependence lies both in the fact that the migrants often cannot be employed should they return to their home countries and in the fact that they constitute a source of income through remittances they sent to their families. For example, unemployment in Turkey was 20 percent and remittances amounted to some $2 billion in 1984.

At the same time, Morocco had some 460,000 migrant workers in France, including their families. Any abrupt return of these workers to Morocco would bring disaster (Ramonet). Morocco has an international debt of $12 billion, 85 percent of its total GNP! (NYT, 28 April 1984). Its urban population (because of drought and because of land modernization in some areas) has expanded enormously between 1936 and 1984, from 20 percent to 45 percent of the total population, with most of the increase moving to the slums and bidonvilles on the outskirts of the cities. Casablanca, one of the grotesque cases of the Third World megalopolis swell, now has a population of 3.5 million, many of them unemployed. Morocco's population has grown from 10 million in 1956, the year it became independent, to 25 in million 1984. Today, one person out of ten is unemployed, a quarter of the children remain unschooled, delinquency and drugs have become a major urban problem, and those living in utter poverty comprise about 45 percent of the population. Adding to Morocco's many difficulties have been periodic droughts in parts of the country; the weakness of the price of phosphates (Morocco's leading export item); the cost of the Saharan War; competition in agricultural goods from Spain and Portugal, both provided with favorable terms by the Common Market; as well as serious problems of student and worker unrest. Morocco is hardly in a condition to sacrifice the $6 million a year she obtains from migrant worker remittances, or to cope with the workers and their families should they be forced to return. In fact, there is evidence that the Moroccan government openly discourages their return by cooperating with French authorities in disciplining labor "agitators" (since Moroccan workers have become among the most militant and aggressive foreign workers in France) and has even had these laborers beaten during return visits to their families (Le M, 3 December 1982; M.E., October 1984, pp. 15–21; MERIP Reports, October 1984).

Migration is therefore a form of dependency—in the case of the migrants' countries of provenance as well as of migrant workers themselves, and this dependence is widespread. James Markham, in the *New York Times* (9 July 1984) painted a vivid picture of migrant workers gaining illegal entry into Western Europe through East Berlin and then into West Germany. Among those smuggling themselves in are "Tamil tea pickers from Sri Lanka, teenagers smuggled out of

Iran to avoid the draft, war-weary Kurds from Beirut, unemployed Ashantis from upcountry Ghana, and Pakistani drug dealers. . . . Poles, Czechoslovaks, and other refugees from Eastern Europe keep arriving as well." Western Europe continues to be a pole of attraction to millions from the Third World as well as from Eastern Europe, just as the United States is to the hungry and unemployed of Latin America.

Particularly damaging to the Third World countries, whose people migrate in large numbers, is the "brain-drain"—the emigration of highly skilled and educated persons. Through such emigration, a Third World nation loses many of its most highly trained and most talented persons to the West. A vicious circle is created that makes matters worse. The outflow of talent creates an increasingly less favorable professional climate within the nation; this, in turn, discourages others from remaining in their home country.

The harmful effects and extent of the "brain-drain" as a contemporary phenomenon are apparent from the following statistics. Estimates show that from the early 1960s to the mid-1970s, 400,000 specialists moved from the developing to the developed nations (Celeste; Le M, 2 July 1982; WPR, September 1983 p. 46). In the 1970s, 50–70% of newly diplomaed medical personnel left Pakistan. In 1975, Haiti had more doctors abroad than at home (93% of them in the United States). In 1980, 13% of Indian doctors, 15,000 in all (representing $144 million in training costs), worked abroad. In 1972, the Congressional Research Service of the Library of Congress estimated that the United States saved $882,820,000, the amount it would have cost to educate the same immigrants as specialists in the United States. The Conference of the United Nations for Commerce and Development (CNUCEDO) has estimated that it cost the Third World $48 billion to train its own emmigrants. Regarding the Arab world in particular, A. B. Zahlan, a specialist in Arab demography, estimates that of 24,000 Arab doctors (in 1976), 59% have migrated to the West; of 17,000 engineers, 23% have emigrated; and of 7500 natural scientists, 15% have emigrated (1980; 1981). Of the 27,000 mostly European- and American-educated Arabs with Ph.D.s (59% of them in science and engineering), half have emigrated to the West. The main reasons for this tragedy, Zahlan has ascertained, is the low level of Arab government support for scientific research and facilities. Zahlan has also noted that hospitals in Egypt and elsewhere in the Third World still depend on foreign expertise and specialization, and that over 90% of the engineering projects in the Arab world are managed by foreign companies. Similar conditions, obtaining throughout the Third World, serve only to reinforce a dependency that, in turn, perpetuates the brain-drain.

Economic dependence has political as well as human implications. To holders of dependence theory, the political is a reflection of the economic; the politics of the periphery are largely a function of the politics of the center, and governments of the former are placed in power and supported by the latter. As it has been argued, such a direct correlation of interests may be too simple, but there is, nevertheless, some truth to the thesis that economic inequality and vulnerability make for a degree of political dependence upon the wealthy and the developed. It is not hard to believe that an international corporation such as General Motors, for example, with a budget larger than that of many sovereign states, might use its influence to defeat radicalism abroad and that ITT has used its influence to stem socialism in a nation like Chile.

The subject of multinational influence has, in recent years, been highly controversial (Sampson, 1974, 1975, 1981; Gilpin). Some students of the multinationals maintain that in an evermore interdependent world, lines of development are being determined by multinationals as nation-states become obsolete, while others maintain that multinationals, in recent years, have become ever more vulnerable to hostile national government action—e. g., the case of Union Carbide after the 1984 disaster of Bhopal. Then there are those who would maintain that the world as a whole will benefit from growing interdependence under the guidance of multinationals; others, to the contrary, maintain that with growing interdependence, dependence will grow and the gap between rich and poor will only widen. Probably, the future will prove both theses partly true, depending upon circumstances and human initiatives in different cases. In any event, there will always be, in one form or another, "centers" and "peripheries" and economic and political dependence for a large part of humanity.

Another type of political influence comes from the pressures placed by the heavily American financed International Monetary Fund (IMF) and the World Bank upon indebted countries in return for financial protection from total collapse (Lacouture and Baumier, pp. 74–75). Such pressures to cut down on social services can have and have had—in Egypt, Brazil, Tunisia, Morocco, and elsewhere—a serious impact on public order and have even threatened the viability of governments.

But it is in black Africa, in particular, that political dependency, largely because of economic dependency, is most flagrantly evident. Julius Nyerere of Tanzania has often talked of African independence as being only "independence of the flag," and it was with more than sardonic humor that a debt-burdened Sengalese peasant is supposed to have asked his superiors, "When will this independence finally end?" The Club of Rome has suggested that unless Africans overcome their fragmentation into so many "micro-states," the world might not "need" Africa by the year 2000 (Le M, 25 December 1986). Meanwhile, defending the pro-French governments of these micro-states in 1987 required 1,200 French soldiers in Senegal; 700 in the Central African Republic; 3,500 in Djibouti; 500 in the Ivory Coast; 500 in Gabon; and in most of the other ex-French states, agreements existed providing for military assistance.

The Ivory Coast, to cite one case, was led to independence by President Felix Houphouét-Boigny with the clear intent that, in virtually every respect, the new nation would be tied to the West in general, to France in particular—culturally, economically, and militarily. Houphouét-Boigny committed himself to this policy in a famous exchange with President Kwame Nkrumah, father of Ghana, in 1957, at a time when Ghana was becoming the first independent ex-colonial black African state and Houphouét-Boigny was still a minister in the French government. On this occasion, he is purported to have said to Nkrumah, ideologue of socialism as well as Pan-Africanism, that he (Houphouét-Boigny) intended to conduct a policy of pro-Western capitalism, that this was the only path to true progress. He challenged Nkrumah and his rival socialism with the remark: "See you in twenty years" (Lamb; Naipaul, 1984; Le M, pp. 29–30). Houphouét-Boigny is also reported to have made another boastful declaration of his pro-Westernism. Of Léopold Senghor, former President of Senegal and a proponent of a synthesis between "négritude" and French culture, Houphouét-Boigny is credited with saying that Senghor "writes about Eurafrica; I am creating it." In 1980, two decades after receiving its independence, the Ivory Coast, a nation of some 8 million persons, enjoyed a per capita income of over $1,000, which is unusually high for black Africa. In spite of its ninety-some tribes, it displayed impressive unity under the leadership of Houphouét-Boigny. Nkrumah, meanwhile, in less than ten years, was overthrown, having left Ghana's economy in shambles (NYT, 12 May 1979; 15 February 1982; 18–19 April 1982). At the same time, there are some 45,000 French in residence, three times as many as before independence, 20,000 of them *coopérants*, mostly teachers, but also technical experts of various sorts. Evidence of French involvement in the economy is that one third of the manufacturing industry is French-owned. Of Abidjan, the capital, Jean-Claude Pomonti of *Le Monde* has commented, "the air-conditioned monster of French-speaking Africa gives a shock; it's like seeing Manhattan on the lagoons of the Gulf of Guinea" (Le M, 29–30 January 1980). The language of administration and education is, of course, French; and the Ivory Coast pays heavily—80% of the salaries of imported French teachers—for the best that France can provide.

Outside of the French-speaking areas, a particularly dramatic case of dependence is that of southern Africa, where states that are deeply opposed to the Republic of South Africa ideologically, are forced, because of her great military and economic superiority, to do business with her often in clandestine ways (Lamb, pp. 316–18); In the 1980s, for example, twenty African countries each year buy $1 billion worth of South African goods; Zaire obtains 50% of her food from South Africa; 80% of Zimbabwe's trade has been with South Africa and three quarters of Zimbabwe's tourist clientele has been South African; South African technicians run the ports and railroads of Mozambique; 182,000 workers from six neighboring countries work in South African mines; and Lilonwe, Malwi's new capital, was built with a South African loan. It was because, in 1987, the countries bordering on South Africa were obliged to send almost 70 percent of their total foreign trade through South African ports that they had been considering renewing an old route through Mozambique to Beira on the Indian Ocean as a way of circumventing South Africa (NYT, 2 February 1987). *Mutatis mutandis,* the ways black Africa has been both economically and politically dependent upon the developed countries, is typical for much of the Third World. This dependency, in turn, has had both social and cultural implications and effects.

8

Society: Women between East and West

Perhaps no other issue arising from the contact between East and West has been more sensitive or more controversial than that of the status of women, and this is especially true in the Islamic context. As Cheryl Benard and Zalmay Khalilzad observe regarding women's social role, both Muslim progressives and conservative militants agree that it is a crucial index of social progress or of social regression (*The Government of God*, pp. 97–98). It is when this particular issue is met that many ideologues of the Third World, including conservative and militant revivalist Muslims, make a clear distinction between modernization, which they would accept, and Westernization, which, in regard to women, they clearly reject. Whether this rejection is possible or desirable, since modernization involves *inter alia* the full mobilization of brains as well as the brawn of a society, women must be given full and equal access to participation in all spheres of society. However, if one maintains that modernization is not identical with Westernization and that a society can be selective in the new it accepts and in the old that it preserves, it seems presumptuous for a Westerner to assume that others should want their women to resemble those of the West. Take the case of Japan, with its obviously successful non-European modernization; women to this day are certainly not socially equal to men, nor, in fact, does society want them to be (Black et al., 1975, pp. 207–08, 221–22, 274–75, 314–15; Hane). Well after the process of modernization had been launched, especially in the '30s when integral nationalism held sway, the wont of some Japanese ideologues was to insist upon the superiority of the Japanese family system (culminating in obedience to the emperor) over Western "individualism"; women in the Japanese system were expected to be wholly obedient to their husbands. Until 1945 when the United States imposed a number of reforms on the status of women along with other revisions of Japanese society, women were excluded from the state university system, and the colleges they could enter provided them largely with training only in domestic skills. Even today, the top strata in the political world are almost all male,[7] with only 3 percent of the national political machinery consisting of women. Polls have showed that 71 percent of the Japanese favor separate roles for the sexes (NYT, 8 April 1984). In 1986, while 40 percent of the labor force consisted of women, only 6.4 percent of professional scientists, 2.4 percent of engineers, 9.3 percent of lawyers, and 6.2 percent of managers or officials were women (Polan).

Changes, to be sure, are occurring; more women are receiving modern industrial training, are entering business as software engineers and are expressing increased dissatisfaction with their traditional status. The case of Japan, however, may not be conclusive one way or the other. All that one can say is that the emancipation of women, according to Western norms, has certainly not kept pace with the rapid modernization of other areas of Japanese society, and that such an emancipation cannot be automatically assumed to be an essential part of any "holistic" process of modernization. The Japanese, apparently, attribute, not always with approval, what advances women have made to "Western influence" (NYT, 9 May 1984).

Within the Islamic world, the reader has already encountered some reformers for whom modernization and Westernization amounted to almost the same thing and who, regarding the question of the status of women, were convinced that part of the success of the West was due to the relative freedom women enjoyed. Thus Atatürk, did not hesitate to provide women with the vote that enabled them to capture seventeen seats in the Grand National Assembly in 1935. Polygamy and the power of men to repudiate their wives easily and at will were outlawed, and women came to enjoy the rights of the new civil code modelled upon the Swiss. In present-day Turkey, on a lower class and provincial level, women are still treated as inferior beings, but the possibility remains for legal change; the law, in fact, facilitates such change as Cigdem Kagitcibasi observes.[8]

Among Muslim Arabs, Egypt took the lead in adopting Western principles regarding the emancipation of women. At the beginning of the nineteenth century, Rifa'a al-Tahtawi expressed admiration for the status of women in France and, toward the end of the century, Amin Qasim had published two books, *Liberation of the Woman* (1899) and *The New Woman* (1901); both defended woman's emancipation as essential for social progress (Haddad, 1982, pp. 54–70; Ibrahim, 1982b, pp. 54–70). Muhammad 'Ali had opened a school for midwives, but a school for girls was not opened until 1874. In 1923, Huda Sha'rawi started her crusade against wearing of the veil. In 1956, women received the vote. In 1976, 1.6 million girls were in primary schools (compared to 300,000 in 1952); 153,000 were in universities (compared to 10,000 in 1952), and in 1962, Durriya Shafiq's long and difficult crusade brought fruit when women were declared equal to men. But in the late 1980s, the tide began to turn.

Personal Status Law (No. 44), ("Jihan's Law" after the name of the sponsor, Sadat's wife), was declared unconstitutional in 1985 because it offered guarantees to women contrary to *Shari'a,* which had been declared in 1980 by constitutional amendment to be the sole basis of law. No longer could an Egyptian woman enjoy the right of divorce should her husband take a second wife, or keep custody of her children (ME, June 1985, pp. 17–20). Cancellation of "Jihan's Law" left matters of family status in the hands of judges applying piecemeal law dating back to 1920; in effect, men's prerogatives were returned to them. But in spite of this setback, Egyptian women, mainly from the upper classes, continue to fight for their rights through organizations such as the Cairo Family Planning Association and the Arab Women's Solidarity Organization. Laila Abu-Saif, a highly regarded theater director, has continued to speak out in favor of a liberalization of the Family Status Law, and Jehan Sadat continues to defy the spirit that contributed to the assassination of her husband.

Elsewhere in the Arab Muslim world, women have followed the lead first taken by Egypt in their struggle for social and political equality. In Lebanon, until other matters absorbed the energies of its citizens, a small galaxy of female novelists wrote about the inferior position of their sex; Latifa al-Zayyat, Layla Ba'albakki, Colette Khuri, and Khalida Sa'id, among others. (Allen, pp. 84–87). In Morocco, emancipated women opposed the Moroccan Family Law of 1957, which in effect condones the interpretation of the Koran that sees women as inferior to men (Mernissi in Barakat, ed.). In Tunisia, the most "liberal" of the ex-North African States, militant conservative Islam has not yet proven strong enough (although it represents a clear threat) to shake the status of women regulated by the Family Code of August 13, 1956. This code guarantees, *inter alia,* that women must consent to their marriage, that they receive larger shares of inheritance than traditionally provided for, that they might marry someone of a faith other than the Muslim, and that polygamy and easy divorce are no longer permitted the male (Perkins, pp. 124–30).

In Algeria, a state that proclaims itself to be socialist and that promised women equality for their faithful services as nurses and bomb planters during the revolution, feminists remain deeply disillusioned with the lack of legislation favorable to them and with the masculine atmosphere in the public sector (Gordon, 1968; McRabet; Minces; Accad). The National Charter of 1976, a basic constitutional document, states that "the emancipation of women does not mean the abandonment of the ethical code deeply held by the people." Most threatening to feminists has been the Family Code that has been in preparation for many years; its earlier version narrowly based the status of women upon Quranic prescriptions. President Chadli Benjedid, however, listened to feminist protestations and proved amenable to reconsidering the document; he has also stood steadfast against pressures from conservative militant groups whose actions and propaganda he has denounced as "distortions of the *Quran*, aiming to 'paralyze' society"—one of these distortions has been, he stated, to claim that Islam favors the "cloistering of women" (Le M, 7 December 1982). The version of the Family Code finally accepted by the National Popular Assembly is less rigidly doctrinaire than had been feared, but it is still very conservative (Le M, 1 June 1984). While based upon the *Quran* and recognizing polygamy and unequal inheritance between daughters and sons as part of law, the new Family Code makes it much more difficult for a husband to take a second wife. He must now prove equal treatment of both wives. The first wife has the right to divorce him if she objects to the new marriage, and the husband can only take a second wife if the first is sterile or incurably ill. The legal age for a girl's marriage is now eighteen, and she has the right to refuse a groom imposed upon her by her family. In the event of a divorce, custody goes first to the mother. However, polygamy is, in principle, accepted (Article 8); Muslim women are not allowed to marry non-Muslims (Article 31); a wife cannot work if her husband, whom she must "respect," does not allow her to (Article 39); and a woman still inherits less than does a man (Vandevelde, ME, April 1985, pp. 54–56). Regarding unequal inheritance, Boualem Baki, Minister of Justice, insisted that it was justified because, whereas a man must work to support his family, a woman *can* work, but she does not have to—this is an argument not likely to impress many feminists (Le M, 20 June 1984).

To militant Algerian feminists, this code, in spite of its being preferable to its earlier versions, is one more confirmation that women are not equal to men in "socialist" Algeria. But the fact that women were able to exert any pressure at all on the final outcome shows that, in Algeria as in most other Islamic countries, including Iran, there are thousands of women, supported by many educated men, who favor a future for women based on the Western pattern.

In the Gulf, the more conservative part of Middle Eastern Islam, women have made surprising progress in Bahrain, where literacy among women has risen to 59 percent, and 45 percent of government employees are women (Ramazani). But Bahrain is remarkably advanced in this respect. There were no universities for women in Saudi Arabia in the early 1970s; by 1985, 12 percent of university students were women, but they had to sit apart from the men students and receive lectures over television, and were still not allowed to drive. In the wake of the dramatic attack on the Grand Mosque of Mecca by religious dissidents in 1979, and because of Iranian pressures, beauty shops and hairdressing salons could no longer be run by women, and women were barred from serving as television announcers.

Outside the Arab world, in Pakistan in the late 1980s, under Zia's dictatorship and his program of Islamization, the lot of women had deteriorated (from a Western vantage). The Women's Action Forum was denounced as "elitist, westernized and anti-Islamic," as was the leader of the opposition to Zia, the Oxford-educated Benazir Bhutto. The Federal *Shari'a* Court was empowered to rule against laws deemed anti-Islamic, and according to the *Zina* (adornment, beauty) ordinance, fornication merited death by flogging and women's testimony was less valued than a man's. Ms. Bhutto, while campaigning, felt obliged to cover her head, wear sunglasses, travel with a chaperon, salute supporters rather than shake their hands—all in conformity to popular susceptibilities (Kronholz). The government obliges radio announcers to wear veils. At one point it forbade the national women's field hockey team from leaving the country lest they expose themselves in their sports' outfits. The *hadd* laws of the *Shari'a* prescribe particular punishments for transgressions such as stoning for adultery and are enforced.

Today, in Iran and in many other Muslim states, partly because of the political pressure of Iran, the trend has been increasingly toward the regulation of women's actions and their relationship to men, according to the norms of the *Quran* and the *Shari'a*.[9]

Regarding the status of Islamic women, scriptures are explicit as to man's superiority and, for this reason, the emancipation of women is a more formidable challenge that in non-Muslim traditional societies where custom rather than precept determine a woman's status (Beck and Keddie, pp. 1–34, 25). Custom, in many parts of the Third World including the Islamic, favors the male, but the burden of protecting the woman's purity and the honor of his family and his own name falls almost entirely on him. Under colonialism, the ability to protect the woman effectively from being encouraged to unveil was taken by many pious and traditional Algerian Muslims as a humiliation, a humiliation that was one cause among many for the revolution against the French (Heggoy; Berque, 1967, p. 307).

In Tayeb Saleh's *Season of Migration to the North*, the desire of a Sudanese Arab male to take revenge upon European society for the humiliation of his manhood, brought in the wake of colonialism, is one of the main themes. His protagonist's revenge takes the form of his seducing and murdering a number of English girls while a student in great Britain. As the author has indicated, the theme is an echo of *Othello*—a play that only makes sense if the factor of Othello's racial humiliation is admitted (ME, June 1979, pp. 66–68; Allen, pp. 131–38).

This view of women as objects of family and personal honor, by Western norms derogatory to women, is often accompanied, according to Fatima Mernissi, by misogyny, and the view that women are by their very nature sexually unreliable. It was this attitude that, in part, led to the overthrow of the Ali Bhutto government in Pakistan in 1977—the prime minister had been too energetic in promoting sexual egalitarianism (Richard Reeves, *New Yorker*, p. 52). It was this attitude that Vivian Gornick, in her fictional account of her amatory adventures in Egypt, found even among the most sophisticated men she met (pp. 292–93). One such friend, Hamdi, is quoted as saying: "I want a woman who can share my life and my work with me. A woman who can give me *understanding*, not this slave-like devotion most Egyptian men want. But how is that possible! For if a woman has understanding, then she has experience, and if she has experience . . ." It is this attitude that constitutes a frequent theme in the novels of many Arab women in North Africa and other parts of the Islamic world (Accad; Gordon, 1968).[10]

Symbolic of the controversies over woman's status has been the "veil"—the term loosely used here to indicate any type of covering of the head or part of the body to show modesty and preserve purity.[11] During the Iranian revolution, the veil has been both a symbol of Islam's integrity and, to Muslim feminists, a symbol of women's subjection; this was also true during the Algerian revolution. In both cases, it represented a challenge to the establishment—to the Shah and to the French—as well as a rejection of the West. In the Algerian revolution, when efforts were made by some French to undermine resistance by encouraging Muslim Algerian women to shed their veils, wearing the veil assumed importance as a way of asserting one's Arab and Islamic identity. According to Malek Alloula, an Algerian idealogue, the French campaign to de-veil Algerian women was part of a policy of "penetrating" and demeaning the culture of Islam. The British used the outlawing of suttee in India and of circumcision in Kenya (in the 1920s) in the same way, he argues. The ultimate purpose in these cases was to humiliate the native man and bend him to the colonial will. In a practical rather than ideological way, the veil, at times, served as a convenient disguise for purposes of espionage and the planting of explosives in enemy establishments. While to a secularist like Fanon (1959, pp. 13–49), the veil served only as a symbol of resistance, one to lose relevance upon independence, to most Algerians the revolution was Islamic rather than Third Worldist, and the veil is still widely worn in Algeria. In the case of the struggle between Iran and Iraq, one accusation the Iranians make against the Ba'th party is that it has encouraged women to work freely and unveiled by the side of men; this is a sign of apostasy. The same accusation was made against the Shah by the present militant Islamic rulers of Iran to whom Muhammad Reza Shah, like his father, was, in fact, behaving as an enemy of Islam by encouraging unveiling as a mark of "progress."

The type of militancy characteristic of the present rulers of Iran can be found in many other parts of the Islamic world, with similar implications for the status of women. In Egypt, for example, Sana Hassan, in an interview with several militants, discovered that their hatred for Sadat, expressed in the epithet "Pharaoh" with its pagan pre-Islamic connotations, resulted from his allegedly being influenced by his wife Jehan to discourage polygamy and ease conditions under which a woman could divorce. One militant told Sana Hassan that Sadat had even disgracefully allowed President Carter and Prime Minister Begin to kiss Jehan! This particular militant's sister, now fully veiled, had taken as her life-model the wife of the Caliph Umar, who, out of respect for him, washed her husband's feet every night.

One must, however, qualify this observation. The return to the veil alone does not necessarily indicate the adoption of revivalist militancy (S. Ibrahim, 1982b., pp. 16–19; Williams). For example, many women in Egypt have taken to the veil defensively, for example, the case of unsophisticated girls who come to Cairo and other cities to study and find the life-style of Westernized girls intimidating and find anonymity in the crowded streets more comfortable. Others adopt the "lawful dress" (covering the body and hair but not the face) to avoid harassment from the militant youth associations (the *gamiat al-islamiyya*) or from a genuine aversion to pornography and other aspects of "Western materialism." Saad Eddin Ibrahim points out that in most cases these veiled students are not against modernity (1982b., pp. 1–25), nor are they in favor of any form of "fanaticism"; they simply feel more comfortable in traditional costume and with traditional ways. Fatima Mernissi reports on a similar phenomenon in Morocco where she discovered village women found greater comfort and help, including medical aid, in a traditional Islamic sanctuary rather than in a public hospital, which, to them, constituted "a strong, alien setting, a modern building full of enigmatic written signs on doors and corridors, white-robed, clean and arrogant civil servants who speak French for all important communications and only use Arabic to issue elementary orders" (p. 22).

Whatever the case might be elsewhere in the Islamic world, militant Islamic revivalism is clearly dominant in Iran for the present, and this means that women have lost the "rights" they won under the Shah. The new mood can be seen in the text of the speech given by the official delegation to the United Nations Decade for Women Conference in Copenhagen (July 1980), a document reflecting some of Shariati's ideas, as well as Khomeini's (Tabari and Yeganeh, pp. 88–93). Under the Shah, the speaker argued women were treated as "Pahlavi dolls," mere sex-objects, encouraged by Western capitalism to indulge in "consumerism" so that they would purchase more Western goods. The Shah's sister, Ashraf, publicly pretended to promote the rights of women, but privately she pushed heroin, pornography, and prostitution. Only the mosque was able to resist this corrupt regime and, now, with victory, women have regained their dignity—they can be the "real" selves that Islam has always preached; they can model themselves upon Quadishah, the first wife of the Prophet, upon Fatima, his daughter, or upon other ideal women of early Islam.

The Imam Khomeini has often spoken about the status of women in uncompromising terms (1981, pp. 171–72). In one case he talked of Iranian women who "have grown up with lechery, treachery, music and dancing, and a thousand varieties of corruption," inspired by the example of Western women who regard "civilization an advancement of the country as dependent upon women's going naked in the streets, or to quote their own idiotic words, turning half the population into workers by unveiling them (we know only too well what kind of work is involved here!)." Iranian women who have been seduced by such behavior have plunged Iran into a "nightmare." With the revolution, Khomeini claimed, women were no longer treated as "objects" (pp. 263–64) or "possessions"; they were now free collaborators with their men in the service of Islam. Violently in disagreement, however, are the Iranian feminists such as Haleh Asfar (Tabari, pp. 75–90), who, in her essay "Khomeini's Teachings and their Implications for Iranian Women," argues that Khomeini wants, in effect, the complete subjugation of women, and even the denial to women of the few rights promised by the *Quran* (Tabari and Yeganeh, pp. 75–90). Khomeini, she insists, believes women to be inferior—he has even written in detail about their "periodic filth" to prove the point—and he simply wishes to use women as Hitler did, to raise children to be martyrs. Equally radical is Azar Tabari who believes that feminine emancipation is only possible outside the bounds of Islam itself, that the *Quran* clearly considers the male superior, the female inferior (Tabari and Yehaneh, pp. 5–25). As evidence, Tabari refers to verses 11 and 28–29 of "Women," 223 and 282 of "The Cow," and suras (divisions) 24 and 31 of the *Quran*. She might also have cited the case of the formal dinner in Zimbabwe when President Ali Khomenei of Iran stalked out in protest because of the presence of wine and women at the head table. He declared that both violated the tenets of Islam (NYT, 26 January 1986).

Between the secular militancy of women like Asfar and Tabari, and the strict orthodox of the Iman Khomeini, is the more moderate, and hesitant, point of view of those Islamic radicals who fought against the Shah under Khomeini's leadership but now oppose him from exile or in the underground—members of the Islamic modernist Mujahidin-e Khalq and the secularist Fidayeen-e Khalq. To Tabari and other militant feminists, these groups have betrayed the cause of women by dismissing the demonstration in Tehran of March 1979, for example, in which several thousand women protested against the compulsory wearing of the veil, as a manifestation of "bourgeois" sentiments and even of "cultural imperialism." This argument that women's emancipation Western style is "bourgeois" is not purely rhetorical. Both conservative militants and Marxists denounced the Shah for his "bourgeois preoccupation" with "women's rights" (Cole and Keddie, p. 25; Yeganeh and Keddie, pp. 120–24). Probably about 80 percent of Iran's women favor the status quo and those who object constitute only 20 percent of the educated classes. In fact, however revolutionary and progressive in other respects these groups might be, they have been hedging in their support for some of the more radical feminist demands. The Mujahidin have taken the line, for example, that to make an issue of the veil now was to serve reaction, that it required time to outlive "imperialist culture." The more radical Fidayeen took the line that the veil should not be forced upon women, but that women of their own free will should adopt the veil to show solidarity with the revolution (à la Fanon). Both groups have drawn inspiration from Ali Shariati, discussed earlier as one of the most influential radical Islamic voices on the eve of the revolution. Regarding the question of women, Shariati tended to be quite vague, and he is sometimes seen as having "desexualized" woman, of having turned her into a loving and "natural" partner of man, rather than a being equal to man in rights and instincts (Yeganeh and Keddie, pp. 130–31). A woman, he maintained should emulate Fatima, the obedient wife of Ali and daughter of the Prophet; beyond the expression of such pieties, he has said little, and as for the question of the veil, he considered that it should be worn, if only out of defiance of the capitalist West (Shariati, 1983; Tabari and Yeganeh, pp. 11–12). This situation would continue, he believed, as long as Iranians remained with no other leaders but the clerical fanatics and the "ultra modern" allies of the Shah. Today, of course, the "clerical fanatics" are in power and, as for the militant secular feminists like Azar Tabari, Shariati's disciples have failed them, even when, in the first months of the revolution, they shared power. To the "ultra moderns" among the women, the revolution has been a double disappointment.

However one might feel about the present regime in Iran, by Western norms women certainly are worse off than they were under the Shah. Doubtless many Iranian women prefer their present status and are convinced that it has divine sanction, but there are women in the thousands who have studied in the West and who once lived wholly Western lives, who remain, however dangerous it is to make themselves heard at present, in opposition to the Imam and to his followers.

Perhaps such women are, as they are accused of being, "bourgeois" relics of the past, selfishly trying to hold on to their Western life-styles, but then again perhaps the future will prove that the demands of modernity and of modernization in regard to women will ultimately justify the Western pattern in the Third World.

9

Culture: The Problematics of Historiography, Language, and Communication

Many Third World ideologues would insist that decolonization cannot be held to be complete until a national cultural identification has been forged, an identification in which citizens have confidence and in which they can recognize themselves and take pride, one that can serve as a basis for a nationwide mobilization of loyalty, energy, and creativity. Until this is accomplished, a nation is likely to remain culturally dependent and incompletely free.

There are many aspects to the subject of the Western imbrication in the cultural heritage and life of many Third World countries. Here the focus will be limited to three dimensions of the cultural life of such Third World countries; historiography, language, and communication.

As many nationalists have struggled to emancipate themselves, so also have they struggled to reconquer the "truth" about their own past, which they claim the colonizer has attempted to destroy (Gordon, 1971a). This concern with the past, a fading reality in the contemporary developed world (Plumb, 1969), has been of visceral as well as propagandistic importance to revolutionaries of the Third World, both during the period of resistance to the colonial power and in the post-colonial period of national reconstruction (or simply construction); to those in a state of tumult and transition, history is often of the essence. Among those who have maintained that only by recovering one's past can one find one's identity in the present are Mohamed Sahli, an Algerian, and Abdallah Laroui, a Moroccan.

Sahli's main thesis has been that the French colonialist historians falsified the Arab Muslim past to justify their right to rule, and to

133

demoralize and dominate the indigenous inhabitants; decolonization, in turn, involves the restoration of the truth about the past, to show that colonialism has been unjustified and unjust, and to restore to the natives their self-confidence and pride (1965). Laroui, while also defending this thesis, goes further to insist that the native must do more than reject the colonizer's falsification of his past; he must also learn to view himself and his past historically in order to rid himself of the weakness Malek Bennabi (an Algerian) has called his *colonisabilité*, his vulnerability to be colonized (1976, 1979). History should teach the North African, Laroui maintains, that much of what he considers to be his cultural heritage consists of frozen and even transformed fragments of his past that the colonizer has preserved in order to maintain the myth of the native's cultural inferiority and to assure his subordination. Thus, many powerful North African chieftans, and even the Moroccan Caliph as hereditary king, obtained their legitimization not from any authentically Moroccan sources but from the French for French purposes; many other institutions and customs were preserved for similar reasons. The value of history then is to help the native rid himself of a baneful "traditionalism," one that has made him exploitable in the past and one that now obstructs his progress into the future (Laroui, 1976, 1979).

Of obvious importance to the leaders of the developing and developed nations is the use of history textbooks to encourage national loyalty and pride among the nation's youth (Gordon, 1971b.; Ferro; Shipler, pp. 169–70, 200–206, 209, 257–58, 319–20). Through textbooks, the past is ideologically manipulated both to build national morale and, alas, to divide humanity against itself by keeping alive memories that foster mutual hatred. There are, however, cases of ex-colonies that allow the colonizer's view of history to persist after independence. For example, Christian Harzo has discovered, through a study of textbooks used in a number of African countries from 1960 to 1977, that the colonial view of history has been only superficially modified, and that students are still imbued with "another's memory." African heroes have been revived, to be sure, but 1492, for example, remains a crucial date in these texts, and periodization in general still follows the Western pattern. But most serious, Harzo discovered, is that these African texts accept the Western view of progress and, by implication, Africa's pre-colonial inferiority and Western superiority. In such cases, Western "cultural neo-colonialism" does, indeed, persist, and historiography continues to bind the ex-colonized and keep him in a condition of dependency, as Wallerstein maintains (1984, pp. 180–81). This is done, Wallerstein says, by convincing (through education among other means) the ex-colonized of the "idea of progress," of history as moving by stages and culminating with the Western model. The means to arrive at this point, the Westerner teaches, is through the "bourgeois revolution" and the institutionalizations of "individual [bourgeois] freedom." This, of course, is the perspective of several modernization theories.

How sensitive Third World scholars and ideologues can be to what they interpret as the Westerner's abuse of history (to continue his hegemony) can be illustrated by the angry revisionism among many Third World historians. To pick only one example at random, the Nigerian scholar Chinweizu takes Roland Oliver to task for his earlier review of *A General History of Africa* (Heinemann) written mainly by African writers (TLS, 27 Sept. 1985). Oliver had maintained that the book under review exaggerated the violence used by the West to conquer Africa in the nineteenth century, made heroes of African villains in some cases, unfairly blamed the West for the decline of traditional culture (which would have come in any case with the Industrial Revolution), and was the main cause of Africa's contemporary troubles (TLS, 6 August 1985). Chinweizu's response was to dismiss Oliver as Eurocentric, as treating Africans with cruel condescension, and to belittle his "attack" as one of the sort "which jaded [historical orthodoxy] is liable to make on its supplanters as it is being pushed from the stage." Such historiographical polemics, marked by bitterness and even personal venom, are likely to continue at least until those of the Third World find their poise in the self-confidence of national identity. Debate will become more academic when many among Western scholars, also traumatized by the experience of the end of Western empire and hegemony, manage to replace injured pride with greater empathy.

Resentment of the ways the West has written the history of the colonized of those of the Third World has been accompanied by a resentment of the manner in which the Western powers have, in many cases, imposed their languages upon the educational and administrative systems of the colonized. Today the quest for national identification often involves a return to the "national" language once disparaged and driven from the corridors of power and, sometimes, of culture (Gordon, 1978).

To ideologues of national liberation, the European language was often a source and a symbol of cultural alienation, its perpetuation an instrument of continuing "neo-colonialist" domination. For many newly independent nations, the elimination of the official use of the European language presented no problem—this was the case with most Arab countries of the Arab Middle East for example. But elsewhere, and for a variety of reasons, the language of the European colonizer continues to be used in the educational system and in administration—in ex-French North Africa, and most black African states, and in some Asian states, including India. To some leaders and ideologues of the new nations this presents no serious ideological problem; such has been the case with Habib Bourguiba of Tunisia, for example, and with Leopold Senghor of Senegal. But to others, the continued use of the European language represents something of a shame and an indignity, and demands are made for "Arabization" and "Africanization" and the elimination of the European language as vehicle of education and culture.

This continues to be a serious issue in ex-French North Africa, an area where French language and culture made a particularly deep impression, one that lasts to today, and one that has involved rivalry to and often displacement of Arabic, the popular language. To North African nationalists, Arabic has been a bearer of a rich culture as well as the language of the *Quran*; a return to the use of Arabic has been of the essence in regard to national pride and piety. But it is striking that even after almost three decades of independence, the French language remains entrenched in the culture and administration of North Africa, particularly in Algeria, the nation that has experienced the French impression longest, most completely and, many would say, most deleteriously.

Algeria fought for over seven years to win its independence and to return to its Muslim-Arab identification. That was the proclaimed goal of the revolution and today Arabic is Algeria's official language and the President of the Republic must be Muslim. French, however, remains the language of the army and of much of the administration (Gordon, 1978; A. Ibrahim; Le M, 7 July 1984; Entelis, 1986, pp. 92–102), and while Arabic is now the principal language during the early years of education, the higher the level, particularly in medicine and the sciences, the more French is used as the language for instruction. In 1980, 25 percent of the 4,000 university professors were French, while four to five thousand Algerian students were studying abroad, mostly in France. The only ministries that conduct their business in Arabic rather than French are those of justice and religious affairs.

Why has Algeria moved so slowly toward her goal of total "Arabization?" Her educational leaders over the years since independence in 1962, Mostefa Lacheraf, Ahmed Taleb Ibrahimi, among others, have proclaimed that while total "Arabization" was the long-term goal, they have cautioned against being precipitous and risking to cut off Algeria's youth from access to modernity (i.e. modern research and professional exposure). They also have been leery of a reaction against Arabic among youths who know only colloquial Arabic or Berber and for whom "classical" written Arabic is very difficult; they want to preserve links with black Africa, many of whose states seem predestined to remain French-speaking; and finally, as leaders, they inherited a generation of French-educated adults whose Arabic was weak or non-existent—a legacy of French colonialist policies. To a novelist like Malek Haddad, his inability to write his novels in Arabic was a source of shame, while to Mouloud Mameri, novelist of Berber background, the fact that he writes in French presents no problem at all; French, to him, can only enrich Algeria's culture (Le M, 29 March 1981). The dispute over Algeria's bilingual status is a subject of passionate debate among Algerians and is likely to remain so for decades to come.

The coexistence of education in both Arabic and French is a source of social tensions within Algeria, tensions that are not unrelated to the militant Islamic movement, a phenomenon now in Algeria as elsewhere in the Muslim world. Clashes between those primarily educated in Arabic and those in French broke out in the city of Constantine in 1974–1976 over whether the civil law should be based upon Islam or not. Subsequently in 1979 students of the "Arabized" Law School led a two-month university student strike to protest the favoritism shown the French-educated in the public sectors of Algerian life and to demand the immediate "Arabization" of all aspects of Algerian life (Le M, 12, 28 December 1979; 27 November 1981). In the riots in Constantine, and in Setif in November, 1986, disturbances included confrontations between French and Arabic educated youth (MEI, 10 December 1986, p. 13).

To the conservative militants, Algeria has been, since the end of the Revolution, overly secular in its "socialism" as well as overly "Westernized" in its reluctance to abandon the French connection. To date, President Chadli Benjedid has stood firm against the *"activistes intégristes"* and condemned what he calls the "false problems" they create by a misinterpretation of the *Quran* (Le M, 7 December 1982). There has been violence, including the burning down of a mosque, whose imam was considered too closely associated with the government, and the killing of four people in Annaba in 1982. A number of long-bearded Islamic youths were detained, and some were tried and imprisoned. As Jean-Claude Vatin points out, while the reformist 'Ulama did provide much of the ideology of the revolution, the final victors, after the revolution was over, were "state reformers," who have managed to date to control the government and to relegate the Islamic leaders to the sidelines (Vatin, 1981, 1983; Sanson). It was they who had directed Algeria's path to industrialization, and they who had dragged their feet on total and immediate Arabization. To many of the militants, drawn largely from recently urbanized peasants, the present establishment, dominated by army officers and technocrats, is unfaithful to Islam. On the other hand, it is paradoxical that feminists and progressive secularists, and many liberal-minded people who simply want more freedom think that the present leaders have "betrayed the revolution." Algeria remains poised uneasily between Mecca and Paris, as much today as on the eve of independence (MD, April 1984, pp. 20–21, 42–43; Entelis, 1986).

In contrast to Algeria, Tunisia had until the late 1970s been relatively relaxed about its French cultural legacy; Habib Bourguiba, architect of the new Tunisia, was convinced that his country should seek a synthesis of its French and Arab heritages, and, in fact, Tunisia remained largely bilingual and bicultural. Arabs visiting from the Middle East are often struck by the manner in which Tunisians cling to their identification with France. Said Hatham Shakra, a Palestinian in Tunisia after the eviction of PLO fighters from Beirut in 1982, said of his hosts: "Their culture is French. Their books, newspapers and films are in French. They may speak Arabic, but they think in French and translate it into Arabic" (Miller, 1985b, p. 63). Halim Barakat, in an analysis of the Arabic language cultural magazine al-Fikr, found the Tunisians (of the establishment at least) as fearful of Easternization (tamashruq) as they claimed to be of Westernization (al-tamaghrub); their preference was for a "Tunisization" (al-tawnasa) distinctly balanced in favor of the West (and France) (Barakat, pp. 50–56). So Western-oriented has Tunisia been according to Le Monde's Paul Balta, that Rached Ghannouchi, leader of the most important conservative Muslim militant movement in Tunisia (the Movement of Islamic Tendency) said that he feels it necessary to couch his language in relatively liberal terms by not insisting on the veil, or on the cutting of the hand for theft; he even talks of favoring the spirit over the letter of the Quran (Le M, 2–3 June 1985). Ghannouchi's colleague on the political bureau of the Movement of Islamic Tendency, Jebali Hamadi, however, is more representative of the general militant conservative Islamic point of view in the Arab world in general than is Ghannouchi. He blamed Bourguiba for trying to destroy Tunisia's Arab-Islamic identity, and for threatening the integrity of the family by freeing women (even for abolishing polygamy) (Le M, 26 November 1986).

Since the later 1970s, in any case, opposition to Bourguibism and a growing emphasis upon Islam and the Arabic language, has presented—particularly with the influence of the Iranian revolution—an ever more serious challenge to the establishment.

In the wake of a perceived serious threat from those, whom some Tunisian modernists called the "turbans," the government has sought to defend itself by suppression, and by a degree of compromise (at least in appearance). The prime minister in the mid-1980s, Muhammad Mzali, was publicly identified with a policy of promoting "Arabization" in education as well as of increasing Tunisian contacts with the Middle East. Then, ironically and to the confusion of many, Mzali was suddenly removed from power in September 1986 and submitted to prosecution on unspecified charges. Without seeking to disentangle the political issues involved, relevant to the present discussion is the accusation made against Mzali that he had promoted "Arabization" to the point that Tunisian students had done miserably on the first (French) baccalaureate examination in 1968. In reaction, a program of "de-Mzalization" has been launched so that French is again taught from the second year of elementary school up, rather than from the fourth year, as had been decreed while Mzali was minister of education. Mzali was clearly being held as scapegoat for Tunisia's educational regression by French "progressive" standards (Le M, 26 November 1986). In his self-defense during an interview from exile in Switzerland, the hounded ex-prime minister asserted his innocence of any charges, including that of having been responsible for any errors Tunisia might have made in its educational policies. He declared, "Even the policy of Arabization of education, with which I am reproached today, was adopted in 1976 with the agreement of Bourguiba" and in accordance with the Constitution that states Islam is the religion and Arabic the language of the nation. In fact, he added, he was by no means "an exclusive, chauvinistic and blind Arabizer" but rather "humanistic and modernist" (Le M, 18 October 1986). No wonder, then, that to the conservative militants there was little difference to choose between Mzali and his replacement. To the militant, Mzali's modest approach to Arabization had only been a trumpery to disguise the establishment's bias towards the West.

As the French presence is still strongly felt in North Africa and in Black Africa, so is the English presence in India, including the English language. The Raj of yesterday is still present in many place names, pig-sticking, sporting clubs, enthusiasm for cricket and for the royal family, civil service, travel laws and codes, press and police; but most important is that the English language is spoken fluently by the top ten percent of India's 730 million people, making India the second largest English-speaking nation in the world. English, as language of communication of much of the elite, serves both to divide this elite from the masses and, on the other hand, more positively, opens India to the rest of the world (Anthony Smith, p. 160). Romesh Thapar, a distinguished contemporary writer, has remarked on this linguistic dependence: "Fortunately it wasn't French, because French would have linked us to France. But English links us to the world" (NYT, 17 November 1983).

Regarding the long history of relations between the Indians and the British, Nirad Chaudhuri observes that once they had decided to rule India and not just profit from it, the British became and remained aloof from their charges—in contrast to the French and their colonized (1953). That the Indian and Briton never really met on intimate terms or came to know one another was recently confirmed by R. K. Narayan, the novelist. In *The English Teacher*, Narayan's protagonist, in response to the horror the English principal of his school expresses when a student misspells "honour," says: "Let us be fair. Ask Mr. Brown if he can say in any one of the two hundred Indian languages: 'The cat chases the rat.' He has spent thirty years in India . . . Why should he think the responsibility for learning is all on our side and none on his? Why does he magnify his own importance?" After independence, Chaudhuri states, Hindus for their part continued to treat the British with "servility and malice" (p. 115) even though Hindu culture, according to him, was becoming ever more Westernized, "the provincial edition of the civilization of Europe, palely reflecting like the moon its borrowed light from the great sun beyond" (p. 452), with Indian creative writers like Tagore only being honored in India after they have been recognized in Europe. Chaudhuri, to be sure, takes a very jaundiced view of his fellow Indians, one closer to that of V. S. Naipaul than, for example, to that of Nehru, who dreamed of a union between the best of India and the best of the West—a proposition that would not have been meaningful to Chaudhuri who considers that Hindu culture is dead (pp. 498–500).

Chaudhuri's pessimism is supported by the findings of a study by

Edward Shils of the intellectual life of India in the 1950s, regarding Indian cultural dependence on the West, Britain, in particular. Shils found that intellectual life in India lacked vitality; that many Indian writers were caught between a feeling of guilt for writing in English and a reluctance to write in their native language for fear of not reaching an international audience; that prestige went to books published in England, not in India; and that more Indian students were studying in England than before independence. Shils wrote: "The sad fact is that India is not an intellectually independent country" (p. 78), and the Indian intellectual is fated "to provinciality, until his own modern culture becomes creative" (p. 87). If V. S. Naipaul is right (1977), Shils's conclusions need not be changed two decades later.

Intellectually provincial as India may be, however, middle-class, English-speaking India thrives. In a recent overview, William Stevens observed that the middle class had grown to 100 million (from some 70 million at independence in 1947); that in India's most prosperous area, the Punjab, there were 5,000 private schools (with English the language of instruction); and that Bangalore boasted one of the most sophisticated satellite programs in the world. On the other hand, among the submerged majority that spoke no English, 300 million lived below the poverty line, and even if life expectancy had risen since independence from 32 to 55, and literacy from 16 to 36 percent, progress had a long way to go. The crucial question, as Richard Nations notes, is whether the "iron hoops"—a legacy of the Raj—would hold the two Indias of rich and poor, and the many Indias of different languages and religions together–the hoops of an independent judiciary, the national police, the Indian Civil Service, the Army, the Congress Party, and, one might add, English as the language of the elite. Nations wonder if the Nehru era, once seen as the dawn of Indian democracy, might not someday seem more like "twilight of the British Raj," a prelude to a future one could hardly even speculate about. The assassination of Nehru's daughter Indira Gandhi in November 1984, did little to encourage optimism, but the Nehru dynasty has survived into the 1980s, as has the English language. In fact, while many Indians clamor for the use of Hindi as the working language of government, or insist on the use of their provincial languages, the editors of the *Hindu* of Madras (January 1984) recently observed that English was experiencing a revival as language of instruction in Sri Lanka (to serve as a bridge between Tamil and Sinhalese speakers), as well as in Burma, and was by way of becoming the sole language of instruction in Singapore. India, the *Hindu*

make it the primary language of instruction, thus enabling itself to communicate better with its neighbors in Asia, as well as to shore up Indian unity (WPR, April 1984, p. 16; William K. Stevens, NYT, 19 March 1984). The fact that some 25 million most influential people of India, Pakistan, Bangladesh, Sri Lanka and Nepal all speak English as a "link" language would seem to confirm the *Hindu*'s case. In this spirit, John Povey, an American professional English teacher, claims that African languages, usually minority languages, are unsuited to be national languages and that English, a unifying factor, is *not* destined to prove transitory. The task ahead, he implies, is to forget the debates over cultural alienation and the like, and concentrate on simply teaching English more effectively and more widely, where no alternative exists, as, he insists, in Africa.

To a proponent of dependence theory this pragmatic approach to language seems cynical and self-defeating. Thus Herbert Schiller insists that the spread of English is a function of "cultural imperialism," a weapon by which the center dominates the core (p. 5). Sharing Schiller's concern is Pierre Maes, a French cultural administrator who insists that the use of French as a national language promotes *élitisme* by dividing the rich, who can afford to learn French really well, from the masses, and serves to impoverish Africa culturally by allowing local languages, some of which are more widely spoken than French at present (Wolof in Senegal, Haoussa in Niger, for example), to wither. A similar point is made by William Bosworth in an article on the "dependency" of many Africans. He observed that French education in Africa is very expensive and that often it has only served to produce unemployable graduates unsuited to the daily life of their countries. French education, Bosworth maintains, plays an "autonomous role," divorced from commonly accepted norms, patterns, and human relations, and is kept only to feed national pride and to protect class interest.

These critics of the "universal" roles of English, and to a lesser extent of French, may be theoretically, even morally right, but present currents seem to move against them. Too many among the ruling elites, for whatever reasons, consider English or French as an essential tool and even an intrinsic part of their individual and national identity. In a sense the reality of interdependence is seen as more important than the need for total independence, and in the long run considerations of pragmatism may win out over those of ideology.

Among the many complaints lodged against the West by the Third World concerns the Western (particularly American) domination of the international media, communication facilities, and the distribution of information. This complaint has become the subject of an important and controversial debate within UNESCO, with the lead being taken by Dr. Ahmadou Mahtar M'Bow of Senegal, director-general of UNESCO from 1974 to 1986; by Séan MacBride, ex-foreign minister of Ireland, winner of both the Nobel and Lenin peace prizes and author of the *New World Information Order*; and by Mustapha Masmoudi, Permanent Representative of Tunisia when, in 1971–1972, he first began the campaign against what he called "cultural alienation" and dependency upon a Western-dominated world communications system. While, in fact, the controversy between the direction of UNESCO and its American opponents involved more than only the issue of the freedom of the media—it also involved financial and administrative matters—the focus here will be on the ideological dimension of the controversy.

Relevant data cited in this controversy by the West's opponents have included the following: nine-tenths of all foreign news is transmitted by the leading Western agencies (Reuter, Associated Press International, Agence France-Presse); U.S. dailies cover events in the industrialized world over those in the Third World by a margin of 11:1; one-quarter of all Third World news deals with disasters and violence—the figure for the industrialized world is 10 percent; further, the private news and advertising agencies, the American ones in particular, are only interested in sensationalism and encouraging consumerism (Anthony Smith; NYT, 15 February 1981; Le M, 9-11 August 1983; Ortega). The net effect, it is alleged, is to swamp the Third World with negative images of herself and a positive image of an alien way of life; both serve to demoralize and to help the spread of a superficial and corrupt cosmopolitanism. Other objections made on behalf of the Third World are that the powerful multi-nationals dominate the "electro-magnetic spectrum" (Anthony Smith, pp. 26–27; WPR, October 1985, p. 34–35) and transmission through satellites; and that 75 percent of the world circulation of television programs, 65 percent of information data programs, 60 percent of discs and cassettes, 82 percent of electronic components, and 65 percent of world advertising are all dominated by United States companies. Among the remedies proposed have been control of foreign journalists through government licensing and the adoption of international regulations to control the present open-ended flow of information. The West has countered by arguing that the measures envisioned would curb the free flow of news and information and would only serve to enable authoritarian governments to oppress their own peoples more easily.

In October 1983, at Talloires, France, representatives of sixty news organizations representing twenty-five nations met to condemn all efforts by the United Nations to try to regulate the flow of international news. Then, in December, 1984, the United States served notice that it was planning to withdraw from UNESCO on January 1, 1985. Great Britain was also, at that time, considering withdrawing.

It is clear that there is merit to both sides in this international dispute. Critics of controls of the media can point to the abuse of freedoms that hardly deserve international sanction; for instance, in Indonesia all publishing houses must obtain licenses to function and prove that they have "sufficient funds" to operate. On the other hand, as Anthony Smith observes, the world interpreted by the international media currently *does* reflect Western values and life-styles (pp. 26–27). There is even a case to be made for the view of a dependence theoretician such as Herbert Schiller—even if one rejects the motives he attributes to Westerners—that the net effect of the Western, particularly the American, domination of world communications is to further the "ideological homogenization of the world" (p. 17).

This cultural imbalance between North and South can only make the Third World more vulnerable, and more bitter. All men of good will agree that the gap must be closed, as it must be, obviously, in the sphere of economics. The question is how to do this, how to respect the cultural integrity of nations and their right to protect the community from cultural "pollution" without denying to individuals the right to see and hear what they will, and to judge for themselves.

The consideration of the status of women, language policy (particularly regarding linguistic minorities), and control of the media and communication has involved the question of human and individual rights, an issue that deserves to be addressed. Human rights, broadly seen as involving respect for individual dignity and security, are universally recognized, if not always with sincerity or in the same applications, and respect for them is not tied to any one particular polity. Many Westerners, nevertheless, tend to associate the maintenance of human rights with the institution of liberal, constitutional, parliamentary government. This institution, it is believed, offers the best guarantee of such rights and the best avenue to express and exercise them. Proponents of the view that the interests of the collectivity must come before those of the individual often argue, however, that the liberal Western view of human rights is often a mask for the domination of the bourgeois class over others. The Iranian intellectual Ali Shariati, for example, would warn against "tricky sociologists" of the West, who preach "internationalism" and other "isms," such as "humanism," to promote the myth of a false partnership that only enables the West to remain dominant (1981, pp. 115–19). Khomeini has referred to Western liberalism as "the bulldozer of colonialism and the steamroller of imperialism," and to the Western judicial system as a "Western sickness" (Bakhash, pp. 62–63, 137).

It has often been remarked that the rest of the world, while quite willing to accept Western technology, has been neither willing nor able (where willing) to accept its liberal and democratic tradition of self-government. As Cyril Black suggests, it is possible that representative government might only be a particular institution limited to the West, and not an inevitable fruit of the process of global modernization (Black, 1966, p. 53). However, even in the case of representative government, Third World voices have expressed dismay that their peoples are thought to be unworthy or incapable of ruling themselves democratically. At the yearly conference of the Middle East Studies Association (Chicago, 1983), the elderly Egyptian writer and diplomat, Tawfiq Yusuf Awad, applauded by Albert Hourani who also spoke, argued that democratic government remained, in spite of all the new " 'isms," the last and best hope for Egypt and for the Arabs. In a similar vein the Peruvian novelist, Mario Vargas Llosa, has stated: "what I want for my country and Latin America is the kind of civilization and well-being that brought liberty to the West" (NYT, 8 April 1984). Perhaps because of voices such as these, the Western ideal of individual and communal autonomy will continue to be an option in the process of global modernization, an option valid and valuable whether the system of government and society be liberal or Marxist. The West can, after all, make the case that it is individual liberty and community autonomy that has accounted for part of its vitality and its radiation to all parts of the world, and has contributed to the breach of yesterday's Chinese Walls, as Karl Marx himself admitted.

10

The West and Four Patterns of Self-Identification: Turkey, Lebanon, Israel, and Japan

The four discussions that follow are not of "test-cases" but are rather of composite perceptions, sometimes oversimplified and stereotypical, held by Third World ideologues both within and outside of the countries discussed. The spectrum of perception is not comprehensive, of course, but represents articulate, vocal, and often, militant opinion; each of the four countries here considered have been perceived as particularly extreme cases of "Westernization."

The Turkish Republic has developed according to the inspiration of Kemal Atatürk, who is more of a Westernizer than any other modern major Muslim leader; Lebanon, now in a state of disintegration, was significantly the creation of a Maronite Christian minority, which has looked to the West for protection and for its identity; Israel, in the eyes of at least some of its founders, was established as a Western state in the East and has been looked upon as being such by Arabs amidst whom it was established; and Japan, an inspiration and a model for many in the Third World, has been alternately admired as the nation *par excellence* to have Westernized itself without losing its identity, or Westernized itself to the extent of sacrificing its own cultural traditions. All four countries are examples of non-Western countries that, to one extent or another, have sought to assimilate or maintain Western values, and have, in fact, consciously made the West part of their identity. Japan and Israel are not Third World countries, to be sure, but they have played a significant part in the quest for full self-determination and self-identification of Third World countries, particularly their neighbors. To be sure, each of these nations has its own historical roots, being, and identity as much as any other nation that might have been picked as an illustration; but these four each in its own way, serve as negative or positive models of what to cultivate or what to avoid in contacts with the West. To militant conservative Muslims in particular, Turkey is often thought to be heretical because of its self-conscious Westernism; Lebanon is perceived by many as a nation whose most influential minority has embraced the West too closely at its own peril; Israel is perceived by Arabs in particular as an "artificial" Western state in an alien environment; and Japan is seen by many fellow East-Asians as having become as materialistic and domineering as any Western nation. In a positive sense, Turkey was once thought to be in the vanguard of Third-World self-moderniza- tion; Lebanon, alas, was seen as a model of multi-ethnic coexistence; and Israel and Japan have been perceived as models of progress and strength because of the virtues of their peoples, virtues to be incul- cated and encouraged among one's own. Japan, in particular, serves as both a positive and negative prototype for new entrants into the industrial world system among the peoples of Taiwan and South Korea, both rapidly advancing in Japan's footsteps.

The Turkish Republic was conceived of and brought into being at a time when the liberal West still rode the crest of prestige, a prestige reinforced by the victory of the Allies in World War I (Lewis, 1968; Kinross; MERIP, March/ April, 1984). But it was brought into being against Western opposition, in spite of military intervention by the Allies with the collapse of the Ottoman Empire, and after a bitter war to drive the Greeks out of the western part of Anatolia. It was only in 1923 that Atatürk's republic was recognized as sovereign by the Treaty of Lausanne. Because of this victory against the West, Atatürk became something of a Third World hero; it is paradoxical that Atatürk reinforced the value and viability of the liberal Western paradigm by adopting the values and institutions of the liberal West. A hero to many non-Westerners, when his secularist reforms were unveiled, Atatürk was anathema to some Muslims and was considered an enemy of Islam (W. Cleveland, pp. 117–19). But to the reform-minded Reza Shah of Iran, Atatürk was a paragon; to Khomeini, he must seem a devil incarnate (Volkan and Itzkowitz, pp. 323-24).

Once independent, Turkey proceeded to abolish the Caliphate, placed church property under the state, rejected the Arabic alphabet in favor of the Latin, and replaced the rule of the *Shari'a* with European legal systems. Atatürk's intent was for Turkey to become fully Western, a policy in direct opposition to traditional Islam and to the ensuing Iranian revolution. One can sense the difference between

Atatürk and Khomeini by juxtaposing two representative statements of ideology made by each.

In August 1925, at Kastamonu, Atatürk said in a speech:

> I flatly refuse to believe that today, in the luminous presence of science, knowledge, and civilization in all its aspects, there exist, in the civilized community of Turkey, men so primitive as to seek their material and moral wellbeing from the guidance of one or another sheikh. Gentlemen, you and the whole nation must know, and know well, that the Republic of Turkey cannot be the land of sheikhs, dervishes, disciples, and lay brothers (Kinross, p. 468).

During the revolution, Khomeini pleaded for support among the educated thus: "So preserve your mosques, O people. Intellectuals, do not be Western-Style intellectuals, imported intellectuals; do your share to preserve the mosques" (Khomeini, 1981, p. 274).

Atatürk died in 1938. In the decades since, it has become clear that while Atatürk won over to his philosophy much of the educated elite of Turkey, he had never converted the masses of still-pious Turks who, while they revered him as a person, neither understood nor appreciated his efforts to secularize and modernize the nation. The game of politics since his death has been played upon the themes of the dichotomies between the religious and the secular Turkey, the urban and the rural, and often, between the rich and the poor. Today, the new civilian government seeks a rapprochement with the Muslim world. It has adopted a more puritanical approach to public morals; even before the military permitted the election of the current Ozal government in 1984, public prayer could be said in Arabic, religion was being taught in schools, Friday had become once again the day of rest, and a number of ideological movements had arisen to challenge the "secular Jacobinism" of Atatürk. In an article entitled "Why Atatürk is turning in his Grave," Thomas Goltz pointed to the fact that Turgot Ozal, prime minister in the late 1980s, was seeking to replace Turkish words, originally introduced as part of Atatürk's nationalistic secularist policy, with Arabic words having an Islamic association. Thus *özgürlük* (freedom) was to be replaced by *hurriyet*, *dogga* (nature) by *tabiyat*, and *yasam* (life) by *hayat*. According to Şerif Mardin, one of the most sensitive students of modern Turkey, Atatürk, in his unqualified embrace of the West, had created a moral vacuum, one that has inspired movements such as that of Necmettin Erbakan whose National Salvation Party won 11 percent of the forty-eight seats in the parliamentary election of 1973. Although a minority party, Mardin suggests that the NSP does speak for the misgivings of many more Turks than those who vote for it. According to Erbakan, Turkey has become too Westernized, family values (respect for elders, separation of the sexes, etc.) have suffered, and dancing, ballet, and theater have polluted society; the Turks must now escape from their dependence upon the "capitalist-Christian West," follow the Japanese paradigm toward industrialization, and revive traditional moral and spiritual values.

The imprint of Atatürk, however, has been too strong to allow for a radical return to traditionalism. "Kemalism" remains of great philosophical importance to many elements of society, including the military officer class. It was not strange, when events in Iran in the late 1970s led to so much talk about the threat of "Islamic revivalism"; two Turks, in letters to the *New York Times* (10 July 1979 and 15 January 1980), insisted that while Turkey might be Muslim, it was secular and liberal in its commitments and values and should not be considered party to any "fanatical" revivalism, and that, in any case, Khomeini's "reactionary" movement would most likely prove ephemeral. But these Turkish correspondents might have protested too much—Turkey once did embrace the West too precipitously and uncritically, in part because it had entered modernity at a time when few saw any alternative to the Western model. Now, many Turks feel, the time has come to continue to modernize while returning to those traditional values that might serve to strengthen the unity and the moral and cultural fiber of the Turkish people, and bring Turkey closer to its fellow Muslims. But in a recent work, *Turkey: Coping with Crisis*, George S. Harris is sanguine about the future of Kemalism. Harris writes: "the main surge of change is directed not toward the pervasive Islamization of the elite, but toward the modernization of traditional Islamic style practiced by the remainder of the populace" (p. 216).

After the end of Western empires, inevitably, there were sequels in the form of communities that, for one reason or another, and to one degree or another, had become intimately involved with the imperial reign and its rulers. Such communities often constituted an anomaly within the succession nations to the imperial power, their prosperity and protection having been dependent upon it. Now adrift, so to speak, in a new world in which they are looked upon as anomalies, or worse, as enemies for having sided with the previous colonialist oppressor, they live a life that is often threatened, and they share an identity that is out of step with the mainstream, especially the radicals.

Such groups were once favorites of empire; they included communities in India from whom prized units were recruited for the British army—the Assyrians of Iraq, victims of a "massacre" after independence, and North African Berbers, the "desert Arabs" who were led by T. E. Lawrence.

Another such group might prove to be the Maronites of Lebanon, once favored by the French as the vanguard of their culture and influence in the Levant. It is this community of uniate Catholics that has, in the main, remained faithful to the problematical "nation" of Lebanon, since 1975 caught in a vicious, internecine war of self-destruction, cruelly sponsored by external powers and interests. In this multi-sectarian state, since 1946 free of French troops (officially independent in 1943), Maronites tended (or at least were perceived by their enemies) to dominate because they held an official plurality and because they controlled both the presidency and the army (Gordon, 1983; Hudson, 1968; Cobban, 1985; Corm, 1986).

It is the Maronites in the main, with some support from other Christian sects and from some non-Christian sects sharing in the prosperity that Lebanon once knew, who have given Lebanon the image among other Arab nations of being something of an outpost, if not a bastion of the West, like Israel. While one group of Maronites have insisted upon a genuine compromise with the Muslims and with the Arabs in general, instransigents have always existed who insist that Lebanon remain isolated from the Arab world and maintain close ties with the West, France in particular. It is only because the first group of Maronites prevailed that Lebanon was able to come into existence as an independent state in 1943. But it is the ultras among the Maronites who have gained the ascendancy among the Maronites and among others who have been fighting against the Palestinians and the Lebanese "Leftists" since the civil war began in 1975. They demand that Lebanon be restored to what it basically was before 1975—an open, free-trade, capitalist state with close links to the West, its sovereignty guaranteed by Maronite Christian political predominance. Needless to say, after a decade of civil war, the Muslims, who now as a whole have a majority of the population—the Shi'ites constitute the largest single Lebanese sect—will never again accept the restoration of the Lebanon that was. A possible prospect is that the present *de facto* partition will, in the course of time, be legalized by prescription.

During its years of prosperity in the 1950s and 1960s, even while both sides abided by the National Covenant (except during the civil war of 1958), Lebanon was already an anomaly: a genuine capitalist republic with a free press and a home to important Western universities in an area of the world that was turning more and more to forms of socialism and authoritarian integral nationalism. Even when this anomalous state was tolerated, prescient observers such as Michael Hudson (1968) predicted trouble and anticipated Thierry Desjardin's comment, made after the start of the civil war in 1975, with Lebanon in mind, that history abhors anomalies.

After the civil war in 1975 and the Israeli invasion of 1982, it is not strange that many Arabs found their worst views confirmed. These were, in effect, that the militant Maronites and the Israelis were party to a Western conspiracy to recolonize Lebanon and to weaken the forces of Palestinian and Arab nationalism, and of Islam. Malcolm Kerr, assassinated on January 18, 1984, was most probably a victim of such feelings; as president of the American University of Beirut he symbolized, to militant Shi'ites in particular, Western civilization itself in its American expression. This was the interpretation made by G. H. Jansen (*Los Angeles Times*, 22 January 1984), Thomas Friedman (NYT, 29 January 1984), and Michael Hudson (1984). Fouad Ajami (1984) suggested that the assassination marked the "end of the affair," meaning the final demise of the perception, once held by most Arabs, of the United States as philanthropic and innocent of the political intrigue associated with Europeans. To Charles Malik, a leading voice of Lebanese Christian nationalism (although not a Maronite), the assassination of Malcolm Kerr was more than a political act. It involved issues of culture and of values. The United States, he argued, under the rubric "The West Misses Its Calling in Lebanon" (WSJ, 28 March 1984), had refused to defend its own liberal values and, by refusing to do so, had betrayed not only Lebanon but itself. Kerr, he implied, was the victim not of Western strength but of its weakness, as revealed by its failure to defend the Lebanon of President Amin Gemayel. It was this rigid identification of Lebanon with the West by leaders of conservative opinion such as Charles Malik that had done so much to fashion the image of Lebanon among many in the area as a perverse curiosity at best, an outpost of Western imperialist designs at worst. The Maronites, if they are finally to be victims of fate, may someday seem to be victims of a self-fulfilling prophecy (the dread many of them had of "Islam") who had loved the West not wisely but too well.

Whatever Israelis might believe today, their state was conceived of as a projection of Europe into the Middle East, at least by some of the founding fathers. Theodore Herzl, for example, saw Israel as having a Western "civilizing mission," and as being "a portion of Europe against Asia, an outpost of civilization as opposed to barbarism," and a "mini-Switzerland in the heart of the Middle East" (Rubinstein, p. 11). The assumption made by many of the early Zionists was that Jewish socialism would undermine Arab feudalism and benefit the Arab workers and that, in their wake, the Jews would bring a prosperity that would deflect Arab hostility (Rubinstein; Hertzberg; Benvenisti, pp. 87–88). In his speech in Israel, accepting a prize for literature, Milan Kundera thought it fitting to state: "Even after Europe so tragically failed them, the Jews nonetheless kept faith with the European cosmopolitanism; thus it is that Israel, their little homeland finally regained, strikes me as the true heart of Europe—a strange heart, located outside the body" (NYRB, 13 June 1985, pp. 11–12).

Amos Elon, in his study of Herzl, places the founding father in the Western utopian tradition (1975, pp. 347–51). His *Altneuland*, published in 1912 in Leipzig, has an epigraph on the title page: "If you will it, it is no fairy tale." This is the Jewish utopia that is technologically developed and cosmopolitan. The Arabs living in it are happy, rich, and enthusiastic citizens. Even to this day there are Israelis who believe that they are a force for modernization and progress among the Arabs (Avineri, 1970; Turner, 1978, pp. 25–32). In fact, the creation of Israel has turned out to be triply offensive to non-Jewish inhabitants of the region, *terra irredenta* to Arab nationalists, a homeland to be reconquered for displaced Palestinians and—Jerusalem being their third holiest city—anathema to Muslims. Because the Jews who created Israel were Westerners to the Arabs of the region and, also because of the support Great Britain and then the United States has given her over the years, Israel has been inevitably regarded by the Arabs as a Western bastion in their midst. The argument sometimes made that Zionism can be seen as the first Third World revolution against Western Christian domination (Robert Wistrich, TLS, 23 May 1980), while persuasive to some Westerners, seems complete sophistry to most Arabs who judge Israel by their own historical experience of her (Haddad in Esposita, 1980; Committee on International Relations).

Kenneth Jacobson, director of Middle Eastern affairs of the Anti-Defamation League of B'nai B'rith, in an opinion piece meant to persuade his audience to continue to support Israel as America's only trustworthy ally in the Middle East, stated: "A common thread running through all these ideological approaches [among Arabs] is the

rejection of Israel as an alien body in the Arab-Islamic Middle East"
(CSM, 16 March 1984). Allowing for some exceptions, this observation is basically correct. Even if pragmatic interest should lead to some
sort of accommodation between Israeli and Arab, Israel will continue
to be regarded by most Arab Muslims as an entity deliberately
implanted by the West to disrupt and undermine Arab civilization
(Ajami, 1981, p. 5) and Zionism as a form, as Maxime Rodinson puts
it, of "Western colonialism" (1968, p. 14). Arabs often draw a parallel
between Israel and the Kingdom of Jerusalem. They believe that
Israel will someday face a new Saladin. To bring peace to the Levant,
enough Arabs need to be persuaded that Israel is not a beachhead of
Western imperialism; the Israelis, need to persuade their neighbors
of this; as for the West, the United States must encourage this
conviction on both sides.

Japan is discussed in the present context, although she is clearly
not part of the Third World. Her experience with the the West bears
some similarity to that of the Third World; she offers a possible
model for modernization by a non-Western people—a synthesis of
the traditional and the Western—and the West still remains in the
consciousness of some of her intellectuals, a factor or even a problem
for Japanese self-identification.

Japan has been of importance to other "Easterners," now members
of the Third World, who have been impressed and often inspired by
her success in avoiding colonization, and then competing successfully
with the West. To the Arab scholar, Hisham Sharabi (1970, p. 129),
the Japanese, unlike his fellow Arabs, have managed to combine the
traditional and the modern without losing their equanimity. Nirad
Chaudhuri spoke for many Asians when he wrote concerning Japan's
victory over Russia in 1904–1905: "After the Japanese victory we felt
an immense elation, a sort of reassurance in the face of the Europeans, and an immense sense of gratitude and hero-worship for the
Japanese" (1953, p. 105). From the 1930s to 1945, Japan's image
changed, but even if, to many Asians, the Japanese appeared as
bullies and imperialists, they were impressed by the rapid demise, at
Japanese hands, of the European empires in Asia. After 1945, many
Asians feared the economic power of the Japanese but were also
impressed by Japan's success in competing not only with the Europeans but even with the formidable Americans.[12] It no longer seems
strange or even presumptuous for Toshi Aoki to say, without apology,
that Japan has caught up with the West economically; that Japanese,
like English, could become an "international vehicle"; and that Japan's

most serious problem, is not to succumb, as many Europeans had, to the arrogant pride of being a major power (Le M, 2 July 1982). Many Westerners today cannot but concur with Aoki. John Ardagh observes that, during the French economic "miracle" of the sixties, some intellectuals feared that the French were becoming too "modernized" and too "Americanized" *or* Japanese-like and that, as "the Japanese of Europe," they were turning into "robots" (pp. 652–54). This concern, almost European obsession with Japan, was played upon by Albert Méglin in an interview in *Le Monde* entitled *"Mme. Butterfly parle,"* which lambasted the West (France in particular) by comparing her to Japan (Le M, 17 March 1983). Speaking through an imaginary young Japanese woman, he describes France as falling victim to decadence, jealousy, *"néantisation,"* of being reduced to nothing, to laziness, incapable of rising above her "Cartesianism" to understand the "subtle Oriental." Now, the civilized people were the Japanese who knew the secret of the union of opposites (Zen), and with this secret would win out over the "colonisable" French. Be advised Lieutenant Pinkerton!

The recognition that Japan was on a par with the West in terms of technology and industrialization, was even superior to it in many ways, is a fairly recent phenomenon, coming well after World War II. As late as 1968 Charles Gallagher still felt compelled to inform his American readers of how "modern" the Japanese had become and, in 1984, *Le Monde Diplomatique*, in a special issue, thought it worthwhile to inform its readers that the Japanese were becoming more individualistic; that the extended family was giving way to the nuclear family; and that one reason new Japanese novels did not receive the attention in France that earlier Japanese novels had, was that they seemed no different in their experimentation from Western novels—the "exotic" was no longer there (February 1984, pp. 21–28). But were the implications of these last observations (of René de Ceccatty's and Ryoji Nakamura's, p. 28) valid? Has Japan indeed become so Westernized that she has lost her uniqueness as a nation and a people between West and "East?" This is a question of concern to many Japanese intellectuals, and it is also a matter of concern to many non-Japanese in the Third World who have been tempted to wonder if the Japanese might not be the most appropriate model for their own modernization.

The Japanese paradigm presents problems. A strong case can be made that Japan is too individual a case to serve others; that, in contrast to the cases of other peoples, factors were already operating

among the Japanese that favor a positive response to the challenge of
the West even before the Western impact was seriously experienced
during the mid-nineteenth century (Issawi, 1982, p. 233). Some
factors were: a tradition of borrowing from others (the Chinese
classics, for example); the coexistence of diverse faiths and philosophical systems (hence tolerance); a high esteem for learning (in 1868
some 50 percent of the male population were literate); relative technological expertise among its artisans; demographic homogeneity,
controlled population growth, and a high level of urbanization; political centralization; an interest in science (the Copernican theory,
through Dutch transmission, was adopted in 1800); an active and
relatively sophisticated trading class; and an isolation from the rest of
the world that helped it to avoid colonization and its related psychological complexes (Black, 1975; Sansom; Kuwabara; Gallagher, 1968).
As Kuwabara observes, (pp. 82–83, 167–68) the Japanese, because
they had never been conquered by another and because their culture
was not dominated by a single jealous and exclusive deity, never felt
the need to cling to "tradition" in order to defend identification or
please a single god. Sansom observes (pp. 310–15) that, unlike the
Chinese and the Indian, Japanese culture has been favorable to
change and has been able to assimilate the Western idea of progress
with relative ease.

After Commodore Perry's flotilla appeared off the shores of Japan
in 1853, to those Japanese who recognized the need for a radical
response to this new challenge, such a response could only take one
form—that of the "Westernization" of Japan, the policy adopted with
the Meiji Restoration of 1868 by those Samurai who now seized power
in the name of the restored emperor. This, after all, was the time in
history when Western civilization was unrivaled in power and in
prestige; Western civilization *was* modernity. Kuwabara goes on to
say, that the clichés of the period, such as "Eastern morality and
Western technology" and "Japanese spirit, Western learning" were
only cases of sugarcoating what was now considered ineluctable—the
emperor himself cut off his top knot, took to eating beef, and donned
Western dress (pp. 134–36).

It is well known that the rapidity of Westernization was impressive
but perhaps its depth, Kuwabara suggests, is not appreciated by non-
Japanese; Western classical music, for example, and not only Western
technology—or baseball—became more widespread and more appreciated among the Japanese than among any other non-European

Japanese a long time to free themselves from "communal frames" (one reason for the disastrous imperialism that ended in 1945), Japanese society today is as egalitarian, classless, and mobile as any in the world—in fact, more so than most European countries (pp. 13, 40, 143, 164–65). Such remarks may be true of Japanese males, but they are not true of Japanese females.

Many Japanese fear they may be losing their particularistic identity in the process of modernization.[13] In 1970, Yukio Mishima, unable to arouse the Japanese Army in defense of the old Japan, committed hara-kiri. After a recent trip to Japan, the veteran British journalist, Peter Jenkins, came to the conclusion that most Japanese didn't really care if their "traditions" were disappearing or not (MGW, 20 May 1984, p. 10). Kuwabara, although he believes that Japan has indeed kept many of its traditions and has been selective in its "Westernization," admits the enthusiasm for things European still continues. He observes the popularity of "horizontal-writing" in advertisements and elsewhere, the use of names like George and Peggy among popular singers, enthusiasm for Western painting, and the persistence of the association of "modern rationalism" with Europe. Even some customs assumed to be traditionally Japanese, the Shinto wedding ceremony for example, are in fact recent imitations of Western practice (pp. 144–47). Among those who have wrestled with the question of Japan's contemporary identity have been intellectuals such as Yoshio Abe and Kinhide Mushakoji who, in 1973, were invited by the French magazine, *Esprit* to express their views on Japan's identity vis-à-vis the West.

According to Mushakoji, since World War II there have been three general attitudes among Japanese intellectuals: the view that Japan should become even more Western (i.e. more democratic and more individualistic); the view in favor of recognizing and preserving specific Japanese values held to be the reasons for Japan's success (e.g., family loyalties and rejecting Westernization); and, third, the view of the mainstream that favors a synthesis of the allogenic (the Western) and the autogenic (the Japanese), using Tadao Umesao's terminology. To Mushakoji, who identifies himself with the third position, the Western component of modern Japanese culture is expressed by the values of individualism and the belief that truth is single, exclusive, and definitive. The Japanese component, on the other hand, involves an emphasis upon the problematical and the belief in the multiplicity of truth and reality—the *ga* (but) and the *shikashi* (however)—and upon the need for mutual accommodation between viewpoints (*jin-rin*: we both). In the West, man distances himself from nature, in Japan man and nature are inseparable. The weakness of the Western viewpoint, Mushakoji holds, lies in the "unrealism and arrogance" of its "mechanical and geometric spirit" and in its claim to "universalism;" the Japanese, in contrast, tends to be "provincial" and not open enough to new experiences and to other peoples.

Abe also remarks on Japanese "provinciality." He points, in particular, to the unwillingness of many Japanese to subject many of their traditional ways to rational analysis for fear that this will undermine their authority. He contrasts this attitude with what he holds to be, paradoxically, a "universal" trait of the West—the courage to see all cultures, including the Western, as particular and as equally subject to critical analysis. Whatever Japan's true identity or identities perhaps might be, Kuwabara points out that for most Japanese the days of awe of the West are long over and they need not feel that Westernization and modernization are the same thing (pp. 140–41). Nevertheless, the West means a great deal to many Japanese—its culture as well as its science. Perhaps one might suggest that because of their success and self-confidence, the Japanese are psychologically better prepared than others to appreciate and assimilate the best the West has to offer, what Abe sees as being of "universal" value, without feeling threatened in their identification.

The four instances, Turkey, Lebanon, Israel, and Japan, each in its own way, have influenced the image of the West in the minds of others; many ideologues of the Third World see in these relatively extreme instances what is possible and what is involved, to one's profit or peril, in Western assimilation. The interpretation of each instance varies widely. But from one generalized Third World vantage point, at least, the perception might be, in summary form, that, in the case of Turkey, Westernization has been precipitous; that in the case of Lebanon blind faith in the West might prove self-destructive; that in the case of Israel, identifying herself with the West inevitably leads to the suspicion of colonialism in any guise; and that in the case of Japan, however fraught with difficulty the journey, it is possible to reconcile East and West.

11

Conclusions: Cosmopolitanism and Pluralism

In this work, much consideration has been given to the dependence of the South upon the North, of Third-World nations upon the industrialized powers, because the former are weaker and poorer. But the terms could be reversed—the core is also dependent on the periphery, creditors upon debtors, as "masters" on their "slaves." R. Buckminster Fuller believed the pictures of the earth sent back by the the astronauts served to visualize in a dramatic way that the earth was a single spaceship hurtling through infinite spaces, and that common survival dictates mutual dependence. Thus, a cliché has gained reality—the earth's future is one.

Two utopian projections into the future, the one as pessimistic as the other is optimistic, are those of Aldous Huxley's *Island* and of H. G. Wells's *Modern Utopia*. In the first, a small utopia, the best qualities of "East" and "West" are blended to provide harmony and peace of mind. In the second, because of modern technology, the utopia is and must be global; through this technology, life under man's management will "stretch its realm amid the stars," and through this same technology "the first achievement of world-wide political and social unity" will be attained. For both Huxley and Wells any human outcome must be global, but their attitudes toward this global future are different. Wells welcomed the technological unification of the world he saw ahead; Huxley, on the other hand, saw the world as likely to be dominated by persons of financial and military greed, which would cause the inevitable destruction of his small island utopia. On one matter, however, they would have agreed: that the triumph of homogenizaton over human variegation, which even Wells in his darker moments dreaded, might make human survival not worth the candle. Here, the West and the Third World need each other.

Assuming the universe is spared a "catastrophic" ending—ecological or nuclear—two possibilities appear to face the human earth: the first, the homogenization of the universe; the second, the growing articulation of the world's various cultures and pluralism within the framework of a common fate, as the U.N.'s membership increases and ethnic groups awakened to nationalism multiply. The first would lead to sameness and ennui, the latter to competition and cooperation of diverse and mutually stimulating modes of expression and styles of life. It is likely that both tendencies will continue to unfold simultaneously, assuring greater interdependence and, one might hope, greater variegation. But whatever the future might hold in this regard, the styles and values West will continue to be a crucial influence and, in most cases, an integral part—if only as a negative challenge—in the lives of others.

In this context, "cosmopolitanism" means the tendency toward sameness of values and ways of living worldwide, derived largely but not entirely from the West as acculturations absorbed into the international institutions of fashion and tourism, exotica uprooted from the cultural soil that once gave them sustenance, meaning, and value. A cynical perspective on the cultural "entropy" under discussion is that of Sabina in Kundera's *The Unbearable Lightness of Being*. "At the time, she had thought that only in the Communist world could such musical barbarism reign supreme. Abroad, she discovered that the transformation of music into noise was a planetary process by which mankind was entering the historical phase of total ugliness. The total ugliness to come had made itself felt first as omnipresent acoustical ugliness: cars, motorcycles, electrical guitars, drills, loudspeakers, sirens. The omnipresence of visual ugliness would soon follow" (p. 93). The reality of the threat of cosmopolitanism is also discussed by Claude Lévi-Strauss—his term is "monoculture."

Historian William McNeill (1985, 1986) has traced the beginnings of the trend toward cosmopolitanism to about 1000 A.D., with the development and extensions of long-range inter-civilizational trade routes. Even at this early stage, he has argued, different civilizations began to significantly influence one another. The process toward "our contemporary ecumenical society" has since grown with increasing rapidity, especially with the spread of the Western empires and the Industrial Revolution (Curtin, 1985). In Wallerstein's language, much of the rest of the world became both material "periphery" or "semi-periphery" to the West, and through the spread of Western values and its rationalistic ideologies, for the first time in history, a "world system" was fashioned (1984). It is in the context of a "world system" that English has become the international language of much of aviation, that one-half of the world's newspapers and 80 percent of all computer data are in English, and that in China one of the most popular television programs is "Follow Me," a series that teaches English to as many as a million people (McCrum et al.).

Lamentation over this phenomenon is widespread. The president of the *Association pour le Défense du Français et du Patrimonie Européen*, has said: "Beware of cultural colonisation! Let us avoid that Anglo-American should become the unique means of communication throughout European institutions" (Le M, 12 June 1985). William Gass, the American author, who warned Chinese writers to stick to their traditions, said "Whatever you do, I hope you will not cover yourself with American filth" (Salisbury). Hassan Fathy, the Egyptian architect who, as dean of the Fine Arts School in Cairo, combatted imitation of the West, declaring: "Our architects are university-trained, and the universities are westernized . . . We have been taught that the Islamic style of architecture is exotic. It's our own architecture—how could it be exotic? Tradition defeats the weak, but the strong will comprehend and use it properly" (ME, August 1986, pp. 31–33).

Spiritual entropy has been the theme of many contemporary dystopians, and it is in confrontation with it that more hopeful souls have proposed defenses and alternatives. T. S. Eliot and Arnold J. Toynbee, for example, have proposed religious revival; Jacques Berque, "an eruption of identities" (1978b., p. 202); Denis de Rougement, a revived synthesis of humanism and of its essential base, Christianity; F. S. C. Northrop, a symbiosis of the highest values of East and West. In the face of this "world-wide cosmopolitan West-centered social process," one that threatens to prove "asphyxiating and empty," William McNeill suggests the likelihood that this cosmopolitan civilization may prove to be as ephemeral as Hellenism once was (1963, pp. 767–830, 565–68; TLS, 27 May 1977, p. 655).

In his survey of the devolution of Third World nations from Western empires, Rupert Emerson has argued that to date it is largely from the cosmopolitan Westernized elites that one has heard—that radically different might be the aspirations of those masses submerged until now but beginning to find their voice (pp. 15–16). But then Hellenism covered only the small rim of the Mediterranean. It is by no means certain that once the submerged masses of Third World humanity enter the cities and the polities of the future that they will want much more than the luxuries and satisfactions of their "betters," or that the enthusiasm of the contemporary militant conservative Muslims will prove to be, in the long run, only an explosion of fury and frustration more than a negative revolt of the have-nots.

In the Arab Islamic context, the issue is raised as to whether the *Nahda* (the liberal, progressive "renaissance" of the late nineteenth century) was only the last of the old (of the Western imprint), an expression of the culture of a Westernized elite rather than of the masses for whom Westernization represented only privilege and alienation. By this perception, the writers and intellectuals of the *Nahda* would seem mere figures of the moment, of the "Liberal Age" as Albert Hourani has put it, destined to fade in importance in the sweep of history. In this future, the imitative and derivative nature of the "West," of the native elites, will be revealed clearly and genuine "renaissance" will be sought in one's own heritage. At the same time, there are those who would maintain, among them many of the "marginals" discussed earlier, that the only hopeful future lies in a blend of the Western sources of genuine value and creativity with the legacy of the native past (Ajami, 1987).

The alternative might well be that in the course of time modernity would offer little more than cosmopolitanism, the rebirth of the past little more than self-defeating fanaticism or, as some would have it, "nativism." Whether cosmopolitanism or a more creative variegation is to characterize the distant future, the West will have played its part and will continue to play a part as setter of patterns or as a stimulus to self-determination and liberty. In either case, it should behoove Westerners to sustain their own "authenticity" rather than to lose heart and faith. They owe this to themselves and they owe it to the Other.

Notes

1. Shiva Naipaul has said sarcastically that the term "Third World" is a term "of bloodless universality which robs individuals and societies of their particularity . . . To blandly subsume, say, Ethiopia, India and Brazil under the one banner of Third Worldhood is as absurd and as denigrating as the old assertion that all Chinese look alike. People look alike only when you cannot be bothered to look at them closely" (1987, pp. 34–35). While recognizing the sensible caveats contained in Naipaul's thought, we will still use the term as a shorthand; even if mythical, it is a myth that is widely believed and used; it is a concept that operates on an ideational and ideological plane of discourse and so is of moment, if not of material reality. In addition, "Third World" designates a condition, not a set of qualities.

2. This optimistic view of the West represents only one tendency in contemporary opinion. An alternative view is that of Arnold J. Toynbee who has referred to Western "cultural narcissism"; one representative feature of this self-adoration has been a monolinear interpretation of history, the notion that all of history moves toward a single goal and that at the head of this line of development is the West which all previous civilizations have served to produce. Toynbee and other students of comparative civilization have rejected this interpretation in favor of a pluralistic view that sees the different civilizations as co-equal and experiencing similar cycles of rise and fall. Of a recent world history text that took the linear view, William McNeill commented, such a "Eurocentric vision seems likely to appear as a quaint monument to the myopia of our age," a vision that, taken seriously, might make us unfit for the future, and one that scholars of civilization since Spengler and including Toynbee had rendered academically obsolete. Such Eurocentrism still, he nevertheless agrees, prevails on a popular level (1977). This debate between Toynbee and Kohn is discussed in vol. 12 of *A Study of History* (Reconsiderations), pp. 528–33.

3. Raspail's book was printed in a new edition in Paris in 1985 (Robert Laffont). In the same year, an issue of *Le Figaro Magazine* appeared with a cover of Marianne wearing an Arab woman's veil and an article co-authored by Raspail entitled "Will France still be French in 2015?" (NYT, 3 November 1985).

4. The term "pieds rouges," for French radicals involved with Algeria, was a play on "pieds noirs," a vulgar term applied to the French settlers in Algeria.

5. Karpat, however, in his presidential address to the Middle East Association in 1985 would not agree with this assessment. After indicating that he believes that militancy "is the beginning of popular participation," he goes on to insist that "the Islamic identity . . . is the bedrock of the Muslim's basic concept of nation and nationality."

6. The present author, parenthetically, has also been tarred with the same accusatory brush as has von Grünebaum (Said, 1978, p. 298). Gordon's response appears in Gordon, 1982.

7. An exception in the late 1980s was the remarkable leader of Japan's Socialist Party, Takaka Doi.

8. Kagitcibasi also points out the dangers of talking of "Muslim culture." Greeks and Turks, he observes, are closer in their sex patterns than are Muslim Turks and Muslim Indonesians (pp. 486–87). Similarly, Suad Joseph cautions that important differences have existed and continue to exist among Muslim women, depending upon geography and chronology.

9. A personal note will be introduced here to illustrate the sensitivities involved in the Third World debate over the status of women in the Islamic context in particular. In 1968, I published a monograph on the role of Algerian women during and after the revolution against the French (1954–1962). My thesis was that while much was promised to women during the revolution, less was granted after independence than hoped for, in part, because Algerian society was deeply Muslim and traditions of male dominance were deeply rooted. Elsewhere in this work, I paid credit to Germaine Tillion, the French ethnologist, for some of her ideas about North African women in the context of colonialism.

Following the publication of Said's *Orientalism* in 1978, a stream of articles appeared in *Arab Studies Quarterly* (organ of the Association of Arab-American University Graduates and the Institute of Arab Studies) and elsewhere denouncing one case after another of "Orientalism among Western and Western-influenced writers." In one such article, written by Rosemary Sayigh, a sociologist and journalist, both Germaine Tillion and I were fiercely attacked for viewing the question of women in Islam from a "Eurocentric" point of view. Out of frustration for the West's defeat in Algeria, Sayigh maintained, Western writers were seeking a sort of revenge by trying to make Muslims feel guilty about their treatment of women. Sayigh's thesis was that Islamic women, far from being "subjugated," played a very important and varied role in the life of the community. In a later issue of *Arab Studies Quarterly*, a progressive Palestinian intellectual, Khalil Nakhleh, wrote a critique of Sayigh's article, not defending those she had attacked but questioning the use made of Said's *Orientalism* to preclude needed self-criticism; and he charged Sayigh as guilty of "the barrenness and futility of functional analysis." A similar point was made by Peter Singer in his review of Germain Greer's *Sex and Destiny* in regard to her argument that one ought not to be critical of the customs of other peoples. "Who are we to invade the marriage bed of veiled women?," asked Greer dramatically (NYRB, 31 May 1984, pp. 15–17). Another problem with the stance taken by Sayigh and of Edward Said also, is that propositions are interpreted not in terms of presumed ideological or factual validity but in terms of presumed ideological bias. This approach is often valid but as a universal rule it would eliminate dialogue.

10. While women are enjoined by the *Quran* to exhibit modesty in public, they are not asked explicitly to veil. Veiling, whether by *hijab* (which covers the head but not necessarily the face), the Iranian *chador* (covering women from head to foot), *purdah* (the seclusion of women from public observation, including the veil or *niqab* [face-veil]), is the result of a combination of interpretation and custom adopted from pre-Islamic cultures.

11. For a psychological study of the traditional view of women in Islam, see F. Sabbah. She points out that women are considered to be the embodiment of the principle of disorder. Hence, they must be subordinated to men, the embodiment of the principle of order. Many educated Muslim women (although by no means all) would agree with Juliette Minces when she declares with no qualification or embarrassment that the condition of women in any culture should be judged by Western standards because the Western woman is the "only democratic, just and forward-looking model" (quoted in S. Joseph). Minces is the author of *The House of Obedience: Women in Arab Society* (London: Zed, 1982).

12. Japan's history abounds with paradoxes: while Japan has been seen with respect by fellow-Asians for having successfully resisted Western imperialism, it joined the imperialist club; and while the revolution of 1868 was seen as a return to traditions against the influence of the West, it was, in fact, a revolution for modernization (Duus, pp. 56–72, 189–90, 134–35). The dislike and distrust of the Japanese by many of her neighbors stems from actions in the 1930s, her behavior in World War II, and now her threat of economic hegemony. See Joel Kotking and Yoriko Kishimoto (MGW, 6 July 1986), and John Dower's *War Without Mercy: Race and Power in the Pacfific War* (New York: Pantheon, 1986).

13. The view that Japan's traditional self has been swept away by a wave of Western materialism, or at least seriously threatened, has been the opinion of some Western observers including Donald Keene and Edward Seidensticker. An article in *Le Monde* referred to contemporary culture in Japan as experiencing "Les Années Zéro" (7-8 July 1985). At the same time, there were indications that Japanese traditionalist nationalism might be experiencing a revival: Prime Minister Yasuhiro Nakasone payed homage to the war dead at the Yasukini Shrine in Tokyo; Lieutenant Onada, who emerged from a Philippine jungle twenty-nine years after the war, became a popular hero; and textbooks were whitewashed to erase Japan's World War II record. Recently, a Japanese professor was quoted as saying: "We were eager to learn from the West in external things, but we tried to keep our own traditions . . . We never opened our hearts. We opened our minds, but not our souls" (NYT, 26 September 1986).

Bibliography

Abdel-Malek, Anouar. "L'Orientalisme en crise." *Diogène* October–December, 1963): 109–44.

———. *La Dialectique sociale*. Seuil: Paris, 1972.

'Abduh, Muhammad, Ishaq Musa'd, and Kenneth Cragg, trans. *Theology of Unity*. London: George Allen & Unwin, 1966.

Abe, Yoshio. "La Culture japonaise à la recherche de son identitè." In *Esprit*, no. 421 (February 1973): 295–314.

Abrahamian, Ervand. *Iran Between Two Revolutions*. Princeton: Princeton University Press, 1982.

Abu-Fadil, Magda. "Ron-bo takes on the Shiites." *Middle East Journal* (August 1985): 19–20.

Abu-Lughod, Ibrahim. *Arab Rediscovery of Europe: A Study in Cultural Encounter*. Princeton: Princeton University Press, 1963.

———, ed. "The Islamic Alternative." Combined issue, *Arab Studies Quarterly* 4 (Spring 1982): 1, 2.

Accad, Evelyn. "The Theme of Sexual Oppression in the North African Novel." In Beck and Keddie, *Women in the Muslim World* (1978): 617–28.

Achebe, Chinua. "Viewpoint." *Times Literary Supplement* (1 February 1980).

———. Interview with Achebe. *Times Literary Supplement* (26 February 1982).

Afshar, Halek. "Women, State and Ideology in Iran." *Third World Quarterly* 7 (2 April 1985): 256–78.

Ahmad, Jalal Al-e, Paul Sprachman, trans. *Plagued by the West* [Gharbzadegi]. New York: Caravan Books, Delmar, 1981.

Ahmed, Abdel Gaffar M. "Some Remarks from the Third World on Anthropology and Colonialism: the Sudan." In T. Asad, ed., *Anthropology and The Colonial Encounter*. 259–70.

Ajami, Fouad. *The Arab Predicament: Arab Political Thought and Practice Since 1967*. London: Cambridge University Press, 1981.

———. "The End of the Affair: An American Tragedy in the Arab World." *Harper's* (June, 1984): 53–63.

167

————. *The Vanished Imam Musa al Sadr and the Shia of Lebanon.* Ithaca: Cornell University Press, 1986.

————. "The Silence in Arab Culture." *The New Republic* (6 April 1987): 27–33.

Akçura, Yusuf, and Lewis V. Thomas, trans. *The Period of the Ottoman Empire's Decline, 18th and 19th Centuries.* Istanbul, 1940, Chap. II, pp. 6–9. Mimeo.

Alatas, Syed Hussein. *The Myth of the Lazy Native: A Study of the Image of the Malays, Filipinos and Javanese from the 16th to the 20th Century and its Function in the Ideology of Colonialism.* London: Frank Cass, 1977.

Allen, Roger. *The Arabic Novel: An Historical and Critical Introduction.* Syracuse, N. Y.: Syracuse University Press, 1982.

Alloula, Malek, Myrna Godzick, and Wlad Godzlich, trans. *The Colonial Harem.* Minneapolis: University of Minnesota Press, 1986.

Amin, Ahmed, and Wolfgang H. Behn, trans. *Orient and Occident.* Berlin: Adiyok, 1984.

Amin, G. A. "Economic and Cultural Dependence." In T. Asad and R. Owen, eds., *Sociology of "Developing Societies":* 54–60.

Amin, Samir. *Imperialism and Unequal Development.* New York: Monthly Review, 1977.

Anders, Jaroslaw. "Voice of Exile" and "An Interview with Czeslaw Milosz." *New York Review of Books* (27 February 1986): 31–35.

Anderson, Perry. *Lineages of the Absolutist State.* London: NLB, 1974.

Andrew, Christopher M. "France: Adjustment of Change." In Bull and Watson, eds., *The Expansion of International Society:* 335–44.

Ansari, Hamid N. "The Islamic Militants in Egyptian Politics." *International Journal of Middle East Studies* 16(1) (March 1984): 123–44.

Antoun, Richard T. "On the Modesty of Women in Arab Muslim Villages: A Study of the Accommodation Society." *American Anthropologist* 70 (4 August 1968): 671–97.

Antun, Richard T. "Presidential Address-MESA 1983: Our Roles as Scholars and Citizens." In *Middle East Studies Association Bulletin* 18 (1 July 1984): 3–10.

Apter, David E. *The Politics of Modernization.* Chicago: University of Chicago Press, 1965.

Arciniegas, Germán. *America in Europe: A History of the New World in Reverse,* translated by Gabriella Arciniegas and R. Victoria Arana. New York: Harcourt Brace Jovanovich, 1986.

Ardagh, John. *France in the 1980s.* New York, N. Y.: Penguin Books, 1982.

Aron, Raymond. *La Tragédie algérienne.* Paris: Plon, 1957.

————. *L'Algérie et la République.* Paris: Plon, 1958.

————. "Les Perspectives d'Avenir de la Civilization Occidentale." In Aron, directeur, *Histoire et ses interprétations* (entretiens autour de Arnold Toynbee). Paris: Mouton, 1961.

————. *Plaidoyer pour l'Europe décadente*. Paris: Laffont, 1977.

————. *Mémoires*. Paris: Julliard, 1983.

Asad, Talal, and Roger Owen, eds. *Sociology of "Developing Societies": The Middle East. Monthly Review* (1983).

Asad, Talal, ed. *Anthropology and the Colonial Encounter*. Atlantic Highlands, N. J.: Humanities Press, Inc., 1973.

Atlas Report. "Africa's Next Liberation Struggle." *World Press Review* (October 1978): 39–45.

Avineri, Shlomo, ed. *Karl Marx on Colonialism and Modernization: His Despatches and Other Writings on China, India, Mexico, The Middle East and North Africa*. Garden City, N.Y.: Doubleday, 1968.

————. "The Palestinians and Israel." In *Commentary* 49 (1970): 31–44.

Awad, Louis. "Freedom and Ideology: The Current State of Political Thought in the Middle East." *Middle East Studies Association Bulletin* 18 (1 July 1984).

al-'Azm, Sadiq Jalal. *Al-Naqd al-Dhati ba'ad-al-Hazimah* (Self-Criticism after the Defeat). Beirut: Dar-al-tali'ah, 1968.

————. *Dirasat Yasariyah hawl-al-Qadiyah al-Filastiniyah* (Leftist Studies on the Palestine Problem). Beirut: Dar-al-Tali'ah, 1970a.

————. *Naqd al-Fikr al-Dini* (Criticism of Religious Thought). Beirut: Dar al-Tali'ah, 1970b.

————. "Orientalism and Orientalism in Reverse." In *Khamsin* (1980): 5–26.

al-Azmeh, Aziz. "The Articulation of Orientalism." In *Arab Studies Quarterly* 3 (4) (Fall 1981): 384–402.

Bakhash, Shaul. "The Outcasts of Iran." In *New York Review of Books* (10 May 1984): 33–36.

————. *The Reign of the Ayatollahs: Iran and the Islamic Revolution*. New York: Basic Books, 1986.

Ballhatchet, Kenneth. "Indian Perception of the West." In B. Lewis et al., eds., "As Others See Us," pp. 158–79.

Barakat, Halim, ed. *Contemporary North Africa: Issue of Development and Integration*. Washington, D.C.: Center for Contemporary Arab Studies, 1985.

Baran, Paul. *The Political Economy of Growth*, 2nd ed. Monthly Review (1962).

Barraclough, Geoffrey. *History in a Changing World*. New York, N. Y.: Penguin Books, 1967.

————. *An Introduction to Contemporary History*. New York, N. Y.: Penguin Books, 1967.

————. *Main Trends in History*. New York: Homes and Meier, 1979.

————. "Waiting for the New Order." In *New York Review of Books*, 26 October 1978, pp. 45–53; 9 November 1978, pp. 47–58.

————. "The Limits of Westernization." Conversation with Takeo Kuwabara in *World Press Review* (March, 1981): 24–26.

Batatu, Hanna. *The Old Social Classes and the Revolutionary Movements of Iraq.* Princeton: Princeton University Press, 1978.

Baudet, Henri, and Elizabeth Wintholt, trans. *Paradise on Earth: Some Thoughts on European Images of Non-European Man.* New Haven: Yale University Press, 1965.

Bauer, P. T. *Equality, The Third World, and Economic Delusion.* Cambridge: Harvard University Press, 1982.

Beck, Lois, and Nikki Keddie, eds. *Women in the Muslim World.* Cambridge: Harvard University Press, 1978.

Béji, Hélé. *Désenchantement national: essai sur la décolonization.* Paris: Fran ois Masperio, 1982.

Bell, Daniel. *The End of Ideology: On the Exhaustion of Political Ideas in the Fifties.* Glencoe, Ill.: Free Press, 1960.

Bellah, Robert N., ed. *Religion and Progress in Modern Asia.* New York: Free Press, 1965.

Bellamy, Edward. *Looking Backward 2000–1887.* Modern Library, 1951.

Ben Jalloun, Tahar. *Hospitalité française.* Paris: Seuil, 1984.

Benard, Cheryl, and Zalmay Khalilzad. *"The Government of God": Iran's Islamic Republic.* New York: Columbia University Press, 1984.

Bennabi, Malek. *Vocation de l'Islam.* Paris: Seuil, 1954.

Bennoune, Mahfoud. "The Industrialization of Algeria: An Overview." In Barakat, *Contemporary North Africa*, 178–213.

Benvenisti, Myron. *Conflict and Contradictions.* New York: Villard Books, 1986.

Berlin, Isaiah. *Four Essays on Liberty.* London: Oxford University Press, 1969.

Berque, Jacques. *Les Arabes d'hier à demain.* Paris: Seuil, 1961.

———. *Dépossession de Monde.* Paris: Seuil, 1964.

———. *French North Africa: The Maghrib Between Two World Wars.* Jean Stewart, trans. New York: Praeger, 1967.

Berque, Jacques. Robert W. Stookey, Basima Bezirgan, and Elizabeth Fernea, trans. *Cultural Expression in Arab Society Today* (Langues arabes du présent). Austin: University of Texas, 1978a.

———. *Arabies: Entretiens avec Mirèse Akar.* Paris: Stock, 1978b.

———. *Arab Rebirth: Pain and Ecstasy*, Quintin Hoare, trans. London: Al Saqui Books, 1983.

Berrada, Mohamed. "The New Cultural and Imaginative Discourse in Morocco: Utopic Change." In Barakat, *Contemporary North Africa*, 231–49.

Bill, James A., and Carl Leiden. *Politics of the Middle East*, 2nd. ed. Boston: Little Brown, 1983.

———. "Resurgent Islam in the Persian Gulf." In *Foreign Affairs* (Fall 1984): 109–27.

Black, Cyril E. *The Dynamics of Modernization: A Study of Comparative History.* New York: Harper & Row, 1966.

Black, Cyril E. *et al.*, eds. *The Modernization of Japan and Russia* New York: Free Press, 1975.

Bloch, Marc, and Peter Putnam, trans. *The Historian's Craft.* New York: Vintage, 1953.

Boehm, Rudolf. "L'Illusion humaniste." In *Le Monde* (19 March 1983).

Booker, Christopher. *The Seventies: Portrait of a Decade.* London: Allen Lane, 1980.

Boon, James A. "Comparative De-enlightenment: Paradox and Limits in the History of Ethnology." In *Daedalus* (Spring, 1980): 73–91.

Bosworth, William. "The Rigid Embrace of Dependency: France and Black African Education since 1960." In *Contemporary French Civilization* 3 (Spring 1981): 327–45.

Bourdieu, Pierre. *The Algerians.* Boston: Beacon Press, 1962.

Boyers, Robert. "Confronting the Present." In *Salmagundi* 54 (Fall 1981): 3–97.

Bozeman, Adda. "The International Order in a Multicultural World." In Bull and Watson, *The Expansion of International Society*, pp. 387–406.

Brandt, Willy. "The North-South Challenge." In *World Press Review* (June, 1984): 21–23.

Braudel, Fernand, and Siân Reynolds, trans. *Civilization and Capitalism 15th–18th Century.* New York: Harper & Row, 1982–1984, 3 volumes.

Brière, C., and O. Carré. *Islam, guerre à l'Occident?* Paris: Autrement, 1983.

Brown, L. Carl. "I: Stages in the Process of Change." In Micaud, Brown, and Moore, *Tunisia: The Politics of Modernization*, pp. 2–66.

———. *The Tunisia of Ahmad Bey: 1837–1855.* Princeton: Princeton University Press, 1974.

———. "Ayatollahs and Abracadabra: What Can the Academic Area Specialist Contribute to U.S. Policy in the Middle East?" *Princeton Alumni Review* (6 October 1980): 23–28.

———. *International Politics and the Middle East: Old Rules, Dangerous Game.* Princeton: Princeton University Press, 1984.

———. "The Middle East: Patterns of Change 1947–1987." In *Middle East Journal* 41–1 (Winter, 1987): 26-39.

Brown, L. Carl, and Norman Itzkowitz, eds. *Psychological Dimensions of Near Eastern Studies.* Princeton: Darwin, 1977.

Brown, Norman O. *Life Against Death: the Psychoanalytical Meaning of History.* New York: Vintage, 1959.

Brown, Peter. "Understanding Islam." In *New York Review of Books* (22 February 1979): 30–33.

Bruckner, Pascal. *The Tears of the White Man: Compassion as Contempt*, William R. Berr, trans. New York: Free Press, 1986.

Brunshchwig, Henri. *French Colonialism 1871–1914: Myths and Realities*, William G. Brown, trans. New York: Praeger Publishers, 1966.

Buheiry, Marwan R. "Colonial Scholarship and Muslim Revivalism in 1900." *Asian Studies Quarterly* 4(1) (Spring 1982): 1–16.

Bull, Hedley "The Revolt Against the West." In Bull and Watson, *The Expansion of International Society*, pp. 217–28.

———. "The Emergence of a Universal International Society." In Bull and Watson, eds., *The Expansion of International Society*, pp. 117–26.

Bull, Hedley, and Adam Watson, eds. *The Expansion of International Society*. Oxford: Clarendon, 1984.

Burckhardt, Jacob, and James Hastings Nichols, eds. *Force and Freedom: An Interpretation of Freedom*. New York: Meridian Books, 1955.

———. *Judgements on History and Historians*. Boston: Beacon Press, 1958.

Burke, Edmund, III. "Frantz Fanon's *The Wretched of the Earth*." *Daedalus* (Winter 1976): 127–35.

Bury, J. B. *The Idea of Progress: an Inquiry into its Origin and Growth*. London: Macmillan, 1928.

Butterfield, Fox. *China, Alive in This Bitter Sea*. New York: Times Books, 1982.

———. "Taiwan: A New Sense of Confidence." *The New York Times Magazine* (6 May 1984): 106–7, 110, 116–17, 120–22, 124.

Canetti, Elias. *The Torch in My Ear*, Joachim Neugroschel, trans. New York: Farrar, Straus & Giroux Inc., 1982.

Carr, E. H. *What is History?* New York: Knopf, 1962.

Cary, Joyce. *The Case for African Freedom*. New York: McGraw Hill, 1964.

Caute, David. *The Decline of the West*. New York: Ballantine, 1967.

Celeste, Marie-Claude. "Quand le tiers-monde exporte ses 'cerveaux.' " *Monde Diplomatique* (March 1981): 15.

Chabod, Federico. *Storia dell'Idea d'Europa*. Bari: (Universale) Laterza, 1964.

Chaliand, Gérard. *Revolution in the Third World: Myths and Prospects*. New York: Viking, 1977.

———. *Les Fauburgs de l'Histoire-Tiers-mondismes et tiers-mondes*. Paris: Calmann-Lévy, 1984.

Chatelus, Michel. "Le Monde arabe vingt ans après." *Monde Diplomatique* (July–September 1983): 5–45.

Chaudhuri, Nirad C. *The Autobiography of an Unknown Indian*. New York: Macmillan, 1953.

———. "Passage to and from India." *Encounter* 2(6) (June 1954): 19–24.

———. "What is Hinduism?" *Times Literary Supplement* (3 February 1978): 145–48.

Chevrier, Jacques. "La Négritude, mythe ou réalite." *Le Monde* (21 June 1969).

Chinweizu, Onwuchekwa Jemie, and Ihechukwu Madubuike. *Toward the Decolonization of African Literature*. Enugu, Nigeria: Fourth Dimension, 1981.

Cipolla, Carlo M. *European Culture and Overseas Expansion*. Penguin Books, 1970.

Clark, Sir George. *The Seventeenth Century*, 2nd ed. London: Oxford University Press, 1961.

Clark, William. *Cataclysm: the North-South Conflict of 1987*. London: Sidgwick & Jackson, 1984.

Cleveland, William L. *Islam Against the West: Shakib Arslan and the Campaign for Islamic Nationalism*. London: Al Saqi, 1985.

Cobban, Helen. *The Making of Modern Lebanon*. Boulder, Colo.: Westview Press, 1985.

Cockroft, James D., André Gunder Frank, and Dale L. Johnson. *Dependence and Underdevelopment: Latin America's Political Economy*. Garden City, N. Y.: Anchor Books, Doubleday, 1972.

Cohen, William B. *The French Encounter with Africans: White Responses to Blacks, 1530--1880*. Bloomington: Indiana University Press, 1980.

Cohen, William I., ed. *Reflections on Orientalism: Edward Said, Roger Bresnahan, Surjit Dulai, Edward Graham, and Donald Lammens*. East Lansing: Asian Studies Center, Michigan State University Press, 1983.

Cole, Juan R.I., and Nikki R. Keddie, eds. *Shi'ism and Social Revolt*. New Haven: Yale University, 1986.

Committee on International Relations (Group for the Advancement of Psychiatry). *Self Involvement in the Middle East Conflict*, vol. X, no. 103, (November 1978). New York, 1978.

Conte, Arthur R. *Bandoung tournant de l'histoire (18 avril 1955)*. Paris: Robert Laffont, 1965.

Corm, Georges. *Le Proche-Orient éclaté*. Paris: Maspero, 1983.

———. *Géopolitique du conflit libanais: étude historique et sociologique*. Paris: Le Decouverte, 1986.

Costa-Lascoux, J., ed. "Vers un droit de cité." In Morsy, *Les Nords-Africains en France*, pp. 165–96.

Costello, Peter. *Jules Verne: Inventor of Science Fiction*. London: Hodder & Stoughton, 1977.

Cousins, Norman. *Modern Man is Obsolete*. New York: The Viking Press, 1945.

Craig, Gordon. *Germany 1866–1945*. New York: Oxford University Press, 1978.

Crapanzano, Vincent. *Waiting: the Whites of South Africa*. New York: Random House, 1985.

Crick, Bernard. *George Orwell: A Life*. Secker & Warburg, 1980.

Cromer, Earl of. *Ancient and Modern Imperialism*. New York: Longmans, 1910.

Crone, Patricia, and Michael Cook. *Hagarism: The Making of the Islamic World*. London: Cambridge University Press, 1977.

Crossman, Richard, ed. *The God That Failed*. New York: Harper and Row, 1949.

Crowl, Philip A. "Alfred Thayer Mahan: The Naval Historian." In Peter Paret, ed., pp. 444–77.

Cudsi, Alexander S., and Ali E. Hillal Dessouki, eds. *Islam and Power*. Baltimore: Johns Hopkins University Press, 1981.

Curtin, Philip D., ed. *Imperialism*. New York: Harper & Row, 1971.

————, ed. *Africa and the West: Intellectual Responses to European Culture*. Madison: University of Wisconsin Press, 1972.

————. *Cross-cultural Trade in World History*. London: Cambridge University Press, 1985.

Curtiss, Richard H. *A Changing Image: American Perceptions of the Arab-Israeli Dispute*. Washington, D.C.: American Educational Trust, 1982.

Dahrendorf, Rolf. *Die Angewandte Aufklärung*. Munich: Piper, 1963.

Dalby, Michael. "Nocturnal Labors in the Light of Day." *Journal of Asian Studies* XXXIX:3 (May 1980): 485–93.

Daniel, Norman A. *Islam and the West: The Making of an Image*. Edinborough: University Press, 1962.

————. *Islam Europe and Empire*. Edinborough: University Press, 1966.

Darnton, Robert. *The Grand Cat Massacre: And Other Episodes in French Cultural History*. New York: Basic Books, 1984.

Dastarac, Alexandre, and M. Levent. "Pakistan: le verrouillage." *Monde Diplomatique* (August 1984): 12–14.

Davies, Norman. *Heart of Europe: A Short History of Poland*. New York: Oxford University Press, 1986.

Dawson, Christopher. "The Relevance of European History." *History Today* (September 1956): 606–15.

Dawson, Christopher, and John J. Mulloy, eds. *The Dynamics of World History*. New York: Mentor, 1962.

Dawson, Raymond. *The Chinese Chameleon: an Analysis of European Conceptions of Chinese Civilization*. London: Oxford University Press, 1967.

Dean, Vera Micheles. *The Nature of the Non-Western World*. New York: Mentor Books, 1957.

Debray, Regis. *Les empires contre l'Europe*. Paris: Gallimard, 1985.

De Mott, Benjamin. "Did the 1960's Damage Fiction?" *New York Times Book Review* (8 July 1984): 1, 26–27.

Denoon, Donald. *Settler Capitalism: The Dynamics of Dependent Development in the Southern Hemisphere*. London: Oxford University Press, 1983.

Desjardins, Thierry. *Le martyre du Liban*. Paris: Plon, 1976.

Dessouki, Ali. *Islamic Resurgance in the Arab World*. New York: Praeger Publishers, 1982.

Djafri, Yahia. "Le Chanson, Miroir de l'Immigration" in Morsy, 1984: pp. 93–101.

Djait, Hichem. *Europe and Islam*, Peter Heinegg, trans. Berkeley: University of California Press, 1985.

Dodd, Peter C. "Family Honor and the Forces of Change in Arab Society." *International Journal of Middle East Studies* 4 (1973): 40–54.

Domenach, Jean Marie. *Le retour du tragique: essai.* Paris: Seuil, 1967.

Donohue, John J., and John L. Esposito, eds. *Islam in Transition: Muslim Perspectives.* New York: Oxford University Press, 1982.

———. "Islam and the Search for Identity in the Arab World" in Esposito, ed., *Voices of Resurgent Islam*, pp. 48–61.

Dore, Ronald. "Unity and Diversity in World Cultures." In Bull and Watson, eds. *The Expansion of International Society*, 407–24.

Donelan, Michael. "Spain and the Indies," in Bull and Watson, eds.; 75–85.

Drouin, Pierre. "Le tour de Babel du tiers-mondisme." *Le Monde* (29 January 1985).

Dufour, Dany. "L'Enseignement en Algérie." *Monde Diplomatique* (April-June 1978): 33–46.

Duignan, Peter, and Lewis Gann. "The Case for the White Man." *The New Leader* (2 January 1961): 16–20.

Dulai, Surjit. "George Orwell's Colonial Days." W. I. Cohen, ed., *Reflections on Orientalism*, pp. 15–30.

Dumont, René. *L'Afrique noire est mal partie.* Paris: Seuil, 1965.

———. *Paysannerie aux abois: peut-on sortir de l'impasse?* Paris: Seuil, 1972.

Dumont, René, with Marie France Mottin. *Le Mal-Développement en Amèrique Latine.* Paris: Seuil, 1981.

Duus, Peter. *The Rise of Modern Japan.* Boston: Houghton Mifflin, 1976.

Easwaran, Eknath. "Rewriting the Raj-an Indian Perspective. *Christian Science Monitor* (11 February 1985).

Echeverria, Durand. *Mirage in the West: A History of the French Image of American Society to 1815.* New York: Octagon Books, 1966.

Ehrard, Jean, and Guy P. Palmade. *L'Histoire.* Paris: Armand Colin, 1964.

Eisenstadt, Shmuel N. "Sociological Theory and an Analysis of the Dynamics of Civilizations and of Revolutions." *Daedalus* 11 (Fall 1977): 59–78.

Eliade, Mircea. *Myth and Reality*, Willard R. Trask, trans. New York: Harper & Row, 1963.

Elliott, J. H. "Mastering the Signs." *New York Review of Books* (19 July 1984): 29–32.

Ellul, Jacques. *The Betrayal of the West*, Matthew J. O'Connell, trans. New York: Seabury, 1978.

Elon, Amos. *The Israelis: Founders and Sons.* New York: Bantam Books, 1972.

———. *Herzl.* New York: Holt, Rinehart and Winston, 1975.

Emerson, Rupert. *From Empire to Nation: The Rise to Self-Assertion of Asian and African Peoples.* Boston: Beacon Press, 1960.

Entelis, John P. "The Political Economy of North African Relations: Cooperation or Conflict?" In Barakat, *Contemporary North Africa*, pp. 112–37.

————. Algeria: *The Revolution Institutionalized*. Boulder, Colo.: Westview Press, 1986.

Escovitz, Joseph H. "Orientalists and Orientalism in the Writings of Muhammad Kurd 'Ali." *International Journal of Middle East Studies* 15(1) (February 1983): 95–109.

Esposito, John L., ed. *Voices of Resurgent Islam*. New York: Oxford University Press, 1983.

————. *Islam and Development: Religion and Sociopolitical Change*. Syracuse, N. Y.: Syracuse University Press, 1980.

————. "Pakistan: Quest for Islamic Identity." In Esposito, *Islam and Development*.

Ewans, Michael Lobe. "Des Intégristes entre le marabout et le prince: la montée du discours fondamentaliste musulman en Sénégal." *Monde Diplomatique* (1 April 1985): 15.

Fanon, Frantz. *L'An V de la révolution algérienne*. Paris: Maspero, 1959.

————. *Les Damnés de la terre: préface de Jean-Paul Sartre*. Paris: Maspero, 1961.

————. *The Wretched of the Earth*, Constance Farrington, trans. Penguin Books, 1967.

Fawaz, Leila Tarazi. *Merchants and Migrants in Nineteenth-Century Beirut*. Cambridge: Harvard University Press, 1983.

Ferdows, Adele K. "Women and the Islamic Revolution." *International Journal of Middle East Studies* 15(2) (May 1983): 283–98.

Ferro, Marc. *Comment on raconte l'histoire aux enfants à travers le monde entier*. Paris: Payot, 1981.

Fieldhouse, D. K. *The Colonial Empires: A Comparative Survey from the Eighteenth Century*. London: Weindenfeld & Nicolson, 1966.

Fischer, Eric. *The Passing of the European Age—A Study of the Transfer of Western Civilization and the Renewal of Other Continents*. New York: Russel & Russel, 1967 (original 1943).

Fogg, Walter J. "Technology and Utopia." In Richter, *Utopia/Dystopia?*, pp. 57–73.

Fabian, Johannes. *Time and the Other: How Anthropology Makes its Object*. New York: Columbia University Press, 1983.

Forster, E. M. "The Machine Stops." In Forster, *The Eternal Moment and Other Stories*. Harcourt Brace Jovanovich, 1928 (original 1909).

Foucault, Michel. *The Order of Things: An Archeology of the Human Sciences*. London: Tavistock, 1970.

Frankel, Glenn. "Tanzania Symbolizes Failed Growth Model." *Manchester Guardian Weekly* (December 1984): 17.

Freud, Sigmund. *The Future of an Illusion*, W. D. Robson-Scott, trans. New York: Liveright, 1955.

————. *Civilization and its Discontents*, Janus Strachey, trans. New York: W. W. Norton, 1961.

Freund, Julien. *The Sociology of Max Weber*, Mary Ilford, trans. London: Allen Lane, Penguin Press, 1968.

Friedman, Thomas C. "The Power of the Fanatics." *New York Times Magazine* (7 October 1984): 32–35, 50–54, 68–75.

Fuller, Richard Buckminster. *Operating Manual for Spaceship Earth*. New York: Simon & Schuster, 1969.

Furet, François. "Les Intellectuels français et le structuralisme." *Preuves* (February 1967): 3–12.

Gallagher, Charles F. *Lessons from the Modernization of Japan*, 3 parts. *American Universities Field Staff Reports*, East Asia Series (1968) XV:2–4.

———. *The Shape of Things to Come. American Universities Field Staff Reports* Reports 33/General (1979a).

———. *Rich Countries and Poor Countries Revisited. American Universities Field Staff Reports* 34/General (1979b).

Gaspard, Armand. "L'Europe de Mythe à la Réalité." *Preuves Informations* (30 January 1962).

Gaspard, François. "L'Immigration maghrebine: réalites et representations." In Morsy, 1984: 51–59.

Geertz, Clifford. *Islam Observed: Religious Development in Morocco and Indonesia*. Chicago: Chicago University Press 1973 (original 1968).

———. "Waddling In." *Times Literary Supplement* (7 June 1985).

Gellner, Ernest. *Thought and Change*. Chicago: University of Chicago Press, 1965.

———. *Muslim Society*. London: Cambridge University Press, 1981.

———. "Stagnation without Salvation." *Times Literary Supplement* (14 January 1983): 27–28.

Gendzier, Irene L. *Frantz Fanon: A Critical Study*. New York: Pantheon, 1973.

Ghareeb, Edmund, ed. *Split Vision: Arab Portrayal in the American Media*. Washington, D.C.: The Institute of Middle Eastern and African Affairs, 1983.

Gibb, H. A. R. *Modern Trends In Islam*. New York: Octagon Books, 1975.

Gibbon, Edward. *The Decline and Fall of the Roman Empire*, three volumes. New York: Modern Library, n.d. (original 1776–1788).

Gibson, Charles. *Spain in America*. New York: Harper, 1966.

Gilpin, Robert. *U.S. Power and the Multinational Corporation*. Princeton: Princeton University Press, 1975.

Glucksmann, André. *Les Maitres Penseurs*. Paris: Grasset, 1977.

Goldthorpe, J. E. *The Sociology of the Third World: Disparity and Development*, 2nd ed. New York: Cambridge University Press, 1984.

Goltz, Thomas. "Why Atatürk is Turning in his Grave." *Middle East* (April 1985): 32–33.

Gong, Gerrit W. *The Standard of 'Civilization' in International Society*. Oxford: Clarendon, 1984.

Goodheart, Eugene. "Naipaul and the Voices of Negation." *Salmagundi* 54 (Fall 1981): 44–58.

Goonetilleke, D. C. R. A. *Developing Countries in British Fiction*. London: Macmillan, 1977.

Gorce, Paul-Marie de la. "Le Recul des grandes espérances révoltionnaires." *Monde Diplomatique* (May 1984): 16–17.

Gordimer, Nadine. *July's People*. New York: Viking Press, 1981.

———. *Something Out There*. New York: Viking Press, 1984.

Gordon, David C. *North Africa's French Legacy 1954–1962*. Cambridge: Harvard Middle Eastern Monographs, IX, 1962.

———. *The Passing of French Algeria*. New York: Oxford, 1966.

———. *Women of Algeria: An Essay on Change*. Cambridge: Harvard Middle Eastern Monographs, XIX, 1968.

———. *Self-Determination and History in the Third World*. Princeton: Princeton University Press, 1971a.

———. "History and Identity in Arab Textbooks: Four Cases." *Princeton Near East Paper*, no. 13, *Program in Near Eastern Studies*, Princeton University Press, 1971b.

———. *The French Language and National Identity (1930–1975)*. The Hague: Mouton, 1978.

———. *Lebanon: the Fragmented Nation*. London: Croom-Helm, 1980.

———. "Orientalism." *The Antioch Review* (Winter 1982): 104–12.

———. *The Republic of Lebanon: Nation in Jeopardy*. Boulder, Colo.: Westview Press, 1983.

———. "The Arabic Language and National Identity: The Cases of Algeria and Lebanon." In William R. Beer and James E. Jacob, eds., *Language and Policy and National Unity*. Totowa, N. J.: Rowman and Allanheld, 1985).

Gornick, Vivian. *In Search of Ali Mahmoud: An American Woman in Egypt*. New York: Warner Paperback, 1974.

Gould, Stephen Jay. *The Mismeasure of Man*. New York: W. W. Norton, 1981.

Goytisolo, Juan. "Captives of Our Classics.'" *New York Times Book Review* (26 May 1985): 1, 24.

Graham-Brown, Sarah. "Orientalism in Color." *Middle East Research and Information Project Reports* (July-September 1984): 56–59, No. 125/126.

Grass, Gunter. *Headbirths or the Germans are Dying Out*, Ralph Manheim, trans. Harcourt Brace Jovanovich, 1982 (original 1980).

Green, Martin. *Dreams of Adventure, Deeds of Empire*. New York: Basic Books, 1979.

Greer, Germaine. *Sex and Destiny: The Politics of Human Fertility*. New York: Harper & Row, 1984.

Grimal, Henri. *La décolonisation: 1919–1963*. Paris: Armand Colin, 1965.

Griswald, William J. *The Image of the Middle East in Secondary School Textbooks.* New York: *Middle East Studies Association*, 1975.

Grose, Peter. *A Changing Israel*. New York: Vintage, 1985.

Grousset, René. *L'Homme et son histoire*. Paris: Plon, 1954.

Grünebaum, G. E. von. *Modern Islam: The Search for Cultural Identity*. Berkeley: University of California Press, 1962.

Gueyras, Jean. "L'Islamisation du Soudan." *Le Monde* (23 August 1984).

Gupte, Pranay. *The Crowded Earth: People and the Politics of Population*. New York: W. W. Norton, 1984.

———. "Germany's Guest Workers." *The New York Times Magazine* (19 August 1984): 86–91, 100–101.

Guérin, Daniel. *L'Algérie caporalisée?*. Paris: C. E. S., 1965.

Haas, William S. *The Destiny of the Mind: East and West*. New York: Norton, 1970.

Haddad, Yvonne Yazbeck. "The Arab-Israeli Wars, Nasserism and the Affirmation of Islamic Identity." In Esposito, *Islam and Development*, pp. 107–21.

———. *Contemporary Islam and the Challenge of History*. Albany: State University of New York Press, 1982.

———. "Sayyid Qurb: Ideologue of Islamic Revival." In Esposito, ed., *Voices of Resurgent Islam*, pp. 67–98.

al-Hakim, Taufik. *Bird of the East*, R. Bayly Winder, trans. Beirut: Khayats, 1966 (original 1925).

Hale, Aron J. *The Great Illusion 1900–1914*. New York: Harper & Row, 1971.

Halecki, Oscar. *The Limits and Divisions of European History*. Notre Dame, Ind.: University of Notre Dame Press, 1962.

Hall, A. R. *The Scientific Revolution: 1500–1800: The Formation of the Modern Scientific Attitude*. Boston: Beacon Press, 1956.

Halliday, Fred. "Iranian Foreign Policy since 1979: Internationalism and Nationalism in the Iranian Revolution." In Cole and Keddie, *Shi'ism and Social Revolt*, pp. 88–107.

Halpern, Manfred. *The Politics of Social Change in the Middle East and North Africa*. Princeton: Princeton University Press, 1963.

El-Hamamsy, Laila. "The Assertion of Egyptian Identity." In Hopkins and Ibrahim, *Arab Society*, pp. 39–63.

Hane, Mikiso. *Peasants, Rebels and Outcasts: The Underside of Modern Japan*. New York: Pantheon, 1982.

Hanson, Brad. "The "Westoxication" of Iran: Depictions and Reactions of Behrangi, Al-e Ahmed, and Shari'ati." *International Journal of Middle East Studies* 15(1) (February 1983): 1–23.

Hargreaves, John D. *France and West Africa: An Anthology of Historical Documents*. London: Macmillan, 1969.

Harlow, Barbara. "Introduction" to Alloula, pp. ix–xxii.

Harmand, Jules. *Domination et colonisation*. Paris: Flammarion, 1910.

Harrell-Bond, Barbara. *The Struggle for the Western Sahara*: Part II, Contemporary Politics, *American Universities' Field Service Staff Reports*, 1981/no. 38/Africa.

Harris, George S. *Turkey: Coping with Crisis*. Boulder, Colo.: Westview Press, 1985.

Harzo, Christian. "Peuples sans passé et nouvel ordre planétaire." *Monde Diplomatique* (March 1981): 28.

Hasan, Sana. "Egypt's Angry Islamic Militants." *The New York Times Magazine* (20 November 1983): 137–47.

Havighurst, Alfred F., ed. *The Pirenne Thesis: Analysis, Criticism, and Revision*. Boston: Heath, 1958.

Hay, Denys. *Europe: The Emergence of an Idea*. Edinborough: University Press, 1957.

Hazard, Paul. *The European Mind: 1680–1715*, J. Lewis May, trans. New American Library, 1963 (original 1935).

Headrick, Daniel R. *The Tools of Empire: Technology and European Imperialism in the Nineteenth Century*. New York: Oxford University Press, 1977.

Hegel, G. W. F. *Hegel's Philosophy of History*, J. Sibree, trans. London: Bohn's Libraries, 1857.

———. *Phenomenology of Spirit*, A. V. Miller, trans. London: Oxford University Press, 1977.

Heggoy, Alf Andrew. "Cultural Disrespect: European and Algeria." *The Muslim World* 62 (1972): 323–34.

Heper, Metin. "Islam, Polity and Society in Turkey: A Middle Eastern Perspective." *Middle East Journal* 35(3) (Summer 1981): 345–63.

Herbert, Jean-Loup. "La force mobilisatrice d'une spiritualité." *Monde Diplomatique* (April 1984): 17–18.

Hermessi, Elbaki. "States and Regimes in the Maghreb." In Barakat, *Contemporary North Africa*, pp. 157–63.

Hertzberg, Arthur, ed. *The Zionist Idea*. New York: Atheneum Publishers, 1969.

Herzl, Theodor. *The Jewish State*, 5th ed. London: Pordes, 1967.

Hexter, J. H. "The Birth of Modern Freedom." *Times Literary Supplement* (21 June 1983): 51–54.

Hobsbawm, Eric J. "Karl Marx's Contribution to Historiography" *Diogènes* 64 (Winter 1968): 37–56.

Hodges, Richard, and David Mohammed Whitehouse. *Charlemagne and the Origins of Europe: Archeology and the Pirenne Theory*. Ithaca, N. Y.: Cornell University Press, 1983.

Hoffmann, Stanley. "An American Social Science: International Relations." *Daedalus* I (Summer 1977): 41-60.

Hoffmann-Ladd, Valerie J. "Polemics on the Modesty and Segregation of Women in Contemporary Egypt." *International Journal of Middle East Studies* 19(1) (February 1987): 23–50.

Holborn, Hajo. "History and the Study of the Classics." *Journal of the History of Ideas* xiv(1) (January 1953): 33–50.

Hopkins, Nicholas S., and Saad Eddin Ibrahim, eds. *Arab Society: Social Science Perspectives*. Cairo: American University in Cairo, 1985.

Hopwood, Derak. "Some Western Views of the Egyptian Revolution." In Vatikiotis, *Egypt*, pp. 181–95.

Hottinger, Arnold. "The Depth of Arab Radicalism." *Foreign Affairs* 51(3) (April 1973): 482–98.

Hourani, Albert. "Islam and the Philosophers of History." *Middle East Studies* (April 1967): 206–68.

———. *Europe and the Middle East*. London: Macmillan, 1980.

———. *Arabic Thought in the Liberal Age 1798–1939*, rev. ed. New York: Cambridge University Press, 1983.

Howe, Irving. *Decline of the New*. London: Victor Gollancz, 1971.

Hudson, Dennis. "The Responses of Tamils to their Study by Westerners 1600–1908" in Lewis *et al.*, *As Others See Us*, pp. 180–200.

Hudson, Michael. *The Precarious Republic: Political Modernization in Lebanon*. New York: Random House, 1968.

———. *Arab Politics: The Search for Legitimacy*. New Haven: Yale University, 1977.

———. "Islam and Political Development." In Esposito, *Islam and Development*.

———. "The Islamic Factor in Syrian and Iraq Politics." In Piscatori, *Islam in the Political Process*.

———. "Letter from Beirut." In *Middle East Studies Association Bulletin* 8(1) (July 1984): 1–2.

Hughes, H. Stewart. *Consciousness and Society: The Reorientation of European Social Thought 1890–1930*. New York: Vintage, 1961.

———. *Oswald Spengler: A Critical Estimate*. New York: Charles Scribner's Sons, 1962 (rev. ed.).

———. *The Sea Change: The Migration of Social Thought, 1930–1965*. Harper & Row, 1975.

Huntington, Samuel P. *Political Order in Changing Societies*. New Haven: Yale University Press, 1969.

Husayn, Taha. *The Future of Culture in Egypt*, S. Glazer, trans. Washington, D.C.: American Council of Learned Societies, 1954 (original 1938).

al-Husry, Khaldun S. *Three Reformers: A Study in Modern Arab Political Thought*. Beirut: Khayats, 1966.

Hussain, Asaf *et al.*, eds. *Orientalism, Islam, and Islamists*. Battleboro, Vt.: Amana Books, 1984.

———. "The Ideology of Orientalism." In Hussain, *Orientalism, Islam, and Islamists*, pp. 5–21.

Huxley, Aldous. *Brave New World Revisited*. New York: Harper & Row, 1958.

Ibrahim, Saad Eddin. "An Islamic Alternative in Egypt: The Muslim Brotherhood and Sadat." In *Arab Studies Quarterly* 4(1, 2) (Spring 1982a): 75–93.

———. *The New Arab Social Order: A Study of the Social Impact of Oil Wealth*. Boulder, Colo.: Westview Press, 1982b.

Ibrahim, Youssef M. "Egypt Contains Islam's Fire." *Wall Street Journal*, 28 May 1985.

Ibrahimi, Ahmed Taleb. *De la décolonization à la révolution culturelle*, 2nd ed. Algiers: *S. N. E. E.*, 1976.

Issawi, Charles. *An Economic History of the Middle East and North Africa*. New York: Columbia University Press, 1982.

———. "Middle East Outlook: Murfi's Law Ensures that More Will Go Wrong." *Princeton Alumni Weekly* (9 February 1983): 29–33.

———. *The Middle East in the World Economy: A Long Range Historical View*. Washington, D.C.: Georgetown University Press, 1985.

Jacobs, Jane. "Why TVA Failed." *New York Review of Books* (10 May 1984): 41–47.

Jahn, Janheinz. *Muntu: An Outline of New-African Culture*, Marjorie Grenem, trans. London: Faber and Faber, 1961 (original 1958).

Jansen, Godfrey. *Militant Islam*. New York: Harper & Row, 1979.

Jansen, Marius B. *Changing Japanese Attitudes Toward Modernization*. Princeton: Princeton University Press, 1965.

Jaspers, Karl. *The Origin and Course of History*, M. Bullock, trans. New Haven: Yale University Press, 1953.

———. *The European Spirit*, R. G. Smith, trans. New York: Macmillan, 1949.

———. *The Future of Mankind*, E. B. Ashton, trans. Chicago: University of Chicago, 1961.

Jawdat, Kumait N. "The Orientalist Painters: Europe's Artistic Fantasy of the Arab World." *Arab Perspectives* (September–October 1984): 18–25.

Johnson, Paul. *Modern Times: The World of the Twenties to the Eighties*. New York: Harper & Row, 1983.

Joseph, Suad. "Study of Middle Eastern Women: Investments, Passions, and Problems." *International Journal of Middle East Studies* 18(14) (November 1986): 501–509.

Jouve, Edmond. *Le Tiers-monde dans la vie internationale*. Paris: Berger-Levrault, 1983.

Julien, Claude. "Une Bête à abattre: "le tiers-mon disme." *Monde Diplomatique* (May 1985): 13–14.

Julliard, Jacques. "For a New 'Internationale.'" *New York Review of Books* (20 July 1978): 3.

Kabbani, Rana. *Europe's Myths of Orient.* Bloomington, Ind.: Indiana University Press, 1986.

Kagitçíbasí, Cigdem. "Status of Women in Turkey: Cross Cultural Perspectives." *International Journal of Middle East Studies* 18(4) (November 1986): 485–99.

Kahn, Herman. *The Emerging Japanese Superstate: Challenge and Response.* Englewood Cliffs, N. J.: Prentice-Hall, 1970.

Kalechofsky, Robertz. *George Orwell.* New York: Frederick Ungar, 1963.

Kane, Cheikh Hamidou. *Ambiguous Adventure,* Katherine Woods, trans. London: Heinemann, 1982.

Karpat, Kemal, ed. *Political and Social Thought in the Middle East.* New York: Praeger Publishers, 1968.

———. "Presidential Address-MESA 1985: Remarks on MESA and Nationality in the Middle East." *Middle East Studies Association Bulletin* 20(1) (July 1986): 1–12.

Kedar, Benjamin Z. *Crusade and Mission: European Approaches Towards the Muslims.* Princeton: Princeton University Press, 1985.

Keddie and Cole. "Introduction." In Cole and Keddie, *Shi'ism and Social Revolt,* pp. 1–29.

Keddie, Nikki R. *An Islamic Response to Imperialism: Political Writings of Sayyid Jamal ad-Din "al-Afghani".* Berkeley: University of California Press, 1968.

———. "Iranian Revolutions in Comparative Perspective." *American Historical Review* 88(3) (June 1983): 579–98.

Kedourie, Elie. *Nationalism.* London: Hutchinson, 1960.

———. *Afghani and Abduh: an Essay on Religious Unbelief and Political Activism in Modern Islam.* London: Frank Cass, 1966.

———. *The Chatham House Version and Other Middle Eastern Studies.* London: Weidenfeld and Nicolson, 1970.

Kelly, J. B. *Arabia, the Gulf and the West.* London: Weidenfeld and Nicolson, 1980.

Kerr, Malcolm H. *Islamic Reform: The Political and Legal Theories of Muhammad 'Abduh and Rashid Rida.* Berkeley: University of California Press, 1966.

———. *The Arab Cold War: Gamal 'Abd al-Nasir and His Rivals, 1958–1970,* 3rd ed. London: Oxford University Press, 1975.

Kerr, Malcolm H., and El Sayed Yasin, eds. *Rich and Poor States in the Middle East: Egypt and the New Arab Order.* Boulder, Colo.: Westview Press, 1982.

Khalaf, Samir. "The Americanization of the World: Western Perspectives on Modernization in Developing Societies." In *The Centrality of Science and Absolute Values,* vol. 2. International Foundation, Inc., 1975, pp. 1071–95.

———. *Persistence and Change in 19th Century Lebanon: A Sociological Essay.* Beirut: American University of Beirut, 1979.

Khatibi, Abdelkebir. "Double Criticism: The Decolonization of Arab Sociology." In Barakat, *Contemporary North Africa,* pp. 9–19.

Khomeini, Ruhollah; Joint Publications Research Services, (trans.). *Islamic Government*. National Technical Information Service, Arlington, Va. 1979.

————. *Islam and Revolution: Writings and Declarations of Imam Khomeini*, Hamid Algar, trans. and annotator. Berkeley: Mizan, 1981.

Kiernan, V. G. *The Lords of Human Kind: European Attitudes Towards the Outside World in the Imperial Age*. London: Weidenfield and Nicolson, 1969.

————. *From Conquest to Collapse: European Empires from 1815 to 1960*. New York: Pantheon Books, Inc., 1982.

Kinross, Lord. *Atatürk: A Biography of Mustafa Kemal, a Father of modern Turkey*. New York: William Morrow & Co. Inc., 1965.

Koebner, Richard, and Helmut Dan Schmidt. *Imperialism: The Story and Significance of a Political Word 1840–1960*. Cambridge: Cambridge University Press, 1964.

Kohn, Hans. *The Age of Nationalism: The First Era of Global History*. New York: Harper, 1962.

Koning, Hans. "Onward and Upward with the Arts: The Eleventh Edition." *The New Yorker* (2 March 1981): 67–83.

Kopf, David. *British Orientalism and the Bengal Renaissance*. Berkeley: University of California Press, 1969.

————. "Hermeneutics versus History." *Journal of Asian Studies* xxxix(3) (May 1980): 495–506.

Kraft, Joseph. "Letter from Turkey." *The New Yorker* (15 October 1984): 134–57.

Kramer, Jane. *Unsettling Europe*. New York: Vintage, 1981.

Kreutz, Andrej. "Marx and the Middle East." *Arab Studies Quarterly* 5(2) (Spring 1983): 155–71.

Krishna, Gopal. "India and the International Order-Retreat from Idealism." In Bull and Watson, *The Expansion of International Society*, pp. 269–87.

Kronholz, June. "Bhutto Daughter Clouds Pakistan Politics." *Wall Street Journal* (23 June 1986).

Krutch, Joseph Wood. *The Measure of Man: On Freedom, Human Values, Survival and the Modern Temper*. Indianapolis: Bobbs-Merrill, 1954.

Kundera, Milan. "The Tragedy of Central Europe." *New York Review of Books* (26 April 1984): 33–39.

————. "The Novel and Europe." *New York Review of Books* (19 July 1984): 15–19.

————. *The Unbearable Lightness of Being*, Michael Henry Heim, trans. New York: Harper & Row, 1984.

Kutschera, Chris. "Nouveaux espoirs pour l'opposition chiite irakienne." *Monde Diplomatique* (April 1984): 12–17.

Kuwabara, Takeo. *Japan and Western Civilization: Essays on Comparative Culture*, K. Tsutomo and P. Murray, trans. Tokyo: University of Tokyo Press, 1983.

Lach, Donald F. *Asia in the Making of Europe*. Chicago: University of Chicago Press, 1965–1977, 2 vols.

Lach, Donald R. "China in Western Thought and Culture." In *Dictionary of the History of Ideas*, Vol. I. New York: Charles Scribner's Sons, 1973, pp. 353–73.

Lacouture, Jean, and Jean Baumier. *Le Poids du tiers monde: un milliard d'hommes*. Paris: Arthaud, 1962.

Lamb, David. *The Africans*. New York: Random House, 1982.

Lamm, Governor Richard D., and Gary Imhoff. *The Immigration Bomb: The Fragmenting of America*. New York: E. P. Dutton, 1985.

Landes, David S. *Clocks and the Making of the Modern World*. Cambridge: Belknap, Harvard University Press, 1983.

Lapidus, Ira. M. "Presidential Address 1984." *Middle East Studies Association Bulletin* 19(1) (July 1985): 1–8.

Lari, Musawi. *Western Civilization Through Muslim Eyes*. Houston: Free Islamic Literature, 1979.

Laroui, 'Abdallah. *The Crisis of the Arab Intellectuals: Traditionalism or Historicism*, Diarmid Commell, trans. Berkeley: University of California Press, 1976 (original 1967).

———. *The History of the Maghreb: An Interpretative Essay*, Ralph Manheim, trans. Princeton: Princeton University Press, 1979 (original 1970).

Lasky, Melvin J. *Utopia and Revolution: On the Origins of a Metaphor, or Some Illustrations of the Problem of Political Temperament and Intellectual Climate and How Ideas, Ideals, and Ideologies have been Historically Related*. Chicago: University of Chicago Press, 1976.

Lawrence, T. E. *Seven Pillars of Wisdom: A Triumph*. London: Jonathan Cape, 1935.

Lawson, William. *The Western Scar: The Theme of Been-to in West African Fiction*. Columbus: Ohio University Press, 1983.

Leca, John. "Le Monde arabe vingt ans après: de Sommet de Caire (1964) au Sommet de fès (1982)." *Monde Diplomatique* 100 (April–June 1983): 5–24.

Leduc, Gaston G. "The Economic Balance Sheet of Colonialism." *Journal of Contemporary History* 4(1) (1966): 37–50.

Lefebvre, Henri. *La Fin de l'histoire: epilégomènes*. Paris: Minuit, 1970.

Lehman, Jean-Pierre. *The Image of Japan: From Feudal Isolation to World Power 1850–1905*. London: Allan & Unwin, 1978.

Léon-Portilla, Miguel, ed. *The Broken Spears: The Aztec Account of the Conquest of Mexico*, Lysander Kemp, trans. Boston: Beacon Press, 1966.

Lerner, Daniel. *The Passing of Traditional Society*. Glencoe, Ill.: Free Press, 1958.

Lévi-Strauss, Claude, interviewed by George Steiner. "A Conversation with Claude Lévi-Strauss." *Encounter* (April 1966): 32–38.

———. *Tristes Tropiques*. Paris: Plon, 1955.

Levitt, Leonard. "Tansania: A Dream Deferred." *New York Times Magazine* (14 November 1982): 138–45, 154, 156, 165–69.

Lévy, Bernard-Henri. *La barbarie à visage humaine.* Paris: Bernard Grasset, 1977.

Levy, Marion J. *Modernization and the Structure of Society: A Setting for International Affairs,* 2 volumes. Princeton: Princeton University Press, 1966.

————. *Modernization: Latecomers and Survivors.* New York: Basic Books, 1972.

Lewalski, Kenneth. "Oscar Halecki." In Hans A. Schmitt, ed., *Historians of Modern Europe.* Baton Rouge: Louisiana State University Press, 1971.

Lewis, Bernard. *The Middle East and the West.* Bloomington: Indiana University Press, 1964.

————. *The Emergence of Modern Turkey,* 2nd ed. London: Oxford University Press, 1968.

————. *The Muslim Discovery of Europe.* New York: Norton, 1982.

Lewis, Bernard., ed. *As Others See Us: Mutual Perceptions, East and West. Comparative Civilizations Review* 13 (Fall 1985), and 14 (Spring 1986).

Lewis, Martin D., ed. *The British in India: Imperialism or Trusteeship?.* Boston: D.C. Heath, 1962.

Liang, Heng, and Judith Shapiro. *Son of the Revolution.* New York: Vintage, 1986.

————. *After the Nightmare: A Survivor of the Cultural Revolution Reports on China Today.* New York: Alfred A. Knopf Inc., 1986.

Lichtheim, George. *Collected Essays.* New York: Viking Press, 1974.

Lieberson, Jonathan, and Sidney Morgenbesser. "The Choices of Isaiah Berlin." *New York Review of Books* (20 March 1980): 31–36.

Lieberson, Jonathan. "Too Many People?" *New York Review of Books* (26 June 1986): 36–42.

Lipset, Seymour Martin, and Sheldon S. Wolin, eds. *The Berkeley Student Revolt: Facts and Interpretations.* Garden City, N. Y.: Anchor, 1965.

Lipton, Michael, and John Firn. *The Erosion of a Relationship: India and Britain since 1960.* London: Oxford University Press, 1975.

Lopez, Robert S. "Mohammed and Charlemagne: a Review." *Speculum* 18 (1943): 14–38.

Louis, William Roger. "The Era of the Mandates System and the Non-European World." In Bull and Watson, 1984, pp. 201–213.

————. *Imperialism at Bay: The United States and the Decolonization of the British Empire: 1841–1945.* New York: Oxford University Press, 1978.

Luis Diez del Corral. *The Rape of Europe.* New York: Macmillan, 1959.

Lukacs, John. *Outgrowing Democracy: A History of the United States in the Twentieth Century.* Garden City, N. Y.: Doubleday, 1984.

Luthy, Herbert. "What Western Colonialism Gave to Asia: The Record as Seen from the East." *Commentary* (June 1955): 588–94.

————. "The Passing of the European Order: Colonialism and the Cargo Cult." *Encounter* 50 (November 1957): 3–12.

————. "La Colonisation inachevée." *Preuves* (August-September 1966): 80–95.

Lyon, Peter. "The Emergence of the Third World." In Bull and Watson, 1984, pp. 229–37.

Mabon, André. "Un foyer de contagion, sous l'oeil vigilant des grandes puissances." *Monde Diplomatique* (April 1984): 12–15.

Macaulay, Thomas Babington. "On Education in India." In D. Curtin, ed., *Imperialism*, pp. 178–91.

Maes, Pierre. "La Nécessaire réforme de l'enseignement primaire: assurer la survie des langues africaines." *Monde Diplomatique* (July 1981): 12.

Mahood, M. M., ed. *The Colonial Encounter*. London: Rex Collings, 1977.

Malewaka-Peyre, Hanna. "L'unité et les différences chez les adolescents immigrés." Morsy, *Les Nord-Africains en France*, pp. 109–19.

Mandrou, Robert. *Introduction to Modern France, 1500–1640: An Essay in Historical Psychology*, R. E. Hallmark, trans. New York: Harper Torchbooks, 1975.

Mannoni, Otto. *Prospero and Caliban: The Psychology of Colonization*, Pamela Powesland, trans. New York: Praeger, 1956.

Mansfield, Peter. *The Arabs*. London: Pelican, 1978.

Manuel, Frank E., and Fritzie P. Manuel. *Utopian Thought in the Western World*. Cambridge: Belknap Harvard University Press, 1979.

Mardin, Serif. "Religion and Politics in Modern Turkey. In Piscatori, *Islam in the Political Process*, pp. 138–59.

Marr, Phebe. *The Modern History of Iraq*. Boulder, Colo.: Westview Press, 1985.

Marx, Karl. *Capital*. London: Lawrence & Wishart, 1970, 3 volumes.

Marx, Karl, and F. Engels. *The Communist Manifesto*. Moscow: Foreign Publishing House, n.d.

————. *Karl Marx on Colonialism and Modernization: His Despatches and Other Writings on China, India, Mexico, The Middle East and North Africa*, Shlomo Avineri, ed. Garden City, N. Y.: Doubleday, 1968.

Maschino, T.M., and Fadela M'Rabet. *L'Algérie des illusions: la révolution confisquér*. Paris: Robert Laffont, 1972.

Mason, Philip. *Patterns of Dominance*. London: Oxford University Press, 1970.

Mattelart, Armand. "L'Informatique dans le Tiers-Monde." *Monde Diplomatique* (April 1982): 14–15.

Matthee, Rudi. "The Egyptian Opposition on the Iranian Revolution." In Cole and Keddie, *Shi'ism and Social Revolt*, pp. 247–74.

Mayness, Charles William. "If the Poor Countries Go Under, We'll Sink With Them." *Manchester Guardian Weekly* (2 October 1983): 16–17.

Mazrui, Ali. "From Social Darwinism to Current Theories of Modernization." *World Politics* (October 1968): 69–83.

———. *The Africans: A Triple Heritage*. London: British Broadcasting Corporation, 1986.

———. "Africa Entrapped between the Protestant Ethic and the Legacy of Westphalia." In Bull and Watson, 1984, pp. 289–308.

McCrum, Robert, William Cran, and Robert MacNeil. *The Story of English*. London: British Broadcasting Corporation, 1986.

McFadden, John H. "Civil-Military Relations in the Third Turkish Republic." *Middle East Journal* 39(1) (Winter 1985): 69–85.

McHale, John. "The Plastic Parthenon." In Alan Toffler (1972): 51–59.

McNeill, William H. *The Rise of the West*. Chicago: University of Chicago Press, 1963.

———. *Plagues and People*. Garden City, N. Y.: Anchor, 1976.

———. "The Imprint of Empire." *Times Literary Supplement* (27 May 1977): 655.

———. *Mythhistory and Other Essays*. Chicago: University of Chicago Press, 1986.

———. "Macrohistory: Civilization or Ecumenical?" Lecture given in Yellow Springs, Ohio, International Society for the Comparative Study of Civilizations (3 May 1985).

Meister, Ulrich. "Africa's Shattered Illusions: Independence Did Not Bring Stability." *World Press Review* (October 1986): 31–32.

Memmi, Albert. *The Colonizer and the Colonized*, H. Greenfeld, trans. New York: Orion, 1965 (original 1957).

———. *L'Homme dominé*. Paris: Gallimard, 1968.

———. *Portrait of a Jew*. New York: Viking Press, 1971.

Mende, Tibor. *De l'aide à la récolonisation: les lecons d'un echec*. Paris: Seuil, 1972.

Merad, Ali. "The Ideologisation of Islam in the Contemporary Muslim World." In Cudsi and Dessouki, *Islam and Power*, pp. 37–48.

Mernissi, Fatima. *Sexe, ideologie, Islam*. Paris: Tierse, 1983.

———. "Women, Saints, and Sanctuaries." *Arab Perspectives* (4) (September 1983): 20–27. ⸖

———. "Women's Work: Religious and Scientific Concept as Political Manipulation in Dependent Islam." In Barakat, *Contemporary North Africa*, pp. 214–28.

———. *Beyond the Veil*. Cambridge, Mass.: Shenkman, 1975.

Meyer, Ann Elizabeth. "Islamic Resurgence or New Prophethood: The Role of Islam in Qaddhafi's Ideology." In Ali Dessouki, *Islamic Resurgence*.

Meyers, Jeffrey. *Fiction and the Colonial Experience*. Totowa, N. J.: Rowman & Littlefield, 1973.

Micaud, Charles A., Leon Carl Brown, and Clement Henry Moore. *Tunisia: The Politics of Modernization.* New York: Praeger Publishers, 1964.

Milbury-Steen, Sarah L. *European and African Stereotypes in Twentieth-Century Fiction.* London: Macmillan, 1981.

Miller, Judith. "The Embattled Arab Intellectual." *New York Times Magazine* (9 June 1985a): 58–60, 64–68, 72–74.

―――. "The P.L.O. in Exile." *New York Times Magazine* (18 August 1985b): 26–29, 63, 66, 71–72, 76.

Minces, Juliette. "Women in Algeria." In Beck and Keddie, *Women in the Muslim World*, pp. 159-71.

Minear, Richard H., ed. *Through Japanese Eyes*, 2 volumes. New York: Praeger Publishers, 1974.

―――. "Orientalism and the Study of Japan." *Journal of Asian Studies* XXXIX(3) (May 1980): 507–17.

Mitchell, Richard P. *The Society of the Muslim Brothers.* London: Oxford University Press, 1969.

Monde Diplomatique. "Une Bête à abattre: le tiers-mondisme." Special issue, (2 May 1985).

Montesquieu, Baron de. *The Spirit of the Laws*, Thomas Nugent, trans. New York: Hafner, 1949.

―――. *Pages Choisies I: Lettres Persanes-Considérations.* Paris: Larousse, 1946.

Montvalon, Robert de. *Ces Pays qu'on n'appelera plus colonies.* Paris: Bibliotèque de l'Homme d'Action, 1956.

Moore, Barrington, Jr. *Injustice: The Social Bases of Obedience and Revolt.* White Plains, N. Y.: M.E. Sharpe, 1978.

Moorhouse, Geoffrey. *India Britannica.* New York: Harper & Row, 1983.

Morazé, Charles. *La Logique de l'histoire.* Paris: Gallimard, 1967.

Morris, James. "Long Live Imperialism." *The Saturday Evening Post* (3 July 1965): 9, 14.

―――. *Farewell the Trumpets: An Imperial Retreat.* Harcourt Brace Jovanovich Inc., 1980.

Morsy, Magali. "La migration: dimension et revelateur de la vie nationale." In Morsy, *Les Nord-Africains en France*, pp. 15–37.

―――, ed. *Les Nord-Africains en France: colloque "Des Étrangers qui font aussi la France."* Assemblés nationale 7–8 Juin, 1984, Paris: Le centre des Hautes Études sur L'Afrique.

Mortimer, Edward. *Faith and Power: the Politics of Islam.* New York: Vintage, 1982.

Mottahedeh, Roy. *The Mantle of the Prophet: Religion and Politics in Iran.* New York: Simon & Schuster, 1985.

M'rabet, Fadela. *La Femme Algériene, suivi de Les Algériennes.* Paris: Maspero, 1969.

Muller, Herbert J. *The Uses of the Past: Profiles of Former Societies.* New York: Oxford University Press, 1952.

Mumford, Lewis. *The Story of Utopias.* New York: Viking Press, 1962, (original 1922).

————. *The City in History: Its Origins, Its Transformations, and Its Prospects.* New York: Harcourt, Brace & World, 1961.

al-Munajjid, Salah-al-Din. *"Amidat-al-Nakbah: Bahth "Ilmi fi Asbab-Hazimat-al-Khamis min-Haziran* (The Pillars of Disaster: A Scientific Study of the Causes of the Defeat of June Fifth). Beirut: Dar-al-Katib al-Jadid, 1967.

Munson, Henry, Jr. "The Social Basis of Islamic Militancy in Morocco." *Middle East Journal* 40(2) (Spring 1986): 267–84.

Mushakoji, Kinhide. "Identité nationale et dialogue culturel." *Esprit* 421 (February 1973): 550–61.

Myrdal, Gunner. *Rich Lands and Poor: The Road to World Prosperity.* New York: Hasper, 1957.

Nachman, Larry David. "The World of V. S. Naipaul." *Salmagundi* 54 (Fall 1981): 59–76.

Naff, William. "Reflections on the Question of 'East' and 'West' from the Point of View of Japan." In Lewis *et al.*, *As Others See Us*, pp. 215–27.

Naipaul, Shiva. *North of South: An African Journey.* London: André Deutsch, 1978.

————. *A Hot Country.* London: Hamish Hamilton, 1983.

————. *Beyond the Dragon's Mouth: Stories and Pieces.* New York: Viking Press, 1985.

————. *An Unfinished Journey.* New York: Viking Press, 1987.

Naipaul, V. S. *The Mimic Men.* Penguin Books, 1967.

————. *In a Free State.* Penguin Books, 1973.

————. *India: A Wounded Civilization.* New York: Alfred A. Knopf Inc., 1977.

————. *A Bend in the River.* New York: Alfred A. Knopf Inc., 1979.

————. *The Return of Eva Peron with the Killing in Trinidad.* New York: Alfred A. Knopf Inc., 1980.

————. *Among the Believers: An Islamic Journey.* New York: Alfred A. Knopf Inc., 1981.

————. "A Conversation with V. S. Naipaul" (May, 1979). *Salmagundi* 54 (Fall 1981): 4–22.

————. *Finding the Center: Two Narratives.* New York: Alfred A. Knopf Inc., 1984.

Nair, Sami. "Du Référent d'origine aux nouvelles identités." Morsy, *Les Nords-Africains en France*, pp. 153–64.

Nakhleh, Khalil. "An Intervention." *Arab Studies Quarterly* 4(3) (Winter 1982): 254–55.

Narayan, R. K. "When India was a Colony." *New York Times Magazine* (16 September 1984): 94–98, 104.

Nations, Richard. "India After Punjab." *World Press Review* (September 1984): 32–33.

Needham, J., and Wang Ling. *Science and Civilization in China.* London: Cambridge University Press, 1945–1959, 3 volumes.

Nehru, Jawarharlal. *The Discovery of India.* London: Meridian, 1951.

Nellis, John R. "A Comparative Assessment of the Development Performance of Algeria and Tunisia." *Middle East Journal* 37(2) (Summer 1983): 370–93.

———. The 1979 International Press Seminar, *The Arab Image in Western Media.* London: Morris International Ltd., 1980.

Nisbet, Robert. *History of the Idea of Progress.* New York: Basic Books, 1980.

Nkrumah, Kwame. *Neo-Colonialism: The Last Stage of Capitalism.* New York: International Publications, 1966.

Northrop, F. S. C. *The Meeting of East and West: An Inquiry Concerning World Understanding.* New York: Macmillan, 1946.

Nouschi, André. "Esquisse d'une histoire de l'immigration maghrebine." In Morsy, *Les Nords Africains en France*, pp. 36–49.

O'Brien, Patrick. "Europe in the World Economy." In Bull and Watson, 1984, pp. 43–60.

Ojo-Ade, Femi. "Lectures poétiques et sociales de la Négritude, ou la mise en questions d'une idéologie dite nègre." *Contemporary French Civilization* (Fall 1977): 41–57.

Ortega, Carlos. "Les Vrais Enjeux de la bataille de l'information." in *Monde Diplomatique* (July 1983): 28.

Orwell, George. *Shooting an Elephant and Other Essays.* Harcourt, Brace & World, 1950.

———. "Rudyard Kipling." In *The Orwell Reader: Fiction, Essays and Reportage by George Orwell*, Richard H. Rovere, ed. Harcourt, Brace & World, 1956, pp. 271–83.

Owen, Roger. "Studying Islamic History." *Journal of Interdisciplinary History* (Autumn 1973): 287–98.

Oz, Amos, and Maurice Goldberg-Bartura, trans. *In the Land of Israel.* New York: Vintage, 1984.

Palmer, Robert R. "The World Revolution in the West: 1763–1801." *Political Science Quarterly* 69(1) (March 1954): 1–14.

———. *The Age of the Democratic Revolution: A Political History of Europe and America, 1760-1800*, 2 volumes. Princeton: Princeton University Press, 1959–1964.

Paret, Peter, ed. *Makers of Modern Strategy: from Machiavelli to the Nuclear Age.* Princeton: Princeton University Press, 1986.

Parker, Geoffrey. *Europe in Crisis 1598–1648.* Ithaca: Cornell University Press, 1979.

Parry, Benita. *Conrad and Imperialism: Ideological Boundaries and Visionary Frontiers*. London: Macmillan, 1984.

Paton, Alan. *Ah, But Your Land is Beautiful*. New York: Charles Scribner's, 1981.

Paul, L. *The Annihilation of Man: A Study of the Crisis of the West*. Princeton: Princeton University Press, 1972.

Perkins, Kenneth J. *Tunisia: Crossroads of the Islamic and European Worlds*. Boulder, Colo.: Westview Press, 1986.

Péroncel-Hugoz, Jean-Pierre. *Le Radeau de Mahomet*. Paris: Lieu Commun, 1983.

Pfaff, William. "Reflections: The Reactionaries." *The New Yorker* (19 February 1979): 106–13.

———. "A Different Place, With a Different Past." *The New Yorker* (10 December 1979): 208–14.

Pickthall, Mohammed Marmaduke. *The Meaning of the Glorious Koran*. New York: Mentor Books, 1953.

Pirenne, Henri. *Mohammed and Charlemagne*, Bernard Miall, trans. New York: W. W. Norton, 1939.

Piscatori, James P., ed. *Islam in the Political Process*. Cambridge: Cambridge University Press, 1983.

Plumb, J. H. *The Death of the Past*. London: Macmillan, 1969.

———. Introduction to Series "The History of Human Society" (Hutchinson, London), C.R. Boxer, *The Dutch Seaborne Empire 1600–1800*. London: Hutchinson, 1965.

Polan, Brenda. "Half a Step Behind." *Manchester Guardian Weekly* (23 March 1986), p. 9.

Polk, William R. *The Arab World*, 4th ed. Cambridge: Harvard University Press, 1980.

Pontecorvo, Gillo. *The Battle of Algiers: A Film Written by Ranco Solinas*. New York: Charles Scribner's, 1973.

Popper, Karl R. *The Open Society and its Enemies*, 2 volumes. Princeton: Princeton University Press, 1966.

Povey, John. "The Role of English in Africa." *The Newsletter of the Teaching of English Abroad*, Special Interest Group, 2: (2 September 1981) (Teaching English to Speakers of Other Languages, University of Michigan Press).

Pruett, Gordon E. "The Escape from the Seraglio: Anti-Orientalist Trends in Modern Religious Studies." *Arab Studies Quarterly* 2(4) (Fall 1980): 291–317.

———. "Islam and Orientalism." In Hussain, 1984, pp. 43–87.

al-Qadhafi, Nuammar. *The Green Book*, 3 volumes. Tripoli, Libya: Public Establishment for Publishing; printed Astmoor, Runcom, England.

Quigley, Carroll. "The Oscar Iden Lectures." The School of Foreign Service, Georgetown University Press, Washington, D.C., (October 1976).

Rabb, Theodore K. *The Struggle for Stability in Early Modern Europe*. New York: Oxford University Press, 1975.

Raeff, Marc. *Understanding Imperial Russia: State and Society in the Old Regime*, Arthur Goldhammer, trans. New York: Columbia University Press, 1984.

Ragin, Charles, and Daniel Chirot. "The World System of Immanuel Wallerstein: Sociology and Politics in History." In Skocpol, ed., pp. 276–312.

Rahman, Fazlur. *Islam & Modernity: Transformation of an Intellectual Tradition*. Chicago: University of Chicago Press, 1982.

Ramazani, Nesta. "Arab Women in the Gulf." *Middle East Journal* 39(2) (Spring 1985): 258–76.

Ramedhan, Erwin. "La Société indonésienne face à la pénetration du monde occidental." *Monde Diplomatique* (June 1981): 21.

Ramonet, Ignacio. "Maroc: L'heure de tous les risques." *Monde Diplomatique* (January 1984): 7–11.

Randal, Jonathan C. *Going all the Way: Christian Warlords, Israeli Adventurers, and the War in Lebanon*. New York: The Viking Press, 1983.

von Ranke, Leopold. "Die Grossen Machte." Hildegarde Hunt von Laue. Trans. In Theodore H. von Laue, *Leopold Rande: The Formative Years*. Princeton: Princeton University Press, 1950, pp. 181–218.

Raskin, Jonah. *The Mythology of Imperialism*. New York: Dell, 1973.

Raspail, Jean. *The Camp of the Saints*, Norman Shapiro, trans. New York: Charles Scribner's, 1975 (original 1873).

Rausch, Donald A. *Zionism Within Early American Fundamentalism 1878–1919: A Convergence of Two Traditions*. New York: Edwin Mellen, 1979.

Reeves, Richard. "A Reporter at Large (Journey to Pakistan)." *The New Yorker* (1 October 1984), pp. 39–105. Published in book form as *Passage to Peshawar: Pakistan: Between the Hindu Kush and the Arabian Sea*. New York: Simon & Schuster, 1984.

Reichard, Herbert. *Westlich von Mohammed: Geschick und Gschichte der Berber*. Berlin: Kiepenheuer und Witsch, 1957.

Renan, Ernest. *Caliban*, Eleanor Frant, trans. New York: Shakespeare, 1898 (original 1878).

Reston, James, Jr. "How Japan Teaches Its Own History: The Nation is Debating Revisions in Its Text-books." *New York Times Magazine* (October 1985): 52–60, 64–66.

Richter, Payton E., ed. *Utopia/Dystopia?* Cambridge, Mass.: Schenkman, 1975.

Roberts, J. M. *The Hutchinson History of the World*. London: Hutchinson, 1977.

Rodinson, Maxime. *Mahomet*. Paris: Seuil, 1961.

———. *Islam et capitalism*. Paris: Seuil, 1966.

———. *Israel and the Arabs*. New York: Pantheon, 1968.

———. *Marxisme et monde musulman*. Paris: Seuil, 1972.

———. *La Fascination de l'Islam*. Paris: Maspero, 1980.

Rosenberg, Nathan, and L. E. Birdzell, Jr. *How the West Grew Rich: The Economic Transformation of the Industrial World.* New York: Basic Books, 1986.

de Rougement, Denis. *L'Aventure occidentale de l'homme.* Paris: Albin Michel, 1957.

Rouquie, Alain. *L'Etat militaire en Amerique Latine.* Paris: Seuil, 1983.

Rouleau, Eric. "La bouée de l'Islam." *Le Monde* (23 August 1984).

———. "La Recherche d'une identité." *Le Monde* (22 August 1984).

Rowe, William T. "Approaches to Modern Chinese Social History." In Zunz, pp. 236–96.

Rubinstein, Ammon. *The Zionist Dream Revisited: From Herzl to Bush Emunin and Beck.* New York: Schocken Books, 1984.

Rushdie, Salman. "Raggedy 'Ghandi'." *The Movies* (July 1983): 112–13.

———. *The Jaguar Smile: A Nicaraguan Journey.* New York: Viking, 1987.

Ruthven, Malise. *Islam in the World.* New York: Oxford University Press, 1984.

Saadawi, Naawal El. *The Hidden Face of Eve*, Sherif Hetata, trans. London: Zed Press, 1980.

Sabbah, Fatna A. *Women in the Muslim Unconscious*, Mary Jo Lakeland, trans. New York: Pergaman, 1984.

Sahli, Mohamed C. *Décoloniser l'histoire.* Paris: Maspero, 1965.

Said, Edward W. "A Palestine Voice." *Columbia Forum: A Quarterly Journal of Fact and Opinion* (Winter 1969): 24–31.

———. *Orientalism.* New York: Pantheon, 1978.

———. *The Question of Palestine.* New York: Times Books, 1980.

———. *The World, the Text, and the Critic.* Cambridge: Harvard University Press, 1983.

———. "The Mind of Winter: Reflections on Life in Exile." *Harper's Magazine* (September 1984): 49–55.

———. *After the Last Sky: Palestinian Lives, with photographs by Jean Mohr.* New York: Pantheon, 1986.

———. Intellectuals in Post-Colonial World." *Salmagundi* 70/71 (Spring-Summer 1986): 44–84.

———. "The Intellectual in the Post-Colonial World: Response and Discussion." *Salmagundi* 70/71 (Spring–Summer 1986): 65–81.

Said, Laila. *A Bridge Through Time: A Memoir.* New York: Summit, 1985.

Salih, Tayeb. *Season of Migration to the North*, Denys Johnson-Davies, trans. London: Heinemann, 1969.

Salisbury, Harrison E. "On the Literary Road: American Writers in China." *New York Times Book Review* (20 January 1985): 3–4.

Sampson, Anthony. *The Sovereign State of ITT.* Greenwich, Connecticut: Fawcett, 1974.

―――. *The Seven Sisters: The Great Oil Companies and the World They Made.* London: Hodder & Stoughton, 1975.

―――. *The Money Lenders, Bankers and a World in Turmoil.* New York: Viking, 1981.

Sansom, G. B. *The Western World and Japan: A Study in the Interaction of European and Asiatic Cultures.* New York: Knopf, 1950.

Sanson, Henri. *Laicité islamique en Algérie.* Paris: Centre National des Reicheiches Scientifiques (CRESM), 1983.

Sarraut, Albert. *La Mise en valeur des colonies fran aises.* Paris: Payot, 1923.

Sartre, J. P. *Réflexions sur la question juive.* Paris: Gallimard, 1962.

―――. Preface, In Fanon's *Les Damnés de la terre* (1981).

Savory, Roger. "Muslim Perceptions of the West: Iran." In Lewis *et al.*, *As Others See Us*, pp. 73–89.

Sayigh, Rosemary. "Roles and Functions of Arab Women." *Asian Studies Quarterly* 3(3) (Autumn 1981): 258–74.

Schell, Orville. *Watch Out for the Foreign Guests! Chinese Encounter with the West.* New York: Pantheon, 1981.

―――. "The New Open Door." *The New Yorker* (19 November 1984): 86–152.

Schiffrin, Harold Z. "The Response and Reaction of East Asia to its Scholarly Study by the West." Lewis *et al.*, *As Others See Us*, pp. 253–65.

Schiller, Herbert I. *Communication and Cultural Domination.* White Plains, New York: M. E. Sharpe, 1976.

Schleifer, Abdullah. *The Fall of Jerusalem.* New York: The Monthly Review, 1972.

Schorske, Carl E. *Fin-de-Siécle Vienna: Politics and Culture.* New York: Knopf, 1980.

Schwab, Raymond, Gene Patterson-Black, and Victor Reinking, trans. *The Oriental Renaissance: Europe's Rediscovery of India, 1680–1880.* New York: Columbia University Press, 1984.

Scudder, Lewis R., Jr. *Arab Intellectuals and the Implications of the Defeat of 1967.* M. A. Thesis. American University of Beirut, 1971.

Segal, Ronald. *The Race War.* New York: Viking, 1967.

Seliktar, Ofira. "Ethnic Stratification and Foreign Policy in Israel: The Attitudes of Oriental Jews towards the Arabs and the Arab-Israeli Conflict." *Middle East Journal* 38(1) (Winter 1984): 34–50.

Sénac, Philippe. *L'image de l'autre.* Paris: Flammarion, 1983.

Shaheen, Jack G. *The Link.* Americans for Middle Eastern Understanding, April/May, 1980.

―――. *The TV Arab.* Bowling Green, Ohio: Bowling Green University Popular Press, 1985.

Sharabi, Hisham. *Modernization of the Arab World.* New York: Van Nostrand, 1966.

————. *Arab Intellectuals and the West: The Formative Years, 1875–1914*. Baltimore: Johns Hopkins, 1970.

Shariati, Ali. *Man and Islam*, Dr. Fatollah Marjani, trans. Houston, Texas: Free Islamic Literature, Inc., 1981.

————. *Histoire et destinée. Introduction aux choix de textes d'A. Shariati*, Jacques Berque, ed. Paris: Sinbad, 1982.

————. *Fatima is Fatima*, Laleh Bakhtiar, trans. Houston, Texas: Book Distribution Center, 1983.

Shawcross, William. *Sideshow: Kissinger, Nixon and the Destruction of Cambodia*. New York: Simon & Schuster, 1979.

Shayegan, Daryush. "Between Mohammed and Freud." *World Press Review* (January 1979): 23–25.

Shils, Edward. *The Intellectual Between Tradition and Modernity: The Indian Situation*. Mouton: The Hague, 1961.

Shinar, Pessah. "The Historical Approach of the Reformist 'Ulamà in the Contemporary Maghrib." *Asian and African Studies* 7 (1971).

Shipler, David K. *Arab and Jew: Wounded Spirits in a Promised Land*. New York: Times Books, 1986.

Skocpol, Theda, ed. *Vision and Method in Historical Sociology*. New York: Cambridge University Press, 1984.

Siegfried, André. *Voyage aux Indes*. Paris: Colin, 1951.

Skinner, B. F. *Walden Two*. New York: Macmillan, 1948.

————. *Beyond Freedom and Dignity*. London: Jonathan Cape, 1971.

Smith, Albert C. "North African Historiography and the Westerner: the Maghreb as seen by David Gordon." In *History in Africa* 5, David Henige, ed., (1978), pp. 187–99.

Smith, Anthony. *The Geopolitics of Information: How Western Culture Dominates the World*. New York: Oxford University Press, 1980.

Smith, Tony. *The Pattern of Imperialism: The United States, Great Britain, and the Late-Industrializing World Since 1815*. New York: Cambridge University Press, 1981.

Smith, Wilfred C. *Islam in Modern History*. Princeton: Princeton University Press, 1957.

Snow, C. P. *The Two Cultures and a Second Look*. New York: New American Library, 1963.

Sorum, Paul Clay. *Intellectuals and Decolonization in France*. Chapel Hill: University of North Carolina Press, 1977.

Southern, R. W. *Western Views of Islam in the Middle Ages*. Cambridge: Harvard University Press, 1962.

Spector, Leonard S. *Nuclear Proliferation Today: the Spread of Nuclear Weapons*. New York: Vintage, 1984.

Spengler, Oswald. *The Decline of the West*, 2 volumes, Charles Francis Atkinson, trans. New York: Knopf, 1980.

Spraos, John. *Inequalising Trade? A Study of Traditional North/South Specialization in the Context of Terms of Trade Concepts.* London: Oxford University Press, 1983.

Stansky, Peter, and William Abraham. *Orwell: The Transformation.* New York: Knopf, 1980.

Stavrianos, L. S. *Global Rift: The Third World Comes of Age.* New York: William Morrow, 1981.

Steiner, George. "The Archives of Eden." *Salmagundi* 50/51, (Fall 1980, Winter 1981): pp. 57–89.

———. "Master and Man." *The New Yorker* (2 July 1982): 102–3.

Stevens, William K. "India's Force March to Modernity." *New York Times Magazine* (22 January 1984), pp. 28, 34–38, 40–41.

Stoianovich, Traian. *French Historical Method: The Annales Paradigm.* Ithaca: Cornell University Press, 1976.

Stokes, Eric. "Images of India." *Times Literary Supplement* (3 February 1978), p. 21.

Stowasser, Barbara F., ed. *The Islamic Impulse.* London: Croom Helm, 1987.

Strachey, John. *The End of Empire.* New York: Praeger, 1964.

Suleiman, Michael W. *American Images of Middle East Peoples: Impact of the High School.* New York: Middle East Studies Association, 1977.

Tabari, Azar, and Nahid Yeganeh, introducers and compilers. *In the Shadow of Islam: The Women's Movement in Iran.* London: Zed, 1982.

Taccoen, Lionel. *L'Occident est nu.* Paris: Flammarion, 1982.

Talmon, J. J. *The Origins of Totalitarian Democracy.* London: Sphere Books, 1970 (original 1952).

Taylor, William B. "Between Global Process and Local Knowledge: An Inquiry into Early Latin American History, 1500–1900." In Zunz, pp. 115–90.

Teilhard de Chardin, Pierre. *The Phenomenon of Man*, Bernard Wall, trans. New York: Harper & Row, 1961.

Tessler, Mark A. "Le Concept de la modernité dans les science sociales." *Revista de Ci2enias Sociais* 2(2) (1971): 148–60.

Thomas, Hugh. *A History of the World.* New York: Harper & Row, 1979.

Thomson, David, ed. *France: Empire and Republic, 1850–1940.* New York: Harper & Row, 1968.

Thornton, A. P. *Doctrines of Imperialism.* New York: John Wiley, 1965.

Tibawi, A. L. "English-speaking Orientalists: A Critique of their Approach to Islam and Arab Nationalism." *The Muslim World* 53 (1963): 185–204.

———. "Second Critique of English-Speaking Orientalists and their Approach to Islam and the Arabs." *The Islamic Quarterly* 22 (1979): 3–54.

Tibi, Bassam. "Islam and Modern European Ideologies." *International Journal of Middle East Studies* 18(1) (February 1986): 15–29.

Tillion, Germaine. "Les femmes et la voile dans la civilisation méditerranéene." In "Etudes Maghrebines: Mélange Charles-André Julien (Paris: Presses Universitaires de France, 1964): pp. 25–38.

————. *Le harem et les cousins.* Paris: Seuil, 1966.

————. Western State-Making and Theories of Political Transformation." In *The Formation of National States*, pp. 601–38.

Tinbergen, Jan. "What Road to Survival?" *World Press Review* (August 1984): 25–28.

Toffler, Alvin. *Future Shock.* New York: Random House, 1970.

————. *The Futurists.* New York: Random House, 1972.

————. *The Third Wave.* New York: William Morrow, 1980.

Toynbee, Arnold J. *A Study of History.* London: Oxford University Press, 1935–1961, 12 volumes.

————. "Encounters between Civilizations." *A Study of History XII*: 518–35.

————. *Reconsiderations. A Study of History XII.*

————. "The History and Prospects of the West." *A Study of History XII*: 518–35.

————. *The World and the West.* London: Oxford University Press, 1953.

————. Turnbull, Colin M. *The Lonely African.* New York: Simon & Schuster, 1963.

————. *The Human Cycle.* New York: Simon & Schuster, 1983.

Turner, Bryan S. *Weber and Islam: A Critical Study.* London: George Allen & Unwin, 1978.

————. "Orientalism and the Problem of Civil Society in Islam." In Hussain et al., pp. 23–42.

Updike, John. *The Coup.* New York: Knopf, 1978.

Vatikiotis, P. J., ed. *Egypt Since the Revolution.* New York: Praeger, 1968.

Vatin, Jean-Claude. "Religious Resistance and State Power in Algeria." In Cudsi and Dessouki, eds., *Islam and Power*, pp. 119–57.

————. "Popular Puritanism versus State Reformism: Islam in Algeria." In Piscatori, *Islam in the Political Process*, pp. 98–121.

Vandevelde, Hélène. "Où en est le problème du Code de la famille en Algérie?"*Monde Diplomatique* (97) (July/August/September 1982): 39–50.

Veyne, Paul. *Comment on écrit l'histoire.* Paris: Seuil, 1978.

Vincent, R. J. "Racial Equality." In Bull and Watson, pp. 239–54.

Volkan, Vamik D. and Norman Itzkowitz. *The Immortal Atatürk: A Psychobiography.* Chicago: University of Chicago Press, 1984.

Von Laue, Theodore H. *The World Revolution of Westernization: The Twentieth Century in Global Perspective.* New York: Oxford University Press, 1987.

Waardenburg, Jean-Jacques. *L'Islam dans le miroir de l'Occident.* Mouton, The Hague, 1963.

Wachtell, Nathan. *The Vision of the Vanquished: The Spanish Conquest of Peru through Indian Eyes 1530–1570*, Ben Reynolds and Siân Reynolds, trans. New York: Harper & Row, 1977 (original 1977).

Wallerstein, Immanuel. *The Modern World System, volume I: Capitalist Agriculture and the Origins of the European World Economy in the Sixteenth Century*, New York: Academic Press, 1974; Volume II: *Mercantilism and the Consolidation of the European World Economy, 1600–1750*, New York: Academic Press, 1979.

———. *The Capitalist World Economy*. London: Cambridge University Press, 1979.

———. *The Politics of the World-Economy: The States, the Movements, and the Civilizations*. London: Cambridge University Press, 1984.

Walsh, Chad. *From Utopia to Nightmare*. New York: Harper & Row, 1962.

Walsh, Judith E. *Growing Up in British India*. London: Holmes and Meier, 1983.

Ware, L. B. "The Role of the Military in the Post-Bourguiba Era." *Middle East Journal* 39(1) (Winter 1985): 27–47.

Waterbury, John. *Egypt: Burden of the Past, Options for the Future*. Bloomington: Indiana University Press, 1978.

———. *The Egypt of Nasser and Sadat: The Political Economy of Two Regimes*. Princeton: Princeton University Press, 1983.

Watson, Adam. "Russia and the European State System." In Bull and Watson, pp. 61–74.

Watson, Walter. "Universals in Intercultural Perception." In B. Lewis *et al.*, pp. 301–10.

Webb, Walter Prescott. *The Great Frontier*. Boston: Houghton Mifflin, 1952.

Weissman, Steve, and Herbert Krosney. *The Islamic Bomb: The Nuclear Threat to Israel and the Middle East*. New York: Times Books, 1981.

Wells, H. G. *A Modern Utopia*. London: Collins, n.d. (original 1905).

———. *Outline of History: Being a Plain History of Life and Mankind* (new and revised). Garden City, New Jersey: Garden City, 1931.

Wheatcroft, Geoffrey. "The Anguish of Africa." *The New Republic* (6 and 16 January 1984): 18–23.

———. "In Search of a Continent." *Times Literary Supplement* (14 November 1986).

Whitehead, A. N. *Science and the Modern World*. New York: Macmillan, 1962.

Willey, Basil. *The Seventeenth Century Background: Studies in the Thought of the Age in Relation to Poetry and Religion*. New York: Doubleday Anchor, 1953.

Williams, John. "Veiling as a Political and Social Phenomenon." In Esposito, *Islam and Development*, pp. 71–85.

Willis, Roy. "The Indigenous Critique of Colonialism: A Case Study." In T. Asad (1973): pp. 245–56.

Wilson, Angus. *The Strange Ride of Rudyard Kipling: His Life and Works*. New York: Viking, 1978.

Wilson, Henry S. *The Imperial Experience in Sub-Saharan Africa since 1870*. Minneapolis: University of Minnesota Press, 1977.

Wittfogel, Karl. *Oriental Despotism: A Comparative Study of Total Power*. New Haven: Yale University Press, 1957.

Wolf, Eric R. *Europe and the People without History*. Berkeley: University of California Press, 1982.

Woodward, C. Vann. "Clio and Crisis." In Fritz Stern, *The Varieties of History: from Voltaire to the Present*, 2nd ed. New York: Vintage, 1973, pp. 474–90.

1983 World Bank Atlas. Washington, D.C., 1983.

Worsley, Peter. *The Three Worlds: Culture and World Development*. London: Weidenfeld, 1984.

World Press Report, "The Population Debate." (October 1984): 37–42.

Yeganeh, Nahid, and Nikki R. Keddie. "Sexuality and Shi'i Social Protest in Iran." In Cole and Keddie, pp. 108–36.

Yu, Beongcheon. *The Great Circle: American Writers and the Orient*. Detroit: Wayne State University Press, 1983.

Zahlan, A. B. "The Problematique of the Arab Brain Drain." *Arab Studies Quarterly* 2(4) (Fall 1980): 318–31.

———. *Science and Science Policy in the Arab World*. London: Croom-Helm, 1980.

———. *The Arab Brain Drain*. Lowell, Mass.: Ithaca, 1981.

Zahlan, Anne Ricketson. *The Burden Slips: The Literary Expatriate in British Fiction, Before and After World War II*. Ph.D. thesis, University of North Carolia, Chapel Hill, 1983.

Zartman, I. William. "Presidential Address-MESA 1982." *Middle East Studies Association Bulletin* xvii:1 (July 1983): 1–7.

———. "Political Dynamics of the Maghreb: The Cultural Dialectic." In Barakat, ed., pp. 20–36.

Zunz, Olivier. *Reliving the Past: The World of Social History*. Chapel Hill: University of North Carolina Press, 1985.

Index

DATE DUE

DEMCO 38-297